BRIGHT STARS
JOHN KEATS, 'BARRY CORNWALL' AND ROMANTIC LITERARY CULTURE

LIVERPOOL ENGLISH TEXTS AND STUDIES, 57

BRIGHT STARS

JOHN KEATS, 'BARRY CORNWALL' AND ROMANTIC LITERARY CULTURE

RICHARD MARGGRAF TURLEY

LIVERPOOL UNIVERSITY PRESS

First published 2009 by
Liverpool University Press
4 Cambridge Street
Liverpool L69 7ZU

British Library Cataloguing-in-Publication data
A British Library CIP record is available

ISBN 978-1-84631-211-3 cased

Typeset in Garamond Premier by
Koinonia, Bury, Lancashire
Printed and bound in the European Union by
MPG Books Group

'Shooting daggers of bright love ...'

Contents

Acknowledgements

The Introduction reprints material first published as "'Amorous Cavaliers": John Keats, Barry Cornwall and Francis Jeffrey', *Notes and Queries*, n.s. 52 (2005), pp. 464–66. Parts of Chapter 1 first appeared as 'In the Temple of Fame: Barry Cornwall and Keats's Reputation', *Times Literary Supplement*, 5 September 2008, pp. 13–15 (a longer version of this commentary was printed in *Keats–Shelley Review*, 22 (2008), pp. 64–81); and as "'Breathing Human Passion": Cornwall, Keats, Shelley and Popular Romanticism', *European Romantic Review*, 19 (2008), pp. 253–73. Material from Chapters 2 and 4 previously appeared as 'John Keats, Barry Cornwall and Leigh Hunt's *Literary Pocket-Book*', *Romanticism*, 7.ii (2001), pp. 163–76; and as 'Keats, Cornwall and the "Scent of Strong-Smelling Phrases"', *Romanticism*, 12.ii (2006), pp. 102–14. Chapter 2 contains sections first published as 'Bright Stars and Bosom-Friends: John Keats and Barry Cornwall', *Notes and Queries*, n.s. 52 (2005), pp. 48–50. I am grateful to the editors of these journals for permission to recast my work here.

Note on Sources

Unless otherwise indicated, all extracts from Keats's poetry are from *John Keats: The Complete Poems*, ed. John Barnard, 3rd edn (Harmondsworth: Penguin, 1991).

All quotations from Keats's letters are from Hyder Edward Rollins, *The Letters of John Keats, 1814–1821* (Cambridge, MA: Belknap Press, 1958), hereafter *LJK*. Keats's original punctuation, spellings and misspellings have been retained.

Quotations from Byron's correspondence, unless otherwise indicated, are from *Byron's Letters and Journals*, ed. Leslie A. Marchand, 12 vols (London: Murray, 1973–1982); hereafter *BLJ*.

Quotations from Coleridge's letters, unless otherwise indicated, are from Samuel Taylor Coleridge, *Collected Letters of Samuel Taylor Coleridge*, ed. Earl Leslie Griggs, 6 vols (Oxford: Clarendon Press, 1959); hereafter *LSTC*.

All quotations from Percy Shelley's correspondence are from *The Letters of Percy Bysshe Shelley*, ed. Frederick L. Jones, 2 vols (Oxford: Clarendon Press, 1964); hereafter *LPBS*.

Preface

I am grateful to Aberystwyth University for research leave to complete this book. I wish to thank my colleagues in the Department of English and Creative Writing, in particular Peter Barry, Damian Walford Davies and Kelly Grovier. I'm also greatly indebted to John Barnard, Jack Stillinger, Charles E. Robinson, David Fairer, James C. McKusick, Alan Bewell, Nicholas Roe and Marjorie Levinson. I wish to acknowledge the staff of the National Library of Wales, Brotherton Library, Leeds, British Library and Bodleian Library (especially staff of the Duke Humphrey's Library). Thanks are also due to the Carl H. Pforzheimer Collection of Shelley and His Circle at The New York Public Library, Astor, Lenox and Tilden Foundations for permission to quote in full from manuscripts of Cornwall letters. I especially wish to express gratitude to Elizabeth C. Denlinger at NYPL for her generous assistance. Finally, I would like to acknowledge Google's magnificent Library Project, and look forward to seeing sections of the current book available on its virtual shelves soon.

Aberystwyth, February 2009

Introduction:
Bubbles or Gold on the Bounteous Tree?
Cornwall's Celebrity

He occupies privileged space in the convivial scene, wedged tightly between Romantic *eminence gris*, Robert Southey, and the fictitious editor of *Fraser's Magazine*, 'Oliver Yorke' (William Maginn's spiky alter ego). Other confrères, contributors and prominent men-of-letters crowded around the table in Daniel Maclise's sketch include elder statesman Coleridge, leaning baggily on a cane, and a pince-nezed Hogg, tartan plaid over his shoulder. Keats's *bête noire*, Lockhart (*Blackwood's* implacable 'Z.'), is also there, as well as Carlyle and Thackeray.[1]

More so, perhaps, in the frontispiece lithograph of the 'Fraserians', printed in Maginn's journal for January 1835, than in Maclise's original pencil drawing, 'Barry Cornwall', literary pseudonym of solicitor Bryan Waller Procter (1787–1874), appears slightly at sea among the illustrious figures. Harriet Martineau's 1876 recollection of Cornwall in the *Fortnightly Review* perfectly captures the man who peers out of *Fraser's* with his 'small figure' and 'head not remarkable for much beside its expression of intelligent and warm good-will'.[2] The original portrait is kinder. Where several of the assembly look forbiddingly insouciant, or in some cases conspiratorial, Cornwall is self-contained, just happy to be there.

But if we look closer, we detect a youthful, energetic quality to Cornwall – well-read by Maclise – that still survives in his late forties, and which shouldn't be underestimated. Indeed, this 'high enthusiasm', which the *Foreign Quarterly Review* judged to support a 'luxuriant imagination', enabled Cornwall to produce a series of accessible, easily digestible volumes, packed with his trademark 'dramatic scenes'. It helped him to become one of the best-selling Romantic writers after Felicia Hemans and Byron in his perihelion of celebrity in the late eighteen-teens and early 1820s.[3]

1. Too Small a Poet

By the 1830s, Cornwall had published five volumes of poetry, three of which appeared in rapid succession between 1819 and 1821, when Cornwall's aesthetic eclipsed that of Keats, his closest rival in terms of style, in the public's eyes. He also composed a tragedy, *Mirandola*, which in 1821 succeeded in securing a run at Covent Garden, unlike plays by Keats and Shelley. As a reviewer for *The Album* put it in 1822: 'Mr. CORNWALL rose to the heights of fame with a rapidity of which we have scarcely any precedent'.[4] Although his poetic reputation declined sharply with the publication of *The Flood of Thessaly* (1823), a misfiring version of the Pyrrha and Deucalion story, causing *Blackwood's* to inveigh against him for his 'affected' diction and nerveless 'Cockney' versification, he enjoyed a brief period of renewed celebrity with the appearance of *English Songs and Other Small Poems* in 1832. While he produced only occasional original work thereafter, by 1835 – as his inclusion in Maclise's group portrait confirms – Cornwall had become, and was to remain for the rest of his long life, part of the furniture in London's literary scene.

If few of his contemporaries mistook the 'amiable' author's talents for authentic 'genius' in the vivid, lived mode of Shelley or Byron, 'Barry Cornwall' quickly became a literary brand. Were we able to canvass early nineteenth-century readers on the best-loved male poet of the day, in all

THE FRASERIANS.

likelihood Cornwall would be second only to Byron. This was after all a
period, Cornwall's friend Alaric Watts (editor of *The Literary Souvenir*)
recalled, when:

> The psychological element in the poetry of Coleridge, the philosophical in that
> of Wordsworth, the poetry of intellect and the free spirit of Shelley, the poetry of
> passion and free humanity of Keats, were, as yet, rather as wine for the few than
> as bread for the many.[5]

As far as the above authors were popular in their own day at all, it was, Watts
points out, for their poetry's 'aspects of sentiment' (which Cornwall's work
possessed in spades), rather than for those more multilayered, self-reflexive
qualities and vital attunement to irony that Romanticists esteem. In one
respect, then, readers who approved of Barry Cornwall were not, by definition, what might be called 'Romantic' readers in the sense of readers who
preferred Keats (in opposition to Cornwall).

Yet for all Cornwall's skill in catching the wave of early nineteenth-
century popular taste, how easy it is to dismiss him now, how difficult to
take seriously an author whose pseudonym, far from representing a paragon
of euphony, is even less promising than his real name. The dispiriting level to
which Cornwall's stock has sunk may be gauged from the single 'hit' of his
surname in Oxford University Press's 410-page *Literature of the Romantic
Period: A Bibliographical Guide* (2001).[6] He is absent altogether from the
eighth edition of the widely used teaching resource, *The Norton Anthology
of English Literature* (2006).[7] When he is referred to at all in mainstream
Romantic criticism, it is usually as a yardstick for mediocrity, or worse.[8]

While Cornwall received career boosts in his own day from a number of
influential supporters, among them Leigh Hunt, William Jerdan, Charles
Lamb and William Hazlitt, the latter praising his friend's poetry in 'On
Ancient and Modern Literature' for eschewing 'fashionable affectation'
and 'false glitter', many of the Romantic writers we now value as the most
gifted literary talents of their age also disliked Cornwall, and professed to
being nonplussed by his success. Inclined to some degree of solidarity with
Cornwall due to a shared Harrow education, Byron nevertheless labelled his
ex-classmate's work a clumsy 'affectation of Wordsworth – and Hunt – and
Moore – and Myself, all mixed up into a kind of Chaos'.[9] Indeed, as I argue in
Chapter 1, it was in large part the antipathy felt by Shelley towards Cornwall's
best-selling 'trash' that spurred him to pen one of the most important justi-
fications of poetry from the Romantic period – indeed, from any period – *A
Defence of Poetry*, largely as a means of persuading himself that poetry had
not wholly relinquished its claim to be considered a still-relevant force for

social transformation. Keats, too, groused about the flimsiness of his rival's volumes, which he grumbled habitually played it safe, being composed solely of 'Amiability' (*LJK*, II, 268).

For edgier, marginalized writers such as Keats and Shelley, frustrated at their inability to commodify their own work and struggling against the maledictions of *Blackwood's* and the *Quarterly Review*, Cornwall's success was an affront – his verses, lacking depth of focus and emotional seriousness, inexplicably popular among readers of both sexes. From Byron's perspective, the fact that public taste could elevate a Cornwall to speedy prominence raised thorny questions concerning the status of his own best-selling poetry. The ability of a minor poet like Cornwall to unsettle major Romantic authors is one of the factors that drew me to him as a focus of study: his work constitutes a site of anxiety – then, and now – casting into relief issues of audience, taste, critical reception, 'high' vs. 'low' culture and literary commercialism.

The prevailing scholarly view of Cornwall has in significant respects been conditioned by Shelley's and Keats's own representations of the poet as a troubling, baffling presence. Richard Willard Armour's critical biography of Cornwall in 1935 marked the highpoint of interest in the poet: it outlines Cornwall's life, offers much perspicuous commentary on his work and collates 89 unpublished letters written across 53 years to correspondents including Southey, Landor, Carlyle and Robert Browning. However, it is questionable whether Armour's study helped or hindered Cornwall's posthumous fortunes. When the once-fashionable poet had most need of a blessing, the 'Amen' seemed to stick in Armour's throat. Cornwall's work, we're told, is 'sweet but forceless', the author himself 'essentially a small poet, although a pretty one'.[10] Armour acknowledges the commercial success of *English Songs*, largely composed in the mid-1820s, but adds that the lyrics 'contain no deep understanding, nothing unexpected' (p. 179). In Armour's estimation, his subject was 'very plainly a hero-worshipper and a satellite – too small a man and too small a poet to be more, if indeed he had wished to be more' (p. 125).

Gill Gregory has done more than most commentators to attempt a rehabilitation of Cornwall's reputation. In her study of his daughter, Adelaide Anne Procter (herself a popular poet in her day), she points out that if Cornwall's work lacks philosophic coherence, it possesses a 'strong affective centre' and is notable for the 'immense sympathy' it shows its female protagonists, particularly fallen women and women pushed into emotional extremes (p. 45). As we'll see at various points in this book, Cornwall was held in particularly high regard by female readers, who delighted in his savvy portraits of women such as Isabel in *A Sicilian Story*, Julia in *Marcian Colonna* and the sexually indomitable queen Lais in *Gyges*.

It's no easy task to reconcile the scale of Cornwall's early nineteenth-century popularity with his subsequent neglect by generations of critics uncertain of his canon and put off by his style. It may be convenient to dismiss the modish writer as flash-in-the-pan, justly forgotten. But how are we to get around the fact that Coleridge regarded him as one of the most promising writers of the age? On 30 July 1819, the elder poet inscribed a vivid endorsement of the solicitor's work in the margins of Charles Lamb's personal copy of *Dramatic Scenes* (1819), pronouncing Cornwall 'a poet, *me saltem judice*: and in that sense of the term, in which I apply it to C. LMB and WW [Charles Lamb and William Wordsworth]'.[11] Heather Jackson suggests that the praise was in all probability meant to reach Cornwall, since Coleridge generally 'knew or suspected that his marginal comments would find their way back' to the author.[12] In fact, the presentation copy itself had returned to Cornwall's hands by 1832, when American celebrity poet and journalist Nathaniel Parker Willis visited Cornwall and remembered seeing the volume among a higgledy-piggledy library closet packed with poetic 'lumber':

> On a blank leaf of ... the Dramatic Sketches, I found some indistinct writing in pencil. 'Oh! don't read that,' said Procter. 'The book was given me some years ago by a friend, at whose house Coleridge had been staying, for the sake of the criticisms that great man did me the honor to write at the end'.[13]

What, too, are we to make of the circumstance that so eminent a Romantic arbiter of taste as Francis Jeffrey, writing encomiastically in the *Edinburgh Review*, deemed Cornwall 'a poet – and one of no mean rate'?[14] Of course, great critics can be 'right' in some cases, and 'wrong' in others. But how do we square the fact that *most* reviewers preferred Cornwall's *A Sicilian Story* to Keats's cognate version of Boccaccio's morbid tale, *Isabella; or, The Pot of Basil*,[15] or that in the same *Blackwood's* paragraph ridiculing 'silly' Keats and his epic *Endymion*, John Wilson lauds Cornwall's own poem featuring the breathless Latmian boy, 'Hymn to Diana'?[16] Even the habitually unimpressed Byron conceded that Cornwall was 'a poet', albeit one who had been 'spoiled by the detestable Schools of the day'.[17]

Some of the most interesting recent studies in Romanticism have focused on the web of poets, editors, publishers, essayists and painters connected with the 'Cockney School of Poetry', a group given political purpose by insurgent editor of the *Examiner*, Leigh Hunt. Notable contributions in this area include suggestive books by Nicholas Roe and Jeffrey N. Cox.[18] A key relationship in what Roe terms a 'culture of dissent' centred on the Cockney School can be traced, I believe, in the interfriction between Keats and Cornwall. Examining a giddy period between early 1818 and Keats's death in February 1821, during which the two poets tussled for the same demography of readers, *Bright Stars* delves into the poetic, political and commercial contexts of the Barry Cornwall 'phenomenon'. By sharpening our view of Cornwall's best-selling work, by determining what large numbers of readers felt they were endorsing so energetically, we gain crucial insights into how Keats imagined he might bridge two seemingly contradictory aspirations: on the one hand, to write high-altitude Romantic poems, works that would place him 'among the English Poets'; and on the other, to reach a wider, more immediately appreciative contemporary audience. As well, then, as constituting a worthy focus of investigation in his own right, Cornwall represents an exciting route into a fuller understanding of Keats's fretful efforts at negotiating prevailing currents of taste and the nascent mass market.

This book constitutes the first full-length study of Cornwall in over seven decades. Its double focus on a major canonical figure and the modalities of his interaction with a closely associated but long-neglected writer who was nevertheless important in his own day sheds new light on the activities of both. I do not mean to suggest that we should read Keats by Cornwallean candlelight. My point is a different one. Namely, that without Cornwall – and this point holds true in a larger sense for other seemingly peripheral writers and their (now) more canonical counter-presences – we lose sight of a decisive factor in the context conditioning how Keats defined and redefined his poetic goals. I want to suggest that Keats and Cornwall can be considered fascinating and reciprocally fascinated literary 'doubles'; that Cornwall and his work participate in significant dialectical exchange with Keats and his publications; that the relationship was complex and mutually energizing. I contend that for Keats, Cornwall is a possible self, his easily digested work a version of what Keats's poetry always threatens to become.

Bright Stars, then, raises questions about canon formation and literary reception, about early nineteenth-century audiences and reading and reviewing practices, about issues of popularity and obscurity, and about the poetry of one of the period's most admired poets in English and one of its most neglected. In particular, it sheds light on the intimate and hitherto overlooked literary and textual relationship between two poets with such differing critical reputations. Expanding our sense of how literary reputations are made and unmade, *Bright Stars* addresses a central conundrum, one that nagged at Keats and Shelley, and which continues to tease us out of thought: why did Cornwall's frequently unremarkable parnassian elicit such enthusiastic or even visceral responses from contemporary readers, while thematically analogous and more finely fretted compositions by better writers were derided or ignored altogether? What was it about the rub of the writing itself that enabled Cornwall's initial and Keats's longer-term, although posthumous, capture of the audience?

2. Keats and Cornwall

American author James Thomas Fields (1817–1881) met Cornwall several times in London. He described him as the 'friend and companion of Keats', marvelling at being able to 'gaz[e] at the man who had looked on Keats in the flush of his genius'.[19] As the owner of a first edition copy of Cornwall's *A Sicilian Story*, inscribed 'from the author' to J. Ferrars, I recognize how Fields must have felt. When I introduce Cornwall to postgraduates on the Romantic Studies programme at Aberystwyth University's Centre for Romantic Studies, I pass this volume around the class and invite students to reflect on the fact that the hand that signed Ferrars's dedication had shaken the hand of Keats. Most modern critics and funding committees, however, are reluctant to pull Keats and Cornwall into dual focus, despite the fact that several of these writers' own contemporaries discerned strong and sugges-tive filaments of connection. Shelley, for one, picked up on Keats's fascina-tion with Cornwall's lucrative, trend-conscious aesthetic. Praising *The Fall of Hyperion* in a letter to Leigh Hunt's wife Marianne, Shelley sniped that other items in Keats's *Lamia* volume were 'written in the bad sort of style which is becoming fashionable', of which 'nothing is worse than a volume by Barry Cornwall' (*LPBS*, II, 239).

Although studying Keats in relation to a once-closely associated yet more immediately successful writer raises intriguing questions about Keats's own projects and career, the social, political and poetical interfriction between the two figures has still to be taken into full account by Romantic scholar-ship. In 1911, Cornwall's first critical biographer, Franz Becker, suspected that 'Procters persönliche Beziehungen zu Keats waren sehr vertraute und trotz der Kürze innige' [Procter's personal relationship with Keats was intimate and despite its brevity very close].[20] Armour's own biography was disbelieving on this count, insisting that while Keats and Cornwall were sufficiently cognizant of each other's existence to have exchanged gift copies of their poems in February 1820, 'their personal contact was little'. It was left to G. H. Ford in 1951 to moot a scenario in which the competitors had at least met socially before swapping volumes; indeed, in his brief but ground-breaking article, Ford remarked – while inviting expansion – that 'an interesting fragment of Keats's biography can be traced in his relations with the poet "Barry Cornwall"'.[21]

For just one example of such 'interesting fragments', in the single surviving letter from Cornwall to Keats (from late June 1820), Cornwall solicits his rival's opinion on whether the 'Greek Deluge' offered a promising theme for a new long poem. Keats's reply, assuming there was one, seems to have been encouraging, since *The Flood of Thessaly* duly materialized in 1823 as the title piece of Cornwall's fourth collection. Cornwall's letter – and the lost reply – thus tantalizingly involves Keats in the early genesis of a volume that, it transpired, marked a disastrous turning point in the voguish poet's reception.[22]

Cornwall's printed testimonies on Keats in the posthumously published *An Autobiographical Fragment* (1877) fail to add much clarity: 'Of Keats I have little to record. I saw him only two or three times before his departure for Italy.'[23] 'Two or three' face-to-face encounters, taken *at* face value, appears to underscore the orthodox view of Cornwall's limited social contact with Keats. And yet, only a few lines further into his account, Cornwall adds a detail redolent of more sharply defined acquaintance: 'He was always ready to hear and to reply; to discuss, to reason, to admit; and to join in serious talk or common gossip.' A 'common gossip', Keats? Leaving that 'aside' to one side, Cornwall's use of the habitual 'always' sits uncomfortably, to my mind at least, with his earlier claim to have sat down with Keats 'only two or three times'. As long ago as 1917, Sidney Colvin suggested that '[Cornwall's] impression of Keats, recorded almost half a century later, read[s] as though he had known him while still in health' (p. 459), at any rate before February 1820, the time frame conventionally given for the pair's first physical encounter. Andrew Motion, indeed, argues that Keats and Cornwall wouldn't have met in the flesh until March 1820, when both attended an exhibition at which their mutual friend Benjamin Robert Haydon was showing off his imposing canvass, 'Christ's Triumphant Entry into Jerusalem'.[24]

Cornwall's non-committal 'little to record' sits all the more uneasily alongside an anecdote included in Fields's *Yesterdays with Authors* (1872), reprinted as a two-part reminiscence in *Harpers New Monthly Magazine*, which also hints at more thorough-going acquaintance. During his fourth trip to Britain in 1869, Fields visited his old friend, the by now elderly

Cornwall. Beckoning his American guest into the library, Cornwall retrieved 'a package of time-stained papers' from a locked drawer:

> 'Ah', said he, as he turned over the golden leaves, 'here is something you will like to handle'. I unfolded the sheet, and lo! it was in Keats's handwriting, the sonnet on first looking into Chapman's Homer. 'Keats gave it to me', said Procter, 'many, many years ago'.[25]

Fields's account is doubly arresting since Cornwall's holograph copy of the Chapman's Homer sonnet cannot be accounted for. Two holographs of the poem are extant, one at Harvard Library, which Jack Stillinger points out may be the original draft rather than a fair copy, and one inscribed in an unknown hand to Marianne Reynolds, John Hamilton Reynolds's sister, in the Pierpont Morgan Library, New York. Neither has any apparent connection to Barry Cornwall. The fair copy of another early Keats sonnet, 'On the Grasshopper and Cricket', now in the Forster Collection at the Victoria and Albert Museum, London, is known to have been in Cornwall's possession, however, and according to Rollins was given to the poet by Keats in 1820, together with a copy of the *Lamia* volume (*LJK*, II, 267). Cornwall endorsed the manuscript with the following inscription: 'This is Keats's writing. B.W.P.' Stillinger notes that the similarity of the wording with Fields's account – 'it was in Keats's handwriting' – may indicate that Fields confused the Chapman's Homer sonnet with Cornwall's 'Grasshopper and Cricket' MS.[26] Weighing against this explanation, perhaps, is the fact that Fields published the account of his meeting in Cornwall's library only a couple of years after the actual event, and seems certain of his facts, reprinting the entirety of the Chapman's Homer sonnet in both *Yesterdays With Authors* and *Harpers New Monthly Magazine*. At any rate, it's a tantalizing thought that Cornwall's copy of the sonnet might still exist, since it opens the fascinating possibility of authorial variants.

Elsewhere, Cornwall gestures even less equivocally at consequential fellowship with Keats. MacGillivray believes Cornwall was probably the author of an anonymous 1828 'recollection' of Keats in *The Olio*, reprinted several times in England and America.[27] The tribute makes for interesting reading alongside Cornwall's claim to have 'little to record' about Keats:

> Poor fellow, I shall never forget him; those who did not know him and who have only read his too early productions may; but those who knew him well never can, if there be any fellowship in man, and human kindness be anything more than a word. He was kind, affectionate, a delightful friend, and excellent companion.[28]

Cornwall was certainly associated with a select group of well-wishers who called on Keats shortly after the near-fatal lung haemorrhage of 3 February 1820, and may himself have visited. An undated letter from Keats to Fanny Brawne, sent during the week following 13 March, records that Cornwall had cried off one appointment: 'I received a Note from Mr. Proctor [*sic*] today. He says he cannot pay me a visit this weather as he is fearful of an inflammation in the Chest' (*LJK*, II, 278). Does the note imply that Cornwall had made previous visits? Whatever the case, in *The Olio* tribute Cornwall muses: 'I never think of John Keats, but I regret that I knew him, for if I had not known him, the sorrow that I feel for his death would have been less' (p. 256).[29]

Willis's recollections, too, point towards closer amity. In *Pencillings by the Way*, which gathers 'letters home' first published in the *New York Mirror*, Willis reminisces about finding the 'shrinkingly modest' Cornwall 'buried in a deep morocco chair' in the library of his impressive Bedford Square 'whereabout' in the early 1830s (pp. 504–05): 'The conversation ran upon various authors, whom Procter had known intimately – Hazlitt, Charles Lamb, Keats, Shelley, and others, and of all he gave me interesting particulars, which I could not well repeat in a public letter' (pp. 505–06). This passage provides another suggestive *aperçu* into the 'particulars' of an altogether different level of acquaintance, the textual contours of which *Bright Stars* explores.

A central strand of argument in this book suggests that Cornwall is remarkably 'interfrictive' for a supposedly 'minor' Romantic figure. He rubs up against various – from a modern perspective – cachet or higher-altitude writers such as Keats, Shelley, Hunt and Hazlitt.

3. Celebrity, Fame

We tend to perceive Cornwall, if we see him at all, as an opportunistic crowd-pleaser, a literary charlatan with no credible claim to lasting relevance. As a fellow protégé of Leigh Hunt, Keats, critics concede, may well have taken a superficial interest in his more popular peer, who had already built up a considerable CV of publications in William Jerdan's *Literary Gazette*.[30] All the same, Keats seems to have greeted Cornwall's overtures of friendship with coolness and detachment. A reference to Cornwall's work in a letter to John Hamilton Reynolds of 28 February 1820 is frequently cited as verification of Keats's aloofness:

I confess they [Cornwall's *A Sicilian Story* and *Dramatic Scenes*] tease me – they are composed of Amiability the Seasons, the Leaves, the Moon &c. upon which he rings (according to Hunt's expression) triple bob majors. However that is nothing – *I think he likes poetry for its own sake, not his.* (*LJK*, II, 268; italics mine)

Sidney Colvin took that final phrase, 'for its own sake, not his', as watery, back-handed praise, and assumed Keats held his rival's work in as little regard as he evidently did. Colvin thought the letter illustrated how Keats 'could not quite conceal his perception of [Cornwall's] prevailing strains of fluent imitative common-place'.[31] I suspect it is Colvin himself who had difficulty in concealing his negative perceptions. In fact, the letter to Reynolds is loaded with ambiguity. Is the initial reference to Cornwall's volumes so unflattering? 'I confess they tease me' might suggest being intrigued, despite one's better judgement. The observation that Cornwall 'likes poetry for its own sake, not his' could just as easily be interpreted as a compliment as a slight. This, at any rate, is Andrew Motion's slant (p. 507). My own sense is that Keats here is attempting to communicate to Reynolds his feeling that while Cornwall engaged in showmanship rather too often, ringing 'triple bob majors' – a triumphant peel of eight bells – on such clichéd or mundane themes as the 'Seasons, the Leaves, the Moon &c.' (none of which are absent in Keats's poetry), at least he didn't allow ego to mar his compositions – unlike Wordsworth, in Keats's estimation.

Some degree of tension in the letter can be resolved into the unstable nature of Keats's relationship with Cornwall. Both were 'pupils' of Hunt with mutual friends closely associated with the 'Cockney School of Poetry' circle; in the immediate aftermath of Peterloo they were fellow political fugitives, both, like Shelley, composing anti-government poems whose dissent was couched in autumnal imagery, as I discuss in Chapter 3. They were also keen poetic rivals. While it may be going too far to say that Keats was jealous of Cornwall's success, he certainly experienced ambivalent feelings about it. Interestingly, Keats appears to borrow the second half of 'his' opinion on Cornwall's work from Francis Jeffrey's appraisal of *Dramatic Scenes* and *A Sicilian Story* in the *Edinburgh Review*, which appeared a month earlier in January 1820.[32] There Jeffrey had remarked: 'We cannot help supposing him [Cornwall] to be a very natural and *amiable* person, who has taken to write poetry *more for the love he bears it, than the fame to which it may raise him*'[33] (italics mine). The opinion on Cornwall passed off to Reynolds as Keats's own is actually stitched together from several sources. Not only does Keats adapt the final phrase from Jeffrey's critique, ringing the changes on Jeffrey's rhetorical peal – given the two poets' professional jealousy, it's hardly surprising to find that Keats had scanned his rival's reviews; but 'Amiability' also seems to have been picked up from the *Edinburgh Review*. Added to which, Keats's phrase 'triple bob majors' is self-confessedly borrowed from Hunt.

Material omitted from a borrowed phrase can, of course, be as revealing as what gets included. In Keats's distilled version of Jeffrey's formula – 'I think he likes poetry for its own sake, not his' – two key words are missing: 'love' and 'fame'. Coming across an overwhelmingly positive evaluation of Cornwall's work in the high-circulation *Edinburgh Review* a whole six months before Jeffrey got around to appraising his own volumes, Keats is hardly likely to have made 'love' a feature of his bearing to the 'amiable' Cornwall. By the same token, he's reluctant to associate yet more 'fame' with his rival's name, even in a letter. In correspondence with Reynolds, Keats purposefully, which is not to say consciously, puts fame beyond the reach of the more successful man. He manifestly uses Hunt and Jeffrey to work out what he thinks about Cornwall's poetry, evidently not wishing to think too much about it himself.

'Barry Cornwall' represented one of the biggest names in late-Romantic literature, achieving the kind of 'branded identity' that Tom Mole discusses in his recent book on Byron and celebrity.[34] Although Becker believed Cornwall 'hat den Ruhm nicht gesucht' [hadn't sought renown] (p. 36), the poet in fact scrupulously policed his 'brand' in the literary marketplace, demonstrating considerable strategic 'nous'. Also, he assiduously protected his identity as solicitor Bryan Waller Procter – on the one hand, happy for readers to speculate about his real name, and on the other, anxious that his legal business might suffer if his 'sin of Poetry' became common knowledge.[35] Corresponding with Sir William Elford in July 1820, Mary Russell Mitford whispered: 'Now "Barry Cornwall" is an alias. The poet's real name is Procter, a young attorney, who feared it might hurt his practice if he were known to follow this "idle trade". ... By whatever appellation he chooses to be called, he is a great poet.'[36]

By keeping his private – in terms of Chris Rojek's celebrity theory, 'veridical' – self at one remove, Cornwall sought to avoid what Keats himself regarded as a form of assault by the reading public that 'robbed' poets of their name's 'maidenhood' ('On Fame').[37] But Cornwall was also well aware that speculation over his real name generated market-valuable literary chit-chat, adding to his allure; he must have been delighted by an aside about the 'mystery' in the *Monthly Review* in 1820:

In our notice of the 'Dramatic Scenes' of this writer ... we hinted that Barry Cornwall was a feigned name, and might possibly mean Mr. C. Lamb. We have now Mr. C.'s own authority for saying he is not Mr. Lamb, but that he still chuses to enjoy the dignity of the mystery under which the acknowledged fictitious appellation of Cornwall yet conceals him. We have heard his real name positively stated, but do not feel ourselves at liberty to print it.[38]

Guessing at the face behind 'Barry Cornwall' became a popular literary parlour game. As we'll see in Chapter 4, even Keats's girlfriend Isabella Jones took educated stabs at Cornwall's real identity.

In September 1820, Charles Lamb's dedicatory sonnet 'To the author of poems published under the name of Barry Cornwall' was printed in the *London Magazine*.[39] Addressing the issue of pseudonymous identity, Lamb worried that his friend ran the risk of being 'by self of fame bereaved':

Let hate, or grosser heats, their foulness mask
Under the vizor of a borrowed name;
Let things eschew the light deserving blame:
No cause hast thou to blush for thy sweet task.
'Marcian Colonna' is a dainty book;
And thy 'Sicilian Tale' may boldly pass;
Thy 'Dream' 'bove all, in which, as in a glass,
On the great world's antique glories we may look.
No longer then, as 'lowly substitute,
Factor, or PROCTOR, for another's gains',
Suffer the admiring world to be deceived;
Lest thou thyself, by self of fame bereaved,
Lament too late the lost prize of thy pains,
And heavenly tunes piped through an alien flute.

In fact, a month earlier in August 1820, Cornwall's identity as Bryan Waller Procter had already been 'outed' by the *Edinburgh Monthly Review*:

To all this controversy, there can *now* be no great evil in putting an end, by informing our readers, that the author of all these productions is a Mr. Procter – a young gentleman who, we believe, has very lately been called to the bar in London.[40]

Cornwall's continued use of his *nom de plume* became a source of reviewing scorn. In 1824, in a purported new *Blackwood's* series entitled 'Letters of Mr Mullion to the Leading Poets of the Day, No. 1', addressed to 'Bryan W. Procter', William Maginn snorted:[41] 'As for styling you Barry Cornwall, for God's sake, drop that horrid humbug. Everyone is laughing at you about it.'[42] Although in Franz Becker's eyes Cornwall had merely stumbled across his luck as a popular writer, the swiftly marketable poet was far from blasé about his success. While he concealed his identity as a London solicitor for as long as he could, he used his connections with the periodical press adeptly to keep his alter ego in the public eye. By the time *The Flood of Thessaly* appeared in 1823, Cornwall's (and his publishers') skill at manipulating the media had raised hackles. *Blackwood's*, for instance, protested darkly:

> We are perfectly well aware that he has allied himself with the glorious army of the Gentlemen of the Press, in such a way, that we shall be sure to see him quoted and lauded in daily, weekly, and monthly columns ... We think, to speak moderately, that there are not many newspapers in existence to which he himself does not occasionally contribute ... He is paid so far as butter goes, most gloriously. Every line of his gets a paragraph, every paragraph a page. He is trumpeted long before he appears in mysterious hints: – 'The literary circles begin to be impatient for Barry Cornwall's new', &c. It is whispered that Barry Cornwall's forthcoming', &c. and then out comes it and the crack bits are kept hid, ready set up, we almost think, in the same types, and sent from one printing-office to another, until the public eye is quite sickened by their repetition. But what is the end of it all? – Does any body read Barry Cornwall? – Does any body remember any three consecutive lines of his? – Did any mortal ever dream of quoting him? – No. –[43]

In the Preface to the new edition of *Dramatic Scenes* in 1857, Cornwall is frank about the vaulting nature of his early ambition, informing readers that 38 years after the volume's first appearance he had at last managed to 'quell those aspirations which are troublesome ... to the young' (p. vi). All the same, one of the new 'scenes' in the volume, 'Michael Angelo', is specifically focused on fame. In it, the painter Raffaelle declares:

> Give *me* fame, on earth;
> And, when I leave sweet earth, a finer sphere,
> Where Beauty breathes[44] thro' endless summer morns.
>   ('To Michael Angelo', p. 189)

The 'scene' had, in fact, first appeared in the *New Monthly Magazine* in 1824, composed in the aftermath of Cornwall's first failure, the almost universally panned *Flood of Thessaly*. Its theme – art contemplating immortality – suggests Cornwall had not quite abandoned his love of stardom, despite his recent setback; nor for that matter had he wholly accepted that his immediate popularity necessarily disqualified him from joining the English poets in a 'finer sphere', or tone, after his death.

Keats pursued his own thoughts on the subject of fame in a second sonnet. However, his insights there are couched in unconvincing, faux-Byronic terms. Fame is now personified as a 'Jilt', an incalcitrant, deceiving lover (whenever Keats talks about his relations with women, he's on sticky ground):

> Fame, like a wayward girl, will still be coy
> To those who woo her with too slavish knees
> ...
> Ye lovesick Bards! repay her scorn for scorn;
> Ye Artists lovelorn! madmen that ye are!
> Make your best bow to her and bid adieu,
> Then, if she likes it, she will follow you.
>   ('To Fame')

Despite such pronouncements, and notwithstanding Keats's disingenuous claim in a letter to J. H. Reynolds not to have written 'one Single line of Poetry with the least Shadow of public thought' (*LJK*, I, 267), Keats craved public recognition as eagerly as his rival.[45] We shouldn't set too much store by Keats's fey posturing to Woodhouse in October 1818 about the 'solitary indifference I feel for applause', or his assurance that even if his 'night's labours should be burnt every morning and no eye ever shine upon them', he would continue to write 'from the mere yearning and fondness I have for the Beautiful' (*LJK*, I, 388).

Cornwall's perspective on the matter was less callow, more distinctly commercial, if anxious in its own way:

> Fame is a bounteous tree:
> Upon its branches hang bubbles and gold.
> Which wilt thou here?
>   ('To Michael Angelo', p. 183)

Cornwall, then, is plainly discomforted by the thought that poetry designed to please a contemporary public is doomed as fleeting, shiny bubbles rather than genuine, durable gold on fame's bounteous tree. This central dilemma, which informs Cornwall's poetry as much as Keats's, is itself inflected by the realization that he was writing increasingly for the deferred audiences of posterity – for post-Romantic readers, in other words.

If Cornwall hoped for a 'finer sphere' of immortal renown, his enviable earthly popularity indeed proved to be an obstacle. The signs were evident from the first flush of his fashionableness. Partly as an expression of the Romantic doctrine of 'genuine' poetry, which declared artistic authenticity and contemporary acclaim to be mutually antagonistic, and partly due to the (related) attempt of writers like Keats and Shelley to compensate themselves for their frustrating inability to reach emerging mass audiences as effectively as authors like Cornwall, a key expression of Romanticism harboured deep scepticism towards 'celebrity', a category then moving into ontological distinctiveness.

We wait until 1849 for a printed instance of 'celebrity' used in the modern sense to denote a category of subjectivity. In Dinah Craik's novel, *The Ogilvies*, a character inquires – quotation marks signifying the word's freshness, but also already imparting modern ambivalence – 'Did you see any of those "celebrities", as you call them?'[46] But as far back as 1808, Coleridge had disparaged the public 'rage for personality – of talking & thinking ever and ever about A. and B. and L. – names, names, always names!'[47] 'Serious' writers sought to rationalize meagre sales by sublimating the ambition of attaining present-day currency into a realm of higher-order 'fame', producing works of genius that were, by definition, inaccessible to contemporary audiences. At the same time, they denigrated popular performances such as Cornwall's *Dramatic Scenes* as ephemeral, celebrity 'trash' – 'amiable' enough, in Keats's possibly frosty phrase, but empty of any real value.

In the first decades of the nineteenth century, broadly interchangeable terms for discussing renown underwent a process of desynonymization. After 1600, and the first printed instance of 'celebrity' in the sense of 'famousness', variants on 'celebrity' and 'fame' had been used more or less interchangeably. The transposability of these terms can be gauged from Percival Stockdale's *Poetical Thoughts, and Views; on the Banks of the Wear* (1792):

> But chiefly souls, fraught with ethereal flame,
> *Born for celebrity, for deathless fame,*
> Whom intellectual force, whom genius fills;
> Should speed their course, regardless of their ills;
>   (ll. 67–78; my italics)

In the fourth edition of his *Dictionary of the English Language* (1773), Samuel Johnson defined 'celebriousness' as 'renown; fame'. 'Fame', in turn – a turn back on itself – was defined as 'celebrity; renown', Johnson presenting a closed circle of self-referentiality.

2002 'Draft Additions' to the online *OED* appear to suggest that the words' double-meaning field continues today, a *celebrity novel* being 'a novel written by or ascribed to a famous person, *esp.* one expected to sell on the strength of his or her fame'.[48] Similarly, Judith Fischer's 2006 article on Maclise's 'Frasererian' engravings and literary celebrity elucidates nineteenth-century renown thus: 'The term "celebrity" applies to a fame that is conferred upon someone, rather than a fame that is actively sought'.[49]

Such recent conflations actually register a process of *re*synonymization, rather than a mutually referential binary relationship that has continued since Johnson's *Dictionary*. In 1821, Shelley's *A Defence of Poetry* made a strategic, conceptual distinction between 'celebrity' and 'fame'. For Shelley, lasting fame could only be achieved by authentic genius, which itself could only be recognized by posterity, judged by the 'selectest of the wise of many generations':

> Even in modern times, no living poet ever arrived at the fullness of his fame; the jury which sits in judgement upon a poet, belonging as he does to all time, must be composed of his peers: it must be impanelled by Time from the selectest of the wise of many generations. A poet is a nightingale, who sits in darkness and sings to cheer its own solitude with sweet sounds.[50]

The most concentrated and influential account of the 'inescapable obscurity of the living genius', according to Andrew Bennett, is Wordsworth's in the 'Essay, Supplementary to the Preface' in *Lyrical Ballads* (1815). There, Wordsworth argues that neglect during a poet's lifetime has always been the fate of true genius, even claiming to derive solace from the fact that his own work had encountered resistance:[51]

> The love, the admiration, the indifference, the slight, the aversion, and even the contempt, with which these Poems have been received ... they are all proofs that for the present time I have not laboured in vain; and afford assurances, more or less authentic, that the products of my industry will endure.[52]

The consolation for disappointing sales was the promise of later, lasting fame. 'Away, then, with the senseless iteration of the word, *popular*, applied to new works in Poetry', Wordsworth exclaims, insisting that 'qualities which dazzle at first sight, and kindle the admiration of the multitude, are essentially different from those by which permanent influence is secured'.[53] ('Dazzle', with its sense of being merely temporarily overcome, is a key term in Romantic anti-celebrity discourse.)

Coleridge agreed in an 1811 letter to Edward Jenner, opposing 'true FAME' with 'the trifle, reputation' (*LSTC*, VI, 1026). Hazlitt, too, addressed the issue of ephemeral celebrity versus lasting renown. In his essay 'On Different Sorts of Fame', published in *The Round Table* (1817), he noted that the 'caprice of fashion' or 'prejudice of the moment' may confer a 'fleeting reputation', but insisted that 'our only certain appeal ... is to posterity'. He added: 'When we hear any one complain that he has not the same fame as some poet or painter who lived two hundred years ago, he seems to us to complain that he has not been dead these two hundred years.'[54] In the end, Keats had little alternative but to extol the virtues of durable renown, looking out hopefully towards futurity rather than around at contemporaneity;

a species of fame that would place him 'Among the English poets'. He dismissed contemporary acclaim 'Mawkish Popularity', exemplified by the runaway success of Cornwall and 'bluestocking' poets Joanna Baillie and Mary Tighe, writers who lived by the pen but whom Keats thought superficial and 'smokeable' (*LJK*, I, 267).

In P. David Marshall's terms, celebrity productions are derided because they are perceived to represent 'false value'.[55] Celebrities are condemned to generate inauthenticity since they fail to supply the gap between art and an authenticating lived experience – an area in which Cornwall was felt to be particularly vulnerable. When Shelley ridiculed Cornwall's attempts at writing Byronic ottava rima in *Gyges* and *Diego de Montilla*, he purposefully invoked the concept of 'genuine' poetry, where life and art were supposed to be contiguous:

> Is not the vulgarity of Cornwall's wretched imitations of Lord Byron carried to a pitch of the sublime? His indecencies, too, both against sexual nature, and against human nature in general, sit very awkwardly upon him. He only affects the libertine: he is really a very amiable, friendly, and agreeable man, I hear. But is not this monstrous? (*LPBS*, II, 240)

The idea of the 'amiable' Cornwall *living* his racy poetry, Shelley sneered, was preposterous.

Once his true identity, his 'veridical' self, became known, Cornwall struggled with charges of inauthenticity: first because he was a 'gentle', shrinking character who only affected the libertine; and second for being a 'Cockney' poet who mooned over Italian landscapes without ever having visited Italy. In the *Edinburgh Monthly Review*, an anonymous reviewer lampooned Cornwall's reliance on books rather than on first-hand experience:

> Mr. Cornwall informs us first that he has always had a prodigious love and veneration for the soil of Italy (as who has not?) and secondly, that the cause of this feeling in his mind is entirely distinct from any recollections of the antique greatness of that country, but depends altogether on her modern poets, painters, and musicians. Now this is *cockneyism*, and the worst kind of *cockneyism* too. It is quite unworthy of any person but Mr. Hunt and Mr. Keats, men who indeed are equally ignorant to all sensible purposes of ancient and modern Italy, but who seem to be very fond of giving themselves airs of a certain sort, merely, we suppose, on the strength of their having been at the King's Theatre pretty often, and perhaps in the habit of living among a set of fifth-rate fiddlers and composers of opera bravouras.[56]

The *Monthly Review* agreed, decrying the *mal d'Italie* the 'fashion of falling into raptures at the mention of a land which the author has never seen'. This 'preposterous' trend, the reviewer laments, was 'in vogue among a knot of writers whose feet, we believe, have been mostly confined to a perambulation of the streets of our metropolis'.[57]

With disarming honesty, Cornwall acknowledged that he lacked experience of the wider world. S. R. Townshend Mayer's wife recalled asking him if he'd ever visited Italy: "'Only in my dreams", he replied; "never actually farther than Boulogne"; adding with a smile "I am the man who never travelled!"'[58] Far from blushing at having to rely on culled sources, in 'The Genealogists' (a *jeu d'ésprit* from *Marcian Colonna* that possesses much in common with Keats's later and unpublished 'The Cap and Bells; or, The Jealousies'), Cornwall even plays self-consciously with recursive models of experience, breaking off from his whimsical tale to descant on Vesuvius's rumblings:

> 28
> That trembling of the ground beneath one's feet,
> As tho' 'twould swallow all in its red fury,
> Is terrible; 'twould stretch a nerve of steel,
> To be thus buried without judge or jury:
> The thing is not fictitious, Sir, but real,
> A truth, a fact, and this I do assure you:
> I learnt it (for I own I'm no unraveller
> Of Nature's secrets) from a friend – a traveller.

It was the cult of Byron that did much to establish a concept of the authentically or sincerely embodied text. To be sure, William Faulkner delayed finishing *The Shipwreck* (1762) until he had actually witnessed a hurricane; but when Samuel Johnson opened *The Vanity of Human Wishes* (1749) with the words 'Let Observation with extensive View, / Survey Mankind, from *China* to *Peru*', no-one supposed that he was claiming to have wandered the globe himself. If anything, within neoclassical frames of authorship too deep a knowledge of a writer's life was likely to be viewed as a potential impediment to enjoying the work, the relationship between author and text being broadly conceived as one of disunity. Readers simply did not expect poets writing about disaster at sea to have been on board when the ship sank.

It's a different story, of course, when Byron begins the first Canto of *Childe Harold's Pilgrimage* (1812), where the reader is encouraged to read the poem through the author's claims of direct experience. In Tom Mole's words, if Byron can't escape from his status as a belated poet, he is able to make crucial new claims for poetic authority based on the circumstance that he's actually 'been to the home of the muse himself' (p. 45):

Oh, thou, in Hellas deemed of heavenly birth,
Muse, formed or fabled at the minstrel's will!
Since shamed full oft by later lyres on earth,
Mine dares not call thee from thy sacred hill:
Yet there I've wandered by thy vaunted rill;
Yes! sighed o'er Delphi's long-deserted shrine
Where, save that feeble fountain, all is still ...
          (*Childe Harold's Pilgrimage*, ll. 1–7; italics mine)

Like Shelley, then, Byron offers himself as an authenticating sign to be read back into his works, investing his textual signature, his authorial imprimatur, with biographical authenticity.[59] In one important sense these authors make similar pleas to today's celebrities, who insist they are vitally self-identical, or 'veridical', whether at home or in front of the cameras.[60]

Byron's astonishing success at presenting himself as a unified, congruent whole can be gauged from John Wilson's review of *Childe Harold*, Canto IV (1818), in *Blackwood's Edinburgh Magazine*. The critique begins with a strikingly modern account of the self-referentiality of the Byronic sign: 'It is impossible to speak of [Byron's] poetry without also speaking of himself, morally, as a man ... In his poetry, more than any other man's, there is felt a continual presence of himself – there is everlasting self-representation or self-reference.'[61] The degree of conflation between Byron's veridical and public faces was such that readers routinely identified the poet with his protagonists, and themselves with aspects of Byron. As Andrew Elfenbein argues, this blurring of persona represents 'a critical turning point in the relations between author, text, and audience, when the text became not merely an author's product but an eroticized expression of the most authentic depths of his or her personality'.[62]

Cornwall's own biography, however, was notable not for its extravagance but 'prudence' – hardly a Byronic quality, and one at troubling odds with the racy, edgily back-lit poetic narratives associated with the 'Barry Cornwall' brand. As the *Fortnightly Review* put it in its tribute to the recently deceased poet in 1876: 'Mr. Procter's life did honor to his poetry, and is in a way in harmony with it; but it is the harmony of contrast, the harmony of the leaf and the flower, one might almost say the harmony of the ashes and the flame'. Read through Cornwall's life, the creative work was always in danger of appearing insipid: 'The poetry of Barry Cornwall is the record of the extravagances of one who was habitually sober, the audacities of one who was habitually cautious, the eloquence of one who was habitually reserved'.

4. Bright Stars

Cornwall exists as an axial figure between 'high' Romantic aspiration, represented by the classical ideal of Keats and Shelley, and a popularized aesthetic
that defined a significant constituency of Romantic taste, and which Keats
sought to enlist at critical junctures in his career. Andrew Bennett catches an
important aspect of this double craving when he suggests that Keats's work
'at once seeks to express the personal, the private, the "inward feel", while at
the same time attempting to appeal, through this very privacy – or privation
– of experience, to a mass audience' (p. 40). To be sure, there is markedly less
of the private, 'inward feel' in Cornwall; his poems typically lobby audiences
through sheer velocity of narrative, through spectacle and pathos, negotiating the increasing heterogeneity of the reading public through a unifying
petition aimed at satisfying the demand of book buyers to be, in simple
terms, entertained.[63] The results could hardly have been at greater variance.
Keats grew exasperated with, then profoundly depressed by, the lack of
public response, blaming reviewers for 'enervating' readers' minds (LJK, II,
65) and theatrically dedicating himself to the ideal audiences of posterity, the
antithesis of fashionability. Cornwall was left to gather the plaudits, demand
for his à la mode poems often outstripping supply.[64]

Objections to Cornwall invariably return to the unevenness of his work,
frequently due to commercialism and haste. His trademark 'dramatic scenes'
still retain something of what Hazlitt labelled their 'fervour', and give an
impression of what it may have been like to read Cornwall in his heyday
of celebrity.[65] But the miscellaneous poetry is often unaccomplished, and
at times anaesthetizingly bad, which has diluted his impact on the modern
critical consciousness. In recollections from 1854, P. G. Patmore suggested
facetiously that one reason why Hazlitt spoke so highly of Cornwall's verses
was that 'he had not read a twentieth part of them'.[66] It would certainly be
difficult, however carefully passages were selected, to suggest the overlooked
value of much of his work. That said, Cornwall at his best outshines any
other 'significant minor' Romantic (including, in my view, the until recently
under-valued Leigh Hunt); and in a study of 'popular' literature in history
he actually presents us with a more illuminating example than Keats. My
aim is rather to show that Cornwall merits our attention as a Romantic
phenomenon, for the scale of his success – won despite open affiliation with
the politically renegade Hunt – and for his complex, under-explored interfriction with Keats.

Between 1819 and 1823, Cornwall was fêted in literary London, enjoying one of the highest profiles of any Romantic author. What little space is accorded him by modern critics, however, is due more or less entirely to his published reminiscences of figures such as Hazlitt, Hunt, Charles Lamb and De Quincey. Chapter 1 seeks to rehabilitate Cornwall as an invaluable context for the receptions of Keats and Shelley, poets whose place within contemporary early nineteenth-century print culture was once more uncertain than his own. I examine Cornwall's dexterity in negotiating popular taste, and explore his complexly dynamic interaction with Keats, who at various points views his rival as a possible version of himself. Discussion also focuses on Shelley's antipathy towards Cornwall's commercial achievements, ill-disposition given crucial shape by Thomas Love Peacock, which played an important part in the genesis of one of Romanticism's most urgent manifestos, *A Defence of Poetry*. Finally, this chapter asks what it was about Cornwall's *au courant* style that gave rise to his popular appeal in contemporary reading culture, and examines the conditions that led to the sudden decline of his reputation after 1823.

Chapter 2 looks at two letters by Cornwall – one obscure, the other never before published – for the information they contain about the hitherto unsuspected shape and character of his bearing to Keats. Although Cornwall is usually seen as an opportunistic beneficiary of the vagaries of Romantic taste, an overlooked letter to the Reverend Morehead, editor of the *Edinburgh Magazine and Literary Miscellany*, reveals that quietly and behind the scenes Cornwall was in fact working harder even than Keats's closest friends and supporters to redeem his more talented but commercially unsuccessful fellow 'Young Poet'. The second chapter also addresses the thorny issue of rivalry between Keats and Cornwall, shedding new light on the equally contentious issue of mutual influence.

Chapter 3 considers Cornwall's ostensibly neutral political polarity, and addresses his role in a post-Peterloo poetic dialogue that was conducted using seasonal imagery. Sonnets on the seasons contributed by Cornwall to Hunt's *Literary Pocket-Book* for 1820 reveal the poet to have been involved in a close-bosom autumnal conspiracy with Keats and Percy Shelley. Focusing on Cornwall's sonnet 'Autumn', Keats's ode 'To Autumn' and Shelley's 'Ode to the West Wind', all three composed in the dangerous weeks following the Peterloo Massacre in 1819, this chapter weighs the possibility that striking parallels between this trio of purposeful poems amount to political conversation. The fugitive dialogue, I argue, requires us to take Hunt's championing of Cornwall more seriously in terms of the poet's contribution to wider Cockney School dissent; once Cornwall's importance to Hunt and to

the oppositional rhetoric of his circle is established, other claims for significant intellectual and poetic exchange between Keats and Cornwall appear in
a more credible light.

Chapter 4 extends this book's attempt to clarify Cornwall's contemporary popularity by exploring what I term his poetics of erotic containment.
By this phrase, I mean work that flirts with the boundaries of indecorum,
titillating audiences without transgressing to the extent that sections of the
readership, especially women, are excluded. Cornwall enjoyed a reputation
for his mature perspective on love and treatment of heightened emotion.
Keats's would-be manly romances, on the other hand, were denounced
by conservative reviewers as onanistically self-referential. In actual fact,
Cornwall's erotic poetry is often deeply subversive, yet on the face of it
manages to appear more strategically aligned to accepted models of decency
than Keats's own. In one respect, we'll discover, it is precisely Cornwall's rival
erotic productions that made Keats's love poetry appear off-puttingly jejune
to contemporary reading audiences.

Cornwall and Keats acquired significant, and at times shared, insights
into emotional disequilibrium through their respective legal and medical
training. In Chapter 5, I'm interested in how these poets attempted to
parlay professional expertise into verse romances expressly designed to sell
in the market for lurid narratives of insanity. While Cornwall exploited his
personal and professional *entrée* into the rhetoric of psychiatry, locating a
set of spectacular chromatic resources to contribute to such crowd-pleasing
literary performances as *Marcian Colonna* and *A Sicilian Story* (1820), works
such as the *Hyperion* poems and *Isabella* display what Emily Sun welcomes
as a never-ceasing 'insist[ence] on the therapeutic function of poetry', a
claim renewed throughout Keats's work – though to the detriment of its
commercial impact.[67]

Whether working behind the scenes, acting as a direct participant in
Romantic debates, or simply being talked about, Cornwall is powerfully interfrictive in late-Romantic literary and political culture. Focusing on a series
of intriguing intersections involving Cornwall with Keats and other major
personages from the period, *Bright Stars* sets out to recuperate the solicitor-
poet as a serious Romantic presence, rather than as simply a phenomenon of
early nineteenth-century taste. Part of my project involves resisting what Greg
Kucich, in a different context, calls 'troubling continuations of Romantic
practice into our own aesthetic'.[68] The situation vis-à-vis Cornwall's reputation, indeed, is closely analogous to that of Felicia Hemans before Susan
Wolfson rescued her 'from the terms of her nineteenth-century popularity'.[69]

Bright Stars explores the reciprocally instructive careers of Keats and Cornwall, identifying key parallels but also telling discontinuities in the efforts of both to attune their work to the prevailing frequencies of taste. It uses the reception of a minor writer to tell us about the projects and career of a major one, spotlighting a specific set of literary anxieties that actuated both poets in their milieu. At certain points, *Bright Stars* takes as its primary focus of illumination the common spurs and imperatives driving the evolution of two poets closely associated with Leigh Hunt's circle, showing how each responded to and sought to exploit – with very different results – a governing set of market conditions. At others, stylistic proximities, rhetorical overlaps and a mutual, tightly prismed political discourse seem to suggest that the relation between Keats and Cornwall was not always only that of fellow 'Cockney' poets with parallel ambitions, but also included a more intriguingly interpersonal dimension, a vital interfriction. Beyond that, this study offers a passport into a wider cultural matrix, populated by a range of cachet Romantic figures, including Hunt, Shelley, Hazlitt, Wordsworth, Coleridge and Lamb, as well as Lockhart, Jerdan, Watts and Jeffrey.

Keats's retreat from his rival's lucrative poetics into a densely signifying art where each word is made to bear the mark of imaginative pressure; Cornwall's conflicted decision to abandon his aspirations to the integrity of Keats's art and write squarely for the market – *Bright Stars* explores a complex field of creative, political and personal tensions. Above all, it makes the case for a rethinking of canonicity to take account of the contemporary importance of a writer such as Barry Cornwall in the context of Keats's relative marginality. It argues for a timely and decisive reinstatement of Cornwall into the conceptual landscape of the literary and political culture of his day.

Notes

1 *Fraser's Magazine*, 11 (1835): frontispiece. Disguised as 'Alfred Croquis', Maclise sketched semi-caricatures of renowned literary figures to accompany William Maginn's series of satirical essays, 'Gallery of Literary Characters'.
2 G. A. Simcox, 'Barry Cornwall', *Fortnightly Review*, n.s. 20 (1876), pp. 708–18.
3 *Foreign Quarterly Review*, 32 (1843), p. 175.
4 'The Augustan Age in England', *The Album*, 1 (1822), pp. 220–21, at p. 220.
5 Alaric Alfred Watts, *Alaric Watts: A Narrative of his Life*, 2 vols (London: Bentley, 1884), I, 146.
6 *Literature of the Romantic Period: A Bibliographical Guide*, ed. Michael O'Neill (Oxford: Clarendon Press, 1998), p. 203.
7 *The Norton Anthology of English Literature, Volume 2: The Romantic Period through the Twentieth Century*, ed. Stephen Greenblatt (London: W. W. Norton, 2006).

8 A notable exception is Gill Gregory's intriguing study of Adelaide Anne Procter, Cornwall's daughter, also a poet, which presents a broadly sympathetic overview of his work. See *The Life and Work of Adelaide Anne Procter: Poetry, Feminism and Fathers* (Aldershot: Ashgate, 1998).

9 Letter to Murray, 4 January 1821 (*BLJ*, VIII, 56).

10 Richard Willard Armour, *Barry Cornwall: A Biography of Bryan Waller Procter* (Boston: Meador, 1935), pp. 142, 145.

11 Samuel Taylor Coleridge, *A Book I Value: Selected Marginalia*, ed. H. J. Jackson (Princeton: Princeton University Press, 2003), p. 115. Also see Armour, *Barry Cornwall*, p. 61.

12 See Heather Jackson, *Marginalia: Readers Writing in Books* (New Haven, CT: Yale University Press, 2001), p. 157.

13 Nathaniel Parker Willis, *Pencillings by the Way: Written During Some Years of Residence and Travel in Europe* (New York: Scribner, 1852), pp. 507.

14 *Edinburgh Review*, 33 (1820), pp. 144–55, at p. 145.

15 *Monthly Magazine*, n.s. 92 (1820), pp. 305–10. In 1857, *Blackwood's Edinburgh Magazine* reviewed Cornwall's *Dramatic Scenes, with other Poems now first Printed* (1857). The reviewer notes that *A Sicilian Story* had been left out of the new edition, and fondly recalled its original appearance: 'We miss, and we are sorry for it, the *Sicilian Story* (which was a worthy rival of Keats's *Isabella*)'; *Blackwood's Edinburgh Magazine*, 81 (1857), p. 360.

16 See Wilson's review of Hunt's *Literary Pocket-Book* for 1819, *Blackwood's Edinburgh Magazine*, 6 (1819), pp. 235–47, at p. 240.

17 Letter to Taylor, 7 June 1820 (*BLJ*, VII, 113). In a letter to Murray of 4 November 1820, immediately after denouncing Keats for the 'mental masturbation' of his poetry, Byron comments 'Barry Cornwall would write well if he would let himself' (*BLJ*, VII, 225).

18 See Nicholas Roe, *John Keats and the Culture of Dissent* (Oxford: Oxford University Press, 1997); and Jeffrey N. Cox, *Poetry and Politics in the Cockney School: Keats, Shelley, Hunt and their Circle* (Cambridge: Cambridge University Press, 1998).

19 James T. Fields, *Old Acquaintance: Barry Cornwall and Some of his Friends* (Boston: Cambridge, MA, 1876), pp. 10, 21.

20 Franz Becker, *Bryan Waller Procter (Barry Cornwall)* (Vienna: Braumüller, 1911), p. 12.

21 G. H. Ford, 'Keats and Procter: A Misdated Acquaintance', *Modern Language Notes*, 66 (1951), pp. 532-36, at p. 535.

22 For a transcript of the letter, see Ford, 'Keats and Procter: A Misdated Acquaintance'.

23 Barry Cornwall, *An Autobiographical Fragment and Biographical Notes, With Personal Sketches of Contemporaries, Unpublished Lyrics, and Letters of Literary Friends* (London: Bell, 1877), p. 201.

24 Andrew Motion, *Keats* (London: Faber and Faber, 1997), p. 510. As Motion notes, the *Morning Post* picked out Lamb, Keats and Cornwall among 'the principal persons distinguished for rank and talent' present at the event.

25 J. T. Fields, Part 1: '"Barry Cornwall" and Some of His Friends', *Harper's New Monthly Magazine*, 51 (1875), pp. 777–96, at p. 780. Part 2: *Harper's New Monthly Magazine*, 52 (1876), pp. 57–65.

26 I am indebted to Professor Stillinger for his generous advice on the provenance and identity of Cornwall's holograph of Keats's poem.

27 *The Olio*, 28 June 1828, I, 391–94. For MacGillivray's identification of Cornwall's authorship, see *Keats: The Critical Heritage*, ed. G. M. Matthews (London: Routledge & Kegan

Paul, 1971), p. 256. See p. 144 for evidence to support MacGillivray's conjecture.

28 *John Keats: The Critical Heritage*, p. 257.

29 Cornwall also remarks that 'it was impossible to look at him, and think him long lived'; despite the 'lustre' of his face, the 'seeds of early death were sown there' (p. 256). Susan Wolfson has discussed the influence of Cornwall's *Olio* tribute in spreading the myth of Keats's cruel neglect and doom of premature death in *Keats and History*, ed. Nicholas Roe (Cambridge: Cambridge University Press, 1995).

30 See Chapter 1, p. 32.

31 Sidney Colvin, *John Keats: His Life and Poetry, His Friends, Critics and After-Fame*, 2nd edn (London: Macmillan, 1918), p. 457.

32 Jeffrey had declared Cornwall a 'poet and one of no mean rate'. Modern Keats critics seem to want to have their cake and eat it, too, since there is surely a contradiction in our praising Jeffrey's judgement for recognizing Keats's talent if the editor also considered Cornwall to be a genuine poet.

33 *Edinburgh Review*, 33 (1820), pp. 144–55, at p. 146.

34 Tom Mole, *Byron's Romantic Celebrity: Industrial Culture and the Hermeneutic of Intimacy* (London: Palgrave Macmillan, 2007), p. 16.

35 See Chapter 2, p. 77.

36 See A. G. L'Estrange, *Life of Mary Russell Mitford*, 2 vols (London: Bentley, 1870), I, p. 340.

37 Chris Rojek, *Celebrity* (London: Reaktion, 2001), p. 16.

38 *Monthly Review*, 91 (1820), pp. 291–96, at p. 291.

39 *London Magazine*, 2 (1820), p. 302.

40 *Edinburgh Monthly Review*, 4 (1820), pp. 176–77, at p. 176.

41 For Maginn's authorship, see Ralph M. Wardle, *Modern Language Notes*, 57 (1942), pp. 459–62, at p. 461n. 9. This was the only letter printed under the series heading: Maginn had mistakenly assumed Cornwall was the author of Hazlitt's *Edinburgh Review* essay praising Shelley's *Posthumous Poems* (1824).

42 William Maginn, *Blackwood's Edinburgh Magazine*, 16 (1824), pp. 285–289, at p. 285.

43 *Blackwood's Edinburgh Magazine*, 13 (1823), pp. 532–541, at p. 333.

44 Printed 'breaketh' in *New Monthly Magazine*, 7 (1824), p. 118.

45 In a letter to Sarah Jeffrey on 9 June 1819, Keats claimed an 'abatement of my love of fame' (*LJK*, II, 116).

46 Dinah Craik [D. M. Mullock], *The Ogilvies* (1849), II, 74. Tom Mole also discusses this first appearance of 'celebrity': see *Byron's Romantic Celebrity*, p. xii.

47 Letter to Matilda Betham, dated 4 April 1808 (*LSTC*, III, 688).

48 Even recent critical studies of celebrity appear to use *fame* as a synonym of *celebrity*, as becomes clear on page 7 (bottom paragraph) of Graeme Turner's *Understanding Celebrity* (London: Sage, 2004).

49 Judith L. Fisher, '"In the Present Famine of Anything Substantial": Fraser's "Portraits" and the Construction of Literary Celebrity; or, "Personality, Personality Is the Appetite of the Age"', *Victorian Periodicals Review*, 39 (2006), pp. 97–135, at p. 99.

50 'A Defence of Poetry', in *Shelley's Prose: or, The Trumpet of a Prophecy*, ed. David Lee Clark (London: Fourth Estate, 1988), pp. 281–82.

51 Andrew Bennett, *Romantic Poets and the Culture of Posterity* (Cambridge: Cambridge University Press, 1999), p. 22.

52 'Essay, Supplementary to the Preface', in *William Wordsworth*, ed. Stephen Gill (Oxford: Oxford University Press, 1984), pp. 657.

53 'Essay, Supplementary to the Preface', pp. 660–61.

54 *William Hazlitt: The Complete Works*, ed. P. P. Howe, 21 vols (London, 1930–34), IV, p. 94.

55 P. David Marshall, *Celebrity and Power: Fame in Contemporary Culture* (Minneapolis: University of Minnesota Press, 1997), p. xi.

56 *Edinburgh Monthly Magazine*, 4 (1820), p. 179.

57 *Monthly Review*, 92 (1820), pp. 310–18, at p. 311.

58 S. R. Townshend Mayer, *Gentleman's Magazine*, 237 (1874), pp. 555–68, at p. 561.

59 Byron carved his name on a stone at Chillon castle – the inspiration for *The Prisoner of Chillon* (1816) – as physical proof of having 'wandered' there. For a theoretically rich discussion of 'imprimatur', see Aaron Jaffe, *Modernism and the Culture of Celebrity* (Cambridge: Cambridge University Press, 2005).

60 Byron's life functions as a quasi-biographical 'paratext' to his writing in a manner akin to Genette's definition: 'The paratext is ... a zone between text and off-text, a zone not only of transition but also of transaction: a privileged place of pragmatics and a strategy, of an influence on the public, an influence that ... is at the service of a better reception for the text and a more pertinent reading of it'. See *Paratext: Thresholds of Interpretation* (Cambridge: Cambridge University Press, 1997), p. 2.

61 *Blackwood's Edinburgh Magazine*, 4 (1818), pp. 216–24, at p. 216.

62 Andrew Elfenbein, *Byron and the Victorians* (Cambridge: Cambridge University Press, 1995), p. 4. Also see Fisher, 'Present Famine', p. 99.

63 For the increasingly diverse educational, class and financial background of Romantic reading audiences, see Donald C. Goellnicht, 'Keats on Reading: "Delicious Diligent Indolence"', in *Journal of English and Germanic Philology*, 88 (1989), pp. 190–210, at pp. 190–93, 209–10.

64 See the letter from the Ollier brothers to George Keats quoted in Walter Jackson Bate, *John Keats* (London: Hogarth, 1992), pp. 150–51.

65 William Hazlitt, 'On the Spirit of Ancient and Modern Literature' (Lecture 7), in *Lectures on the Dramatic Literature of the Age of Elizabeth* (1820); see *William Hazlitt: The Complete Works*, ed. P. P. Howe, 21 vols (London, 1930–34), VI, pp. 346–47.

66 P. G. Patmore, *My Friends and Acquaintances*, 3 vols (London: Saunders and Otley, 1854), III, p. 163.

67 Emily Sun, 'Facing Keats with Winnicott: On a New Therapeutics', *Studies in Romanticism*, 46 (2007), pp. 57–75, at pp. 57, 69.

68 Greg Kucich, 'Gendering the Canons of Romanticism' in *Romantic Masculinities*, ed. Tony Pinkney, Keith Hanley and Fred Botting (Keele: Keele University Press, 1997), p. 26.

69 Susan J. Wolfson, *Felicia Hemans: Selected Poems, Letters, Reception Materials* (Princeton: Princeton University Press, 2000), p. xiv.

'Breathing Human Passion':
Cornwall and Popular Romanticism

Recent scholarship has done much to crystallize our sense of coterie culture in the Romantic period. Jeffrey N. Cox's *Poetry and Politics in the Cockney School* (1998) rehabilitated a number of Romantic figures long considered peripheral, and new digital resources such as the *Romantic Circles* hypertext editions archive are currently returning a host of interesting characters to view. Nicholas Roe's recent studies of Leigh Hunt, including his superb biography *Fiery Heart* (2005), have similarly pulled a major Romantic presence into sharper definition.[1] Not so Cornwall, scarcely less a phenomenon in his own day, and arguably a better poet. After almost two centuries of neglect, Cornwall – often considered inassimilable into orthodox narratives within Romantic Studies – has yet to be rescued from time's wallet. In stark contrast to his high profile in Hazlitt's 1824 anthology of Romantic poets, he's represented by a single sonnet in Jerome McGann's *The New Oxford Book of Romantic Period Verse* (1993); is not, and has never been, included in *The Norton Anthology of English Literature*, which in 2006 reached its eighth expanded incarnation; he's absent from Anne Mellor's and Richard Matlak's non-canonically focused, gender-conscious *British Literature 1780–1830* (2000); also from the second edition of the *Longman Anthology of British Literature* (2003); and two poems printed in previous editions of Duncan Wu's magisterial, canon-expanding *Romanticism: An Anthology* (1994) recently dropped out of the 'thoroughly revised' third edition of 2005.[2] Cornwall, then, belongs to those other 'minor men [who] have fallen out of anthology pages', as Susan Wolfson calls his fellow non-canonical male poets, Beddoes, Praed and Hood.[3] Once the doyen of literary London, now consigned to footnotes, Cornwall is literally passed over – 'wannabe' Romantic poet at one end of the century, ageing Metropolitan Commissioner for Lunacy and model for 'Beaver' in Lewis Carroll's *The Hunting of the Snark* (1876), at the other.[4]

Considered now as irredeemably abject, in its own day Cornwall's poetry was eminently saleable. While *Marcian Colonna*'s extraordinary first day's sales figures may not compete with the 10,000 copies of *The Corsair* Byron is reputed to have sold in a comparable period in 1814, they firmly established Cornwall as a bona fide literary phenomenon. The rising poet not only enjoyed healthy approval ratings among the reading public, but also secured the support of reviewers on both sides of the political divide. In an otherwise arch 1819 *Blackwood's* critique of Leigh Hunt's *Literary Pocket-Book*, Wilson praised Cornwall's sonnets as 'perfect in their beauty and majesty'.[5] The fact that Cornwall's first two volumes, the 7s *Dramatic Scenes* (1819) and the 7/6d *A Sicilian Story* (1820), had become 'speedily popular' was welcomed by the *New Monthly Magazine* as growing evidence of a salutary 'taste for pure beauty'.[6] Within a year, Cornwall's first two books of poetry sped into second editions, and *Mirandola's* successful Covent Garden staging in January 1821 confirmed Cornwall's status as one of the most celebrated writers of his day.

At the same time, despite being singled out by the *Eclectic Review* as Cornwall's chief 'poetical rival' in terms of style – akin, perhaps, to a contemporary British crime-writer being identified as Ian Rankin's closest competitor – Keats struggled to find readers.[7] Two years after Keats's death, when the poet's friends were debating whether to erect a monument in England, Charles Brown wrote to Joseph Severn observing that '[Keats's] fame is not sufficiently general ... his name is unknown to the multitude'. 'When I quitted England', he informed Severn, 'his works were still unsaleable' (letter dated 7 February 1823), before adding: 'I think that prior to his name being somewhat more celebrated, a monument to his memory might even retard it, and it might provoke ill nature, and (shall I say it?) ridicule'.[8]

In important respects, Keats's early literary career plots an inverse graph of his more successful contemporary's. In 1821, the *Asiatic Journal and Monthly Miscellany* observed, with Cornwall specifically in mind, that 'the trade of a popular poet now-a-days is very profitable'.[9] In 1822, however, John Taylor, publisher of the 9s *Endymion* (1818) and *Lamia ... and other Poems* (1820), significantly cheaper at 7/6d, complained that Keats's lifetime sales numbered no more than 500 copies.[10] Charles and James Ollier, visionary but impecunious publishers who took on Keats's first volume *Poems* (1817) for 10% commission, likewise grumbled about poor sales.[11] When George Keats complained to Charles Ollier that his brother's work had not been marketed properly, the piqued publisher parried that he regretted ever having had anything to do with Keats; one disgruntled customer, he announced, had returned *Poems* (1817) to his London shop as 'no better than a take in', and demanded his money back.[12]

Keats faced a welter of criticism for his idiosyncratic diction and was publicly castigated for flaunting his 'Cockney School of Poetry' connections with radical editor of the *Examiner*, Leigh Hunt. Yet Cornwall, who shared Keats's 'Cockney' affiliations as well as Hunt's 'fatal patronage',[13] was garlanded with praise for his 'winning strains'.[14] While Keats was regularly characterized as 'vulgar' or 'puerile', the epithet most commonly applied to Cornwall was 'amiable'. In 1819, *Blackwood's* reviewer 'Christopher North' (John Wilson) remarked that 'every body seems to think kindly and hopefully' of the poet.[15] Years later, recalling the poet's rapid rise to celebrity, William Jerdan, editor of the influential *Literary Gazette*, pronounced Cornwall 'deservedly popular',[16] while in *Homes and Haunts of the Most Eminent English Poets* (1847), William Howitt remembered the crowd-pleasing, 'genial' Cornwall holding a 'firm ... place in the public heart'. By contrast, Howitt pointed out, Keats's 'vivid orgasm of the intellect' had been misinterpreted as 'madness', and his 'unworldliness' as 'effeminacy'.[17]

Cornwall proved spectacularly adept at negotiating popular taste, producing a series of works that captured the public's imagination. Keats's own best efforts to shape his poetry to prevailing trends in literature – and his letters reveal that he was self-laceratingly focused on this task – resulted in ignominious failure. What was it, then, that contemporary audiences responded to so powerfully in Cornwall's work, yet didn't find in Keats's? Equally, why do we react so strongly today against an aesthetic that between 1818 and 1823 seemed to sweep other artistic considerations before it? What can Cornwall tell us about the way in which more accomplished writers like Keats and Percy Shelley imagined their relationship to the literary market-place? Cornwall's first flush of celebrity in 1819 and 1820 is a suitable place to begin in expanding our field of vision in respect of significant currents in late-Romantic literary culture.

1. Cornwall and Popular Print Culture

Cornwall and Keats each sought to capitalize on the vogue for medieval romance, and like many popular, or would-be popular, writers of the day they found Greek mythology to be rich creative ground. But where Keats, who at crucial junctures in his career was simultaneously 'in flight' from Cornwall's grandstanding style and drawn to emulate its more accessible, best-selling hallmarks, struggled to make an impression on metropolitan literary culture, Cornwall quickly became a household name. In 1822, just three years after the appearance of his debut full-length collection and only an astonishing five years after his first poem was printed in Jerdan's *Literary Gazette*, he celebrated the publication of his three-volume *Poetical Works*. Cornwall saw what was in effect another edition of his collected works included as the fourth part of a single large volume, *The Poetical Works of Milman, Bowles, Wilson, and Cornwall*, published in Paris by Galignani in 1829. Keats also featured in a Galignani edition that year, *The Poetical Works of Coleridge, Shelley and Keats*; Keats, then, found himself in a distinctly more accomplished pantheon of authors. But it was Cornwall's 'presence' that was more vivid in the popular reading consciousness.

In addition to four volumes of poetry, *Dramatic Scenes* (1819; new edition 1820), *A Sicilian Story* (1819; new editions 1820, 1821), *Marcian Colonna* (1820; new edition 1821), *The Flood of Thessaly* (1823), and a tragedy, *Mirandola* (staged in 1821, reprinted three times in the space of a year), Cornwall placed numerous signature 'dramatic scenes' and dozens of shorter poems in various widely circulated periodicals and newspapers, including the *Examiner, Indicator, Annals of Fine Arts, Literary Gazette* and *London Magazine*. He was also a regular contributor to the popular annuals and albums that flourished in the late eighteen-teens and 1820s, notably Leigh Hunt's *Literary Pocket-Book*, William Fraser's *Bijou*, Frederic Shoberl's *Forget-Me-Not*, Thomas Hood's *The Gem*,[18] and Alaric Watts's *Literary Souvenir* and *Poetical Album and Register of Modern Fugitive Poetry*.[19] It's worth pausing at the *Poetical Album* (1828), since Watts – whose own poetry the *Eclectic Review* compared to Cornwall's in 1824 – included both Keats and Cornwall in it, moreover in instructive relation.[20] Watts's miscellany showcases previously published but as yet uncollected work by contemporary poets, providing an index of poetic taste in the period from which items are culled. Though substantially ready for press 'as early as 1824', publication was delayed until 1828 due to publishing disputes, as Watts explains in a prickly preface.[21] His selection includes some 77 authors, among them Byron, Hemans, L.E.L. (Letitia Elizabeth Landon), Scott, Leigh Hunt and Percy Shelley. Two hundred and ninety poems are listed in the contents pages; 80 of these are unattributed, leaving an average tally of 3 attributed poems per author. Predictably, Landon throws everybody into the shade with her 28 entries; and Byron and Hemans also do significantly better than the mean, each represented by 8 poems. But Cornwall is also allocated 8 poems (one of them, 'The Marriage of Peleus and Thetis', is discussed in Chapter 2). This figure is double Percy Shelley's share of the available space. Keats's contribution, at the other end of the spectrum of distribution, is a single sonnet, 'To Ailsa Rock'.

The statistics of poems included in the *Poetical Album* offer an *aperçu* into the kind of 'fugitive' poetry considered (re)saleable in the late-Romantic era. Watts had an established pedigree in gauging the popular literary market – as well as editing the *Poetical Album*, he was also in charge of the *Literary Souvenir* (1825–35), a 'superior' Christmas annual in the *British Critic's* opinion, which turned a healthy profit in a congested market and reputedly sold 6000 copies within just two weeks of its first appearance.[22] In 1829, Wilson dubbed Watts the 'Father of the Annuals.'[23] The fact that the *Poetical Album* finds room for no fewer than eight previously uncollected poems by Cornwall confirms the writer's saleability – especially since in private letters to publishing magnate William Blackwood, Watts confessed to harbouring reservations about Cornwall's character due to the poet's links with the 'villainous depravity' of Hunt's Cockney circle: 'It is a curious fact that all this class of persons, are entirely without any religious creed whatever. Chas Lamb, Procter, Hazlitt, Hunt, Peacock, Chas Ollier, Talfourd, Reynolds *cum multis aliis* all boast of their freedom from the shackles of religious sentiment of every kind.'[24]

The *Poetical Album's* list of contents also serves as a guide to the frequency with which individual Romantic authors published in literary journals and newspapers. Cornwall's remarkable rate of output is confirmed by Jerdan, his early promoter in the weekly 8d *Literary Gazette*. Jerdan's quirky 1852 autobiography records that over a three-year period beginning in November 1817, Cornwall's 'graceful effusions ... adorned the "Gazette", averaging about a poem for every fortnight or three weeks of the publication, signed B., or W., or O., or X. Y. Z., &c'.[25] There were enough uncollected poems from this early period, Jerdan suggests, to 'form a delightful volume' on their own. Until Hemans burst onto the scene, Jerdan's magazine had 'no more constant and prolific supporter than Barry Cornwall' (III, 230). The contents pages of the *Poetical Album* gesture, too, at the relative public profiles of the period's most fashionable writers. Landon's tally reflects both her prolificness and popularity, while Keats's single sonnet correlates with the relatively small body of work he published outside his three volumes, and – since few people bought these – with the public's corresponding lack of familiarity with his poetry. Keats contributed just 14 separately printed poems in his lifetime, spread over 6 different journals, annuals or newspapers (*Examiner, Champion, Indicator, Annals of Fine Arts, London Magazine* and Hunt's *Literary Pocket-Book*).[26] Most readers, it is worth remembering, encountered Keats via strategically selected excerpts in hostile magazines such as *Blackwood's* and the *Quarterly*.

Cornwall's much-anthologized work, by contrast, found a wide readership in a number of different formats. A crucial factor in his success was his ability to keep reviewers across the political divide 'on message'. Unlike other known associates of Hunt, pariah editor and 'hierophant' of the Cockney School, Cornwall had (as *Blackwood's* put it) managed to 'smooth the raven face of periodical criticism until it had smiled'.[27] Considered capable of 'profundity of feeling' by the *Edinburgh Monthly Review*,[28] felt by the *Salt-Bearer* to have 'claims of rivalry' even against Coleridge's mercurial genius,[29] Cornwall speedily became a watchword for easily digestible and above all stirring narrative poetry. From one perspective, then, it's remarkable that modern Romantic scholarship should all but dismiss a writer whose work reviewing *eminence gris* Francis Jeffrey recommended for its 'unalloyed sweets',[30] to discount a figure whom '*Blackwood's* berserker', the implacable John Wilson, pronounced a poet 'of no ordinary genius'.[31]

Reviewing Hunt's 5s *Literary Pocket-Book* for 1819, Wilson demands to know: 'Why should Leigh Hunt and John Keates [*sic*] have a higher opinion of themselves, than Barry Cornwall? One "dramatic scene" – even the very tamest ... is worth both "the two dead Eternities of the Cockneys"'.[32] Cornwall's own contribution to Hunt's volume, 'Hymn to Diana', is presented as a corrective to the 'two feats of Johnny Keates', sonnets on 'The Human Seasons' and to 'Ailsa Rock' (p. 239). Wilson reserved his warmest approbation for a critique of Cornwall's second volume, *A Sicilian Story* (1820). Maga's readers are given a series of lengthy passages, including the last 100 lines of the title piece, with the recommendation: 'We cannot forbear quoting the whole of the remainder of the poem ... [to] enabl[e] our readers to judge for themselves of the power and tenderness of Mr Cornwall's genius'.[33] Wilson's willingness to cede to *Blackwood's* subscribers responsibility for assessing Cornwall's merits serves to reinforce his cultural authority, and thus the sagacity of his judgement in the first place. Such reviewing strategies form a powerful part of a set of authorized responses to Romantic poetry that, Barbara M. Benedict has shown in a different context, 'define contemporary cultural literacy and the attitude of the reader of printed literature'.[34]

A similar strategy, although more malevolent in intent, is evident in the *Eclectic Review's* 1820 appraisal of *Lamia*. Feigning a desire to take a 'fresh and final estimate of [Keats's] talents and pretensions', Josiah Conder offers extracts on the pretext of enabling potential book-buyers to make up their own minds. After reproducing the passages, Conder states: 'We have laid before our readers these copious extracts from Mr. Keats's present volume, without any comment, in order that he might have the full benefit of pleading his own case'. He then delivers his own verdict: 'Mr. Keats has given his whole soul to "plotting and fitting himself for verses fit to live;" and the consequence is, that he has produced verses which, if we mistake not, will not live long, though they will live as long as they deserve'.[35] Like Wilson, Conder not only rejects Keats's poetics, but seeks to influence, by anticipating its reception, its impact on wider spheres of reading culture.

Cornwall cannot, however, be recuperated wholly on his own terms. His initially smooth ride in *Blackwood's* can be partially accounted for by the friendship of Charles Ollier with the Tory magazine's proprietor, William Blackwood. This strategically valuable acquaintance had already secured favourable attention for inflammatory work by an even more obviously contentious member of the Olliers' stable, Percy Shelley. However, unlike Shelley's, Cornwall's poetry sold like hot cakes. Blackwood wrote twice to Ollier, on consecutive days, in July 1820 requesting extra copies of *A Sicilian Story* and *Marcian Colonna* to replenish swiftly depleted stock at his Edinburgh shop.[36] Other factors may also have contributed to the conservative press's initially positive response to Cornwall, compared with the hostility shown to Keats. For a start, there's the important issue of different class status between Cornwall, a Harrow-educated solicitor, and Keats, widely perceived as a jejune pretender to culture. Although *Blackwood's* essayists eventually balked at Cornwall's over-familiar Cockney 'Greekisms' following the publication of the 7s *The Flood of Thessaly* (1823), a piece of 'exquisite trash' that marked a difficult crossroads in Cornwall's career and literary reputation, they initially countenanced his freedom with classical material as in some way legitimated by his Harrow schooling.[37] Keats, on the other hand, was attacked in *Blackwood's* for knowing only as much Greek as he had stumbled on in Chapman, and was emphatically denied any latitude in his treatment of classical sources. In addition, Cornwall's social and professional status possibly blunted his political challenge in the eyes of establishment reviewers, encouraging Wilson and Croker to seek ways of extricating him from the Cockney School's imbricated political and aesthetic agendas – despite the fact that Cornwall's preface to *Dramatic Scenes* openly re-circulates the provoca-tively pro-Wordsworthian rhetoric of Hunt's own politically freighted preface to 1816's cause célèbre, *The Story of Rimini*. Cornwall's call in 1819 for poetic language to be reformed so as to adopt 'a more natural style' would have been recognized as linked to a desire for the reform of wider political structures.[38]

By now it should, I hope, be clear that continued neglect of Cornwall threatens to dull our appreciation of significant aspects of popular Romantic style emergent over the period of his celebrity. In particular, interaction between Keats and Cornwall – primarily literary and imaginative, although at crucial junctures also personal – discloses valuable information about the relationship between two *types* or related *aspects* of Romantic poetry in the marketplace (a concern running throughout this book). Pierre Bourdieu refers to the literary or artistic field as 'at all times the site of a struggle between the two principles of hierarchization' – the 'heteronomous principle' ('bourgeois', or popular art), and the 'autonomous principle' (art for art's sake). Writers 'least endowed with specific capital', Bourdieu argues, 'tend to identify with a degree of independence from the economy, seeing temporal failure as a sign of election and success as a sign of compromise.'[39] Taking Bourdieu as one of my points of departure, I explore as historical embodiments of the phenomenon he describes the mutual bearing of two expressions of Romanticism: a high-ceilinged, intellectually rigorous articulation in Keats, and its more popular anti-type in Cornwall. And yet, the division is uneasy, since each 'type' of Romanticism simultaneously attracts and repulses its counterpart. Keats, desperate to find an idiom that would sell, even beginning a draft of his unstaged tragedy *Otho the Great* in the manner of Cornwall's fashionable dialogue, before rewriting it in the style of Massinger,[40] is most 'Keatsian' when he retreats, at times reluctantly, from the kind of poetry epitomized by Cornwall's popular volumes, from the crowd-pleasing aesthetic of his literary 'double', his unacknowledged or possible self. By the same token, Cornwall is most successful in poetic terms, seen through a modern lens, when he shapes his idiom around more distinctly 'Keatsian' tones. Reversing our perspective, we could also say that Keats is least successful in terms of sales figures when he rejects Cornwall's voguish idiom. Similarly, when Cornwall attempts to reproduce a 'classical' (rather than 'medieval') version of Keats in *The Flood of Thessaly*, his thus far seamless success came to an abrupt end – audiences deserted him and reviewers were emboldened to attack his 'Cockney' pretensions. A finer understanding, then, of the pressures exerted bi-directionally by Keatsian and Cornwallean style discloses important information about the formation of, and writerly responses to, wider paradigms of public taste and poetic appetites in the period.

2. 'Whom can I place beside thee – not descending?'

It's well known that 'Ode on a Grecian Urn' first appeared in January 1820 in the prestigious journal, *Annals of Fine Arts*. A less remarked fact is that it was printed opposite a sonnet by Barry Cornwall.[41] Moreover, like the ode, Cornwall's sonnet also ruminates on the theme of immortality and genuine art:[42]

> 'To Michel Agnolo'[43]
> Michael! thou wast the mightiest spirit of all
> Who taught or learned Italian art sublime:
> And long shall thy renown survive the time
> When Ruin to herself thy works shall call.
> One only, (and he perished in his prime,)
> Could mate with thee; and in one path alone.
> Thou didst regenerate art; and from the stone
> Started the breathing image, perfect great;
> And such as haply, in his first state,
> Man shall attain: And thou could'st trace the rhyme 10
> That lifts its parents to the skies, thus bending
> To thy resistless powers the sisters three,
> Painting, and Sculpture, and wing'd Poetry.
> – Whom can I place beside thee – not descending?

Curiously, in a critical milieu long-attuned to the significance of historical context, co-texts and adjacent texts, the joint dissemination of sonnet and ode has escaped sustained commentary. Cornwall's sonnet, on the other hand, is keenly conscious of its place in the ode's reception, its 'place beside' Keats (l. 14). On first sight at least, Cornwall's poem has little to recommend it to modern readers. Architect James Elmes, influential editor of *Annals*, prints one of Keats's most accomplished poems alongside one of Cornwall's least impressive. That the contrast is so stark today serves to throw issues of taste into bold relief, prompting us to ask why early nineteenth-century audiences so categorically elected Cornwall's aesthetic over that of his rival. Despite its gaucherie, 'To Michel Agnolo' provides clues that help to account for this now scarcely comprehensible preference; indeed, Cornwall's flat sonnet has several things to tell us about Keats's famous ode.

'Art' in Keats's ode-aesthetic is complexly situated in the cold, unyielding marble, an aesthetic that doesn't simply postpone the anguish of mortality but defers it indefinitely ('she cannot fade', 'for ever wilt thou love', ll. 19–20). The carved figures on the 'leaf-fring'd legend' – the 'fair youth' and the young lover, their kiss frozen – for all that they appear to offer humanity a degree of compensation in the face of death's certainty, remain 'far above', detached from 'all breathing human passion' (l. 28). They may be undying, but at the same time, and for all time, are unable fully to engage in the more satisfying, fleshed-out business of living. Cornwall's sonnet also pursues a discernibly late-Romantic agenda, reflecting voguishly in the aftermath of the arrival in Britain of the 'Elgin Marbles' on artistic value and the concept of authenticity. Again like Keats's ode, the sonnet is preoccupied with 'renown', with tantalizing gleams of futurity. Yet Cornwall's sonnet evades Keats's more discomforting, dislocating questions about the imaginative, fictive status of statuary, offering an easier, altogether less critical, aesthetic which blandly asserts that great art can aspire to, be reified into, living existence. Keats, by comparison, scrutinizes the relationship between life and life-in-art more rigorously, crucially stopping short of Cornwall's convivial conclusion. Where for Keats the imaginative act of breaking through into eternal life ends in the frigidity of heat-death – the young lovers never can complete that kiss – Cornwall's sonnet conspires with Romantic ideology, seeking to convince readers through the breath of its colloquial immediacy that the imaginative act alone is sufficient to transform obdurate stone into 'breathing image' (ll. 7–8). It is precisely through its immediacy, its chatty, comparatively untroubled humanity – notwithstanding the stylistic awkwardness that frequently arises – that Cornwall's work finds a winning formula. In this manner, Cornwall's accessible aesthetic was able to overwhelm more durable work such as Keats's.

Interestingly enough, in the second edition of *Dramatic Scenes* (1820), Cornwall included an 'Advertisement' re-emphasizing his commitment to an easily comprehensible 'colloquial spirit' in poetry (p. vi). As we know, Cornwall's 'conversational ease' delighted readers:[44] the influential *New Monthly Magazine*, for example, declared that his poems 'breathe[d] forth human passion'. This phrase intriguingly echoes line 28 of Keats's 'Ode on a Grecian Urn' ('all breathing human passion'), and gestures at the extent to which reviewers considered the poets in the same conceptual breath.[45]

If contemporary scholarship is reluctant to construe Cornwall as a meaningful facet of Keats's reception, as part of a set of circumstances of taste that made Keats's acceptance by the reading public such a thorny issue, Romantic audiences were accustomed to thinking about the pair in related contexts. As well as being published by the same journals, even printed alongside each other as in *Annals of Fine Arts*, the aspiring poets were frequently mentioned in the same sentence by reviewers. Francis Jeffrey, for example,

paused to note 'something very curious ... in the way in which [Keats] and
Mr Barry Cornwall ... have dealt with the Pagan Mythology, of which they
have made so much in their poetry'.[46] Authors, too, made the connection.
In volume 2, chapter 3 of Letitia Elizabeth Landon's novel, *Romance and
Reality*, we find two epigraphs, the first taken from Keats's *Endymion* and the
second from Cornwall's *Marcian Colonna*.[47] There were compelling reasons
for viewing the poets through the same lens. Quite apart from their shared
stylistic tics, it was common knowledge that Keats and Cornwall were both
affiliated with Leigh Hunt's radical coterie.[48] Cornwall first met his poetic
mentor in summer 1817, and with Hunt's encouragement embarked on a
writing career.[49] His literary trajectory echoed Keats's own social and poetic
drift into Hunt's giddying orbit a few months earlier in October 1816. Both
men published early work in Hunt's *Examiner*, and both benefited from
the sophisticated, battle-savvy circle of writers gathered around the belea-
guered editor, whose members included other 'Young Poets', John Hamilton
Reynolds and Percy Shelley.[50] This was the group from which Hunt supplied
his subversive annual, the *Literary Pocket-Book*. Hunt himself publicly forged
a link between his two protégés in an *Examiner* review of *Dramatic Scenes*
(1819), where he remarked that Cornwall reminded him of the 'young poet
Keats'.

Cornwall's links to Hunt were always likely to prove troublesome. In
1819, at the beginning of the 'Barry Cornwall' phenomenon, the *Edinburgh
Monthly Review* warned the modish writer against the 'quaintness and idle
peculiarity of a modern school of poetry', lumping him with other 'ingenious
theorists' who wished to transform poetic diction, an ambition roundly
condemned as a 'great piece of impertinence'.[51] In 1820, the *Edinburgh Review*
was still trying to lift Cornwall away from Hunt, determined to save him
from the seditious editor's blandishments. In a message plainly intended for
Cornwall's benefit as much as to reassure readers, Jeffrey insisted that while
the 'natural bent of [Cornwall's] genius [was] more like that of Leigh Hunt
than any other author', he was happily invested with 'better taste and better
judgement'.[52] *Blackwood's*, scourge of the 'Cockney School', also employed a
disconsolidating rhetoric in an attempt to turn Cornwall from the company
of Hunt and Keats, rather than damning him out of hand for his radical
allegiances:

> We cannot help bearing our testimony to [Cornwall's] simple, manly and digni-
> fied modesty ... a modesty which forms a most pleasing contrast to the ignorant
> arrogance and sottish self-sufficiency of the Cockney School, who, we hear, are
> desirous of investing Mr Cornwall with the insignia of their order.[53]

The *Monthly Magazine* was more caustic and followed the *Edinburgh Monthly* in denouncing both Cornwall and Keats as 'fellow pupil[s]' of a political outcast.[54]

It would be misleading to suggest that Keats's unpopularity compared with the wide appeal of his stablemate can be wholly explained by undesirable connections with Hunt. The painter Benjamin Robert Haydon was right when he claimed in his autobiography that '[Keats] ... by his connection with the *Examiner* clique ... bought upon himself an overwhelming outcry of unjust adversion.'[55] (*Blackwood's* critic 'Timothy Tickler' insisted that Keats would have received a rough ride from reviewers even if he had publicly dissociated himself from Hunt.)[56] But Cornwall also laboured under suspicion of association with the recent resident of Horsemonger Lane Gaol, and his work nevertheless sold in enviable quantities.

3. Cornwall's à la mode Romanticism

Sharing his enthusiasm for Cornwall's work with Lady Blessington, Walter Savage Landor gushed: 'Today I finished a second reading of Barry Cornwall's poems. Scarcely any tether can bring my nose down to that rank herbage that is springing up about us in our walk of poetry. But how fresh and sweet is Barry Cornwall's.'[57] Since Cornwall's last two 'extant' poems fell out of the third edition of Wu's *Romanticism: An Anthology* (2005), it's not easy for twenty-first-century readers to appreciate Landor's passion. We lose sight of the fact that Cornwall's volumes, unlike more determinedly 'esoteric' Romantic works like Shelley's *The Revolt of Islam* (1818) and *Prometheus Unbound* (1820), are committed to a poetic aesthetic predicated on accessibility and inclusion, whose generous politics self-consciously key into Wordsworth's 1802 Preface and Appendix to *Lyrical Ballads*, and also link to Hunt's own Wordsworthian preface to *The Story of Rimini* (1816). Hunt's articulation of 'Cockney School' philology was based on liberal 'principles', which demanded that modern poetry should be composed in a 'freer spirit of versification', deploy a 'free and idiomatic cast of language', and 'use as much as possible an actual, existing language'.[58] A receptive reader of Hunt, Cornwall announced similarly bold intentions in his own manifesto preface to *Dramatic Scenes* (1819). The liberal import of this document would have been widely comprehensible in the context of the bad-tempered 'Cockney School of Poetry' controversy: 'One object that I had in view, when I wrote these "Scenes", was to try the effect of a more natural style than that which has for a long time prevailed in our dramatic literature. I have endeavoured to mingle poetic imagery with expressions of natural emotion' (p. vii).

Cornwall's claim to utilize a more 'natural' mode of expression, a poetics that everyone was in principle qualified to enjoy, amply illustrates what Jon Klancher in *The Making of English Reading Audiences* views as a collective project by Romantic authors to 'elaborate new relations *between* the individual reader and the collective audience'.[59] Cornwall interpellates his readers, configuring them as constituents of a mass audience. His work reassures book-buyers about their competency as readers. As we shall see, Peacock accused Cornwall of peddling 'easily-intelligible ... mawkish sentiment' to an undiscerning public.[60] But this charge misses the point, since in addition to boosting sales, Cornwall's 'easily-intelligible' mix of impassioned dialogue, fruity badinage and gothic schlock was conceived within the context of a wider anti-élitist 'Cockney School' literary project, a solemn undertaking in which Hunt and at various junctures Keats are also enrolled. Cornwall's liberal aesthetic could be said to offer an antidote to the rarified cultural and semantic fields favoured by Shelley and Peacock, for whom the political and imaginative liberation of readers often appears as an ideal to be imposed from above, rather than negotiated from a popular base. Shelley famously envisaged the audience of *Prometheus Unbound* as comprising at most half a dozen (II, 388). These select readers, as Klancher points out, could only include those whose intertextual frame was 'Aeschylean mythography rather than plebeian radical journalism'.[61] Cornwall, on the other hand, unabash-edly aimed at, even as he sought in the process to constitute, emerging mass audiences, selling large numbers of 'easily-intelligible' texts to an eager public, confident that a reformed poetic language would have beneficial workings out among its readers. Echoing Peacock's condescension, Ayumi Mizukoshi dismisses Cornwall's works as 'easy to read' – as if ease of consumption in itself somehow removes art from serious consideration.[62] Cornwall would not have objected to such descriptions of his poetry.

We gain an insight into Cornwall's extraordinary attraction for early nineteenth-century readers by considering a pair of tour-de-force cadenzas from the title piece of *Marcian Colonna* (1820). The first extract opens Part 7:

> O thou vast Ocean! Ever sounding Sea!
> Thou symbol of a drear immensity!
> Thou thing that windest round the solid world
> Like a huge animal, which, downward hurl'd
> From the black clouds, lies weltering and alone,
> Lashing and writhing till its strength be gone.
>   (*Marcian Colonna*, p. 73)

A critic for the *New Monthly Magazine* rhapsodized that Cornwall's lashing apostrophe to the ocean was the 'finest, vastest piece of contemplative imagination ever embodied' by the poet, and professed to prefer its weltering sublimities even to those of Byron's *Childe Harold*.[63] (A critic for the *Monthly Review*, on the other hand, worried that the lines were 'far-fetched and over-charged'.)[64] The address is a striking instance of Cornwall's skill in handling sublime register. If the lines recall the frequencies of Keats's own work, they illustrate my earlier point that Cornwall lodges his strongest appeal to modern audiences when he approaches the hallmarks of Keats's own style – a version of Keats evacuated of any troubling 'boyishness'; we often forget that even when book-sellers received copies of Cornwall's third collection, *Marcian Colonna*, the most *maturely* 'Keatsian' author available to early nineteenth-century readers was 'Barry Cornwall'. Keats's *Lamia* volume didn't appear for another couple of months, and until then 'Keats' signified either the juvenilia of *Poems* (1817) or the failed 'adolescent' experiment of *Endymion* (1818), with its bafflingly daedal plot.

Although *Blackwood's* initially presented Cornwall's volumes as a tonic for performances such as *Endymion*, Cornwall was a responsive reader of his rival's work. For all Cornwall's insistence in a letter to Charles Ollier that he was innocent of plagiarizing *Endymion* in 'The Marriage of Peleus and Thetis', key words and phrases from Keats's poem re-surface in the celebrated apostrophe to the ocean in *Marcian Colonna*.[65] For instance, Keats had already coupled 'immensity' and 'sea' (a Cockneyish rhyme, certainly) in *Endymion*, and had similarly centred his couplet on a 'symbol':

> Be still a symbol of immensity;
> A firmament reflected in a sea
>   (*Endymion*, I, 299–300)

> O thou vast Ocean! Ever sounding Sea!
> Thou symbol of a drear immensity!
>   (*Marcian Colonna*, p. 73)

In 1935, Armour observed that Cornwall often 'came close to the manner of Keats, either through conscious imitation or through the coincidence of poetic training based on the same models' (p. 153). As he points out, a miscellaneous Cornwall poem, 'A Voice', included in the *Marcian Colonna* volume, but first printed in Hunt's *Indicator* as 'Vox et Praeterea Nihil' (signed 'XXX'), was included by Harry Buxton Forman in his 1883 edition of Keats as a note to *Endymion*, Book 2, lines 849–50. Confused as to the provenance of the 34 lines, and failing to notice their appearance in *Marcian*

Colonna – by the 1880s, Cornwall's early poetry was practically invisible –
Forman glossed the lines as a passage rejected by Keats for final inclusion in
his epic apprentice piece.[66]

We might consider in a similar light a second, now equally obscure
Cornwall poem, 'The Fall of Saturn: A Vision', published in the poet's
ill-received fourth volume, *The Flood of Thessaly* (1823). Inscribed to Charles
Lamb, it reworks the same classical myth that inspired both Keats's attempts
at the Hyperion story:

> A dream? – what is it – a birth or death
> Of thought? – 'tis whatever the poet saith:
> A figure (a prophecy) dark or dumb
> Yet breathing a tale of the vast 'to come' –
> ('The Fall of Saturn', pp. 165–66)

These lines converge sonorously with Keats's *The Fall of Hyperion*, and can be
compared with the dreamer-poet's first encounter with Moneta:

> Who alive can say,
> 'Thou art no Poet – mayst not tell thy dreams'?
> Since every man whose soul is not a clod
> Hath visions, and would speak, if he had loved
> And been well nurtured in his mother tongue.
> (*The Fall of Hyperion*, I, 11–15)

Both men ruminate in similar interrogative mode on poetic articulacy,
dumbness, prophecy and vision. Intriguingly, *The Fall of Hyperion* did not
appear in print until Richard Monckton Milnes published it as 'Another
Version of Keats's Hyperion' in *Biographical and Historical Miscellanies of
the Philobiblon Society*, 1856–57 (1856). The poem was 'given up' at some
point around 21 September 1819, although Keats probably tinkered with it
after this date.[67] There's no evidence that Cornwall read Keats's manuscript
fragment before embarking on his own treatment of the overthrown Titans'
plight; none the less, suggestive parallels between the two passages at
least leave open the possibility that he may have seen Keats's poem as an
inner-circle member of the 'Cockney School' coterie described by Roe and
Cox. Quite aside from the issue of whether Cornwall had access to Keats's
poems in manuscript, it becomes clear that Keats's early style was not only
modulated around Hunt's Cockney aesthetic in poems such as *The Story of
Rimini* (1816), but that his work throughout his career was also conditioned
by the successful cadences of other writers associated with the radical editor,
key among them 'Barry Cornwall'.

Returning to the subject of Cornwall's popular appeal, a further highlight in *Marcian Colonna* occurs at the opening of Part 8, which supplies a lurid description of the protagonists's ill-fated flight by sea:

8
And now – wither are gone the lovers now?
Colonna, wearest thou anguish on thy brow,
And is the valour of the moment gone?
Fair Julia, thou art smiling now alone:
The hero and the husband weeps at last –
Alas, alas! and lo! he stands aghast,
Bankrupt in every hope, and silently gasps
Like one who maddens. Hark! the timbers part
And the sea-billows come, and still he clasps
His pale pale beauty, closer to his heart,   10
The ship has struck. One kiss – the last – Love's own.
– They plunge into the waters and are gone.
The vessel sinks, – 'tis vanished, and the sea
Rolls boiling o'er the wreck triumphantly,
And shrieks are heard and cries, and then short groans,
Which the waves stifle quick, and doubtful tones
Like the faint moanings of the wind pass by,
And horrid gurgling sounds rise up and die,
And noises like the choaking of man's breath –
– But why prolong the tale – it is of death.
        (*Marcian Colonna*, p. 76)

Armour experienced his own sinking feeling on encountering this passage. He judged line 6 only the worst of several instances where 'words are unnecessarily repeated to fill up the metre' (p. 151; although he avoids mentioning Keats's similarly lamenting line from *Isabella*: 'I am a shadow now, alas! alas!', l. 305).

Armour's condescension stems in part from an insensitivity towards Cornwall's stylistic trademarks. What Armour interprets as a capsizing inability to locate synonyms could equally be perceived as a deft manoeuvre aimed at conveying Julia's and Marcian's disorientation in the storm's teeth. Another way of looking at things would be to say that Cornwall is willing to countenance a certain amount of semantic redundancy to sustain dramatic momentum, a compromise often struck by Byron, his poetic hero, whose epic tale of jeopardous love, *Don Juan*, abounds with similar instances of metre-filling and contingent or near-arbitrary rhymes.[68] Besides, Armour fails to pick a convincing example of Cornwall's 'fault'. Line 6 is *anything*

but redundant, fizzing with sibilant slant-rhymes ('alas'/'aghast'), and conso-
nance ('l' sounds in 'alas' and 'lo'), where Armour's repeat offender 'alas' also
echoes the preceding line's plangent (and doubly) final phrase 'at last'.

In the *Edinburgh Review*, Jeffrey cooed that *Marcian Colonna*'s shipwreck
scene with its dramatic shifts was 'the most powerful piece of poetry that
has yet proceeded from Mr Cornwall's pen – and might do honour to any
name that now graces our literature'.[69] It is perhaps still possible to appreciate why this plungingly elegiac passage received plaudits from public and
critics alike. The rapidly unfolding disaster at sea, narrated to convey an
impression of 'real time', showcases Cornwall's facility with narrative tempo.
Even the punctuation at lines 13–20 is virtuosic: readers, forced to snatch
breath in the staccato pauses, are virtually obliged to perform the drowning
lovers' 'choaking'. Cornwall is also singularly adept at handling mobility of
viewpoint. His cinematic eye pans and zooms energetically, focusing on the
heroine's smile, then moving to capture the cracking timbers of the vessel,
returning for a close-angled view of the couple's farewell kiss, before pulling
perpendicularly above the scene to gaze down on the ship as it vanishes
beneath the waves, the rolling sea 'boiling o'er the wreck triumphantly'. The
scene's aural textures are similarly arresting. Cornwall regales the ear with
'shrieks' and 'cries', which 'are heard' passively, making the protagonists seem
even further out of reach and beyond help. To this melancholy cacophony
Cornwall adds a variety of 'short groans', 'doubtful tones' and the gothicky
sensational 'horrid gurgling sounds'. At this point the narrative persona inter-
jects – although without interceding – to pose rhetorically: 'why prolong
the tale'? With perfect timing, Cornwall prolongs it just long enough.

The success of this passage derives from Cornwall's skill with poetic narrative at a time when an increased demand for poetry was steadily cohering
around the popularity of long poems and verse romance.[70] As Andrew
Bennett suggests, late-Romantic authors were 'consciously and explicitly
concerned ... with the nature of story-telling and of both the poet's and
the readers' relationship with the poetic story'.[71] The excerpt from *Marcian
Colonna* illustrates how Cornwall is deftly attuned to this relation. Where
Keats petulantly accused readers of failing to respond 'properly' to his
work, Cornwall obviates such fundamental problems with a range of narrative strategies expressly aimed at keeping audiences correctly aligned to his
story. He supplies 'locating' questions ('whither are gone the lovers now?'),
interlacing into the narrative what are essentially stage directions ('shrieks
are heard and cries') to gate readers into an appropriate gothic mode of
enjoying his tale. *Marcian Colonna* is closely focused on what Bennett

calls the 'inescapable function of audience in narrative'. Keats, who found himself operating within Bourdieu's 'autonomous' category, also wanted to provide reading pleasure; but this desire is 'fissured' in Bennett's terms by an overwhelming consciousness of an audience that 'does not or will not read the poems of Wordsworth, Coleridge, Shelley and Keats, and which these poets tend increasingly to think of as degraded and therefore unworthy anyway' (p. 24). We get little sense of such fissuring in Cornwall's shipwreck scene. On the contrary, *Marcian Colonna* seems acutely self-conscious of its status as a text conceived for, and explicitly designed to facilitate its own, popular consumption.

There's an irony attached to Cornwall's success in the literary market, viewed against Keats's failure. Whether due to conscious imitation of Keats or analogous contact with a set of related ideas and themes associated with Hunt's literary and political circle, Cornwall offered reading audiences stylistic features that were closely confluent with Keats's own poetics. By assimilating more acceptable components of Keats's challenging style, by investing figures from classical mythology with human traits and emotions, deploying a more colloquial diction, and incorporating and developing elements of Hunt's (and Wordsworth's) experiments with speech representation and other technical aspects of composition, Cornwall successfully commodified 'Cockney School' aesthetics. In stark contrast, Keats was rejected by wider audiences and critics alike for his 'vulgar' innovation and juvenile breaches of taste. By popularizing a filtered version of 'Cockney' Romanticism, Cornwall rendered Keats's exaggerated form of what now looked to early nineteenth-century readers like 'Cornwallean' style ludicrous, affected or simply beyond the pale. In a direct sense, then, Cornwall's fashionability had the effect of helping to exclude writers like Keats and Shelley from literary commodity culture. It wasn't until Cornwall's modish cadences had paled decisively in readers' eyes that Keats's more vibrant poetry began to take hold in the public's imagination.

4. 'The Pictured Scene': A Sicilian Story and Isabella

If Keats longed to reach the purchasing power of mass audience – Charles Brown's last letter to Keats gamely reassures his dejected friend that the *Lamia* volume was at last beginning to 'increase in sales' – he was in two minds about what participating more fully in the commercial culture embraced by Cornwall would mean for the status of his art. The self-sabotaging effects of his ambivalence are thrown into bold relief in *Isabella*, read against the hurtling poetics of Cornwall's cognate transposition of Boccaccio. Revelling in its theme of exhumation and derangement, while strategically toning down aspects of the original narrative, Cornwall's *A Sicilian Story* culminates spectacularly in Isabel's trepidatious journey through lava-strewn landscapes to recover her lover's mangled body. With its sensational lexis, the poem caught the mood of the moment, prompting *Monthly Review* eulogies on Cornwall's 'splendid imagery'.[72]

Kurz Heinzelman's essay on *Isabella* and 'self-interest' conducts a rare side-by-side analysis of Keats and Cornwall. However, by ignoring the question of why Cornwall was able to steal Keats's plaudits, moreover in a straight contest, Heinzelman's discussion is locked into the consensus of critical opinion vis-à-vis assumptions of Cornwall's insignificance in Romantic literary culture. Heinzelman adheres to a familiar narrative, dismissing *A Sicilian Story*'s 'simple moralizing' at the same time as he discovers value-added layers of complexity in Keats's parallel work.[73] Unlike *Isabella*, then, which offers a critique of the 'economics of literary modernity', we're told that *A Sicilian Story* is 'little concerned with socioeconomic arrangements' (p. 172). From an important perspective, Heinzelman is absolutely right: not only is Cornwall uninterested in the socioeconomic tensions between Guido and Isabel's brother, but in a review of his rival in the *Edinburgh Magazine and Literary Miscellany* (examined in Chapter 2), Cornwall, in concert with several Romantic as well as more recent commentators, specifically objected to Keats's 'bad taste' in deploying terms such as '"money-bags," "ledger-men," &c. which injures, in some respects, this delightful story'.[74] All the same, the grounds on which Cornwall's poem engages *Isabella*, the work Keats both hoped would and would not represent his market breakthrough after the disastrous reception of *Endymion*, is precisely the crude economic question of the marketplace.[75] Heinzelman may be right to ascribe greater self-recursive density to Keats's poem.[76] Nevertheless, *A Sicilian Story* also reflects on its status within Romantic print culture, carefully calibrating its narrative to prevailing tastes. Cornwall's talent for communicating the right *kind* of 'feeling' is abundantly evident in the oneiric scene where Guido's ghost instructs Isabel to retrieve his battered body:

> Her sleep that night was fearful, – O, that night!
> If it indeed was sleep: for in her sight
> A form (a dim and waving shadow) stood,
> And pointed far up the great Etna's side,
> Where, from a black ravine, a dreary wood

Peeps out and frowns upon the storms below,
And bounds and braves the wilderness of snow.
It gazed awhile upon the lonely bride
With melancholy air and glassy eye,
And spoke – 'Awake and search yon dell, for I,
'Tho' risen above my old mortality,
'Have left my mangled and unburied limbs
'A prey for wolves.'[77]

Blackwood's applauded the agreeably horrid scene, slipping enthusiastically into the vivid heat of Cornwall's gothic idiom:

> A murdered body never lay in a more fitting place. There is something mean and miserable about an outstretched corpse lying bloody and gashed and mangled on the common earth. Murder *ought* to be perpetrated in such wild and savage solitudes ... Places of fear – the haunts of wild beasts – of men more fell than they – of the wild agencies of nature.[78]

Maga also endorsed Cornwall's treatment of Isabel's eventual discovery of her lover's corpse:

> Every step Isabel took farther down and down into this ravine, must have dashed her soul with deeper terror. Yet even there she must have imagined that hope could dwell. – And our readers will not fail to be delighted with the knowledge that Mr Cornwall here shews of the human heart. Love will not believe in death until she sees it in his own glazed eyes. (p. 645)

The banked-down emotions of Cornwall's centrepiece scene are similarly impressive, and the 'pay-off' disclosure of the body's mangled condition skilfully deferred. With perfect timing, the second iteration of 'And there she saw him –' ends with a single word: 'dead' (the dolorous 'd's at the end of 'sod' and 'trod', and at the beginning of 'dell', proleptically preparing readers for the fatal syllable):

> Down the slippery sod
> With trembling limbs, and heart that scarcely beat,
> And catching at the brambles, as her feet
> Sunk in the crumbling earth, the poor girl trod;
> And there she saw – Oh! till that moment none
> Could tell (not she) how much of hope the sun
> And cheerful morning, with its noises, brought,
> And how she from each glance a courage caught;
> For light and life had scattered half her fright,
> And she could almost smile on the past night;

So, with a buoyant feeling, mixed with fear
Lest she might scorn heav'n's missioned minister,
She took her weary way and searched the dell,
And there she saw him – dead. Poor desolate child
Of sixteen summers, had the waters wild
No pity on the boy you loved so well!
There stiff and cold the dark-eyed Guido lay,
His pale face upwards to the careless day,
That smiled as it was wont; and he was found
His young limbs mangled on the rocky ground,
And, 'midst the weltering weeds and shallows cold,
His black hair floated as the phantom told,
And like the very dream his glassy eye
Spoke of gone mortality.
          (*A Sicilian Story*, p. 19)

And yet, for all the gothic accoutrements of 'glassy eyes', 'mangled' limbs
and sleep-disturbing 'phantoms', which do an effective job of eliciting a
grisly *frisson*, Cornwall's narrative skirts any genuinely unsettling territory.
From the outset, Cornwall has sanitized Boccaccio's tale, substituting the
original's buried head with a sentimental buried heart ('effortlessly' removed
from Guido's body, as Ralph Pite points out), diluting Boccaccio's original to
standard-issue melodrama:[79] 'I have ventured to substitute the heart for the
head of the lover. The latter appeared to me to be a ghastly object to preserve.'
Even Cornwall's tableau of Isabel's final psychological breakdown is cannily
decolourized. Lacking the visceral power to disturb of Wordsworth's étude
in mental anguish, 'The Thorn', it rarely threatens to perturb conventional
tropes of Ophelia-like love–madness:

And then into the dreary wilderness
She went alone, a craz'd, heart-broken thing;
And in the solitude she found a cave
Half hidden by the wild-brier blossoming,
Whereby a black and solitary pine,
Struck by the fiery thunder, stood, and gave
Of pow'r and death a token and a sign:
And there she lived for months: She did not heed
The seasons or their change, and she would feed
On roots and berries as the creatures fed
Which had in woods been born and nourished.

Once, and once only was she seen, and then
The chamois hunter started from his chace,

And stopped to look a moment on her face,
And could not turn him to his sports again.
Thin Famine sate upon her hollow cheek,
And settled Madness in her glazed eye
Told of a young heart wrong'd and nigh to break,
And, as the spent winds waver ere they die,
She to herself a few wild words did speak,
And sung a strange and broken melody;
And ever as she sung she strew'd the ground
With yellow leaves that perished 'ere their time,
And well their fluttering fall did seem to chime
With the low music of her song: –
    (*A Sicilian Story*, pp. 23–24)

The sonorousness of these lines is purposefully flattening, the effect being to aestheticize (and anaesthetize) psychic damage.

Heinzelman does, however, isolate an important reason why early nineteenth-century readers elected the 'simplistic' Cornwall over his more sophisticated peer. While he insists that Cornwall 'dulls' the 'politico-economic aura' of Boccaccio's tale by collapsing the original's three brothers into one villainous sibling (a gross simplification of Boccaccio, in his opinion), he acknowledges that by rationing the poem's characters in this way Cornwall generates a significant gain in emotional dynamics: 'Because of the brother's singular relationship to his sister ... the murder of her beloved becomes shaded with incestuous jealousy' (p. 172). From a narrative point of view, also, a single brother is arguably more effective than the pair opted for by Keats. In Maurice Ridley's view, Keats, with his long preamble, has in any case already fluffed the most basic element of *Isabella*: the storytelling. Kelvin Everest agrees that Keats's narrative is 'oddly proportioned', devoting 'too much time to the opening introductory account of the young lovers' (p. 109). By telling contrast, Cornwall's *in medias res* opening plunges pell-mell into the torrid tale. When we consider the confident forward dynamics of *A Sicilian Story* next to Keats's less assured treatment of Boccaccio, it becomes clearer why audiences put aside *Isabella* for the more immediate gratifications of Cornwall's tale. And yet, in an otherwise very good book focused on Romantic verse narratives, Hermann Fischer finds space for just one, brief and disparaging footnote on Cornwall's once-celebrated romance.[80]

Just as Cornwall's erotic verse titillated audiences without ever, quite, offending decorum, his similarly soft-focused portrait of madness and murder in *A Sicilian Story* excited readers while insulating them from the real and dislocating horrors of mental infirmity, the gothic shocks always tempered, as Jeffrey reassured *Edinburgh Review* subscribers, by Cornwall's customary pitch-perfect 'taste and judgement'.[81] Keats was more than half in love with Cornwall's style, but experienced cold feet when it came to pursuing a popularist aesthetic to its logical conclusion, anxious that too much syrupy sentiment in *Isabella* could do no more than win for his poem a 'mawkish popularity'. This mode of acclaim he professed to despise, invoking myths of higher calling, deferred audiences and fantasies of 'being among the English Poets' after his death (*LJK*, I, 267). Although *Isabella* had the potential to be his most marketable poem to date, Keats's feelings towards it were conflicted; he believed it guilty of emotional string-pulling and began, as George Yost notes, 'to distrust its emotional impact on the reader'.[82] For his part, Richard Woodhouse, Keats's go-between with publisher John Taylor, was unable to detect any 'sugar & butter sentiment'. None the less, for Keats the 'weak-sided' *Isabella* was an artistic compromise that he quickly came to resent.

If Keats clung to an ideal of elevated art, his conviction of superior calling was lost on the majority of Romantic reviewers. Charles Lamb may have thought *Isabella* the 'finest thing' in the *Lamia* volume (*New Times*, 19 July 1820), but in the *Eclectic Review*'s adjudication Cornwall's transposition of Boccaccio contained 'better poetry and more feeling' (p. 333). The anonymous critic gave short shift to the 'high'/'low' cultural division that overshadows modern, Keats-oriented evaluations:

> There are some persons, we understand, who, indignant at the comparison, will have it that the [*sic*] Keats is the unspeakably loftier poet, the more classical genius of the two ... We must remark that, on the one hand, the name of Barry Cornwall has not yet been affixed to anything half so absurd as Endymion, and that, on the other hand, the author of Endymion has never yet produced anything comparable in genuine delicacy, sweetness and pathos to the following stanzas [reprints Cornwall's 'Woman'] [83]

The *Monthly Review* saw things similarly. In a back-to-back review of the *Lamia* volume and *Marcian Colonna*, *Isabella* was pronounced the 'worst part' of Keats's 1820 collection. Ill-aligned towards all faux-Italian romances, especially those by 'Cockney' writers, the reviewer nevertheless recommended Cornwall's reworking of Boccaccio's fable as 'superior to Mr. Keats's attempt'.[84]

Keats was ideally placed to write about women whose senses were deranged through grief. After 1793, Guy's Hospital Committee only admitted female patients to the lunatic ward; Keats, as Goellnicht points out, 'was required to treat these women in his capacity as dresser' in the hospital (p. 191). To be sure, *Isabella* registers Keats's interest in mental ailments typically associated with women, such as the newly coined 'monomania', a category of melancholia with features of what would now be classed as 'obsessive compulsive disorder':

> Piteous she looked on dead and senseless things,
>   Asking for her lost basil amorously:
> And with melodious chuckle in the strings
>   Of her lorn voice, she oftentimes would cry
> After the pilgrim in his wanderings,
>   To ask him where her basil was, and why
> 'Twas hid from her: 'For cruel 'tis', said she,
> 'To steal my basil-pot away from me'.
>
> And so she pined, and so she died forlorn,
>   Imploring for her basil to the last.
> No heart was there in Florence but did mourn
>   In pity of her love, so overcast.
> And a sad ditty of this story born
>   From mouth to mouth through all the country passed:
> Still is the burthen sung – 'O cruelty,
> 'To steal my basil-pot away from me!'
>   (*Isabella*, ll. 489–504)

Medically informed though this passage is, however, Keats actually presents a conventionally sentimental treatment of the familiar 'Orphelia' motif. Wordsworth does far more to open salutary ironic distance from the trope in 'The Thorn'. On the other hand, it's precisely when Keats departs from normative gothic and sentimental templates that his bid for commercial success falters most decisively. Take the loamy details that come to light with Isabella's discovery of the murdered Lorenzo, whose gradual unearthing is narrated with what Kelvin Everest acknowledges as a 'frank eroticism' (p. 122) – of a different genus altogether from conventionally horrid descriptions of 'yawning' tombs, the passage shifts the poem into hitherto unprepared for territories:

> Then with her knife, all sudden, she began
> To dig more fervently than misers can.
>
> Soon she turned up a soilèd glove, whereon
>   Her silk had played in purple phantasies,
> She kissed it with a lip more chill than stone,
>   And put it in her bosom, where it dries
> And freezes utterly unto the bone

> Those dainties made to still an infant's cries:
> Then 'gan she work again; nor stayed her care,
> But to throw back at times her veiling hair.
> (*Isabella*, ll. 367–76)

Jack Stillinger notes that *Isabella* is really an anti-romance, 'an attempt at a tough-minded modern recasting' of his Italian source, where 'courtly love gives way to psychology'.[86] Expanding this insight, Andrew Bennett identifies a curious 'pathology' at the poem's 'hidden centre': 'Inside both the pot of basil and "The Pot of Basil" [Keats's original name for his romance] is an uncontainable, scandalous, terrifying, and gruesome secret'.[86] This secret, I suggested in *Keats's Boyish Imagination* (2004), is nothing other, or nothing less 'other', than Isabella's genital reality, which forces Keats to confront his own, rather than just his poem's, 'inexperience of life'. Goellnicht argues that Isabella's decapitation of Lorenzo 'smacks of anatomical dissection' (p. 113). To rehearse my earlier argument in a new context, traces of surgical procedure are if anything more disturbingly evident in Lorenzo's second exhumation:

> ... they contrived to steal the basil-pot,
>   And to examine it in secret place:
> The thing was vile with green and livid spot
>   (*Isabella*, ll. 473–75)

These lines have a specific, if surprising, medical 'source'. In Chapter 3 of *The Dissector's Manual* (1820) compiled by Keats's anatomy instructor, Joseph Henry Green – his last name is significant – immediately following a full-page engraving of a dissected vagina, we find the following description: 'The vagina is lined by a *mucous membrane* of a greyish colour, often interspersed with livid spots' (*The Dissector's Manual*, p. 189). Keats used Green's 1815 *Outlines of a Course of Dissections*, rather than his expanded volume of 1820, and the above citation is absent from *Outlines*. All the same, given that the *Dissector's Manual* simply comprises a more comprehensive version of Green's anatomy lectures at Guy's, it is entirely possible, likely even, that Keats heard and mentally noted Green's description of the vagina as it would shortly appear in his manual. Line 475 of *Isabella*, I suggest, owes a great deal to Green's lectures; Keats even mischievously acknowledges the debt by incorporating his demonstrator's name into it: 'vile with *green* and livid spot' (my emphasis).

Whereas Cornwall successfully parlays his legal expertise on the subject of love-derangement into saleable portraits of lunacy, Keats's medical knowledge opens a more troubling window into areas of human psychology from which audiences seemed to have recoiled queasily and instinctively. Modern criticism generally takes Lorenzo's severed head to be an image of phallic castration; the possibility that the head for Keats is freighted with the memory of a medical description of the vagina, as I first suggested in *Keats's Boyish Imagination*, throws things in a rather different light. 'Vile with green and livid spot' becomes (in both senses) a Guy's in-joke, marking a troubling locus of anxiety. Even though *Isabella*'s readers can hardly be supposed to have been familiar with Green's dissection primer, the semantic environment alone in one of the poem's pivotal stanzas, with its furtive examinations, secret places and vileness, communicates something unmistakably disconcerting. At any rate, echoes of genital anxiety in *Isabella* – whether heard or silently audited – radically complicate the ways in which the public could enjoy, or fail to enjoy, Keats's 'commercial' romance, whose double-mindedness about its own bid for popular appeal is encoded at a number of reciprocally complicating levels.

5. 'Drivelling Doggerel': Cornwall and Shelley's *A Defence of Poetry*

Even in its heyday, not all readers were smitten with the popular panache of Cornwall's poetry. Thomas Love Peacock, with whom Keats spent an evening at Hunt's house in February 1818, regarded the *au courant* poet as the prime example of a new breed of writer whose success was due to, as well as an exacerbatory factor in, the vitiated condition of public taste. Peacock elaborated his aversion in a spiky epistle to Percy Shelley on 4 December 1820:

> Considering poetical reputation as a prize to be obtained by a certain species of exertion, and that the sort of thing which obtains this prize <is> the drivelling doggerel published under <the name of> Barry Cornwall, I think <the> conclusio<n is inevita>ble, that to a rational ambition poetical <reputation> is not only not to be desired bu<t most> earnestly to be deprecated. The truth, I <am co>nvinced, is, that there is no longer a poetical audience among the higher class of minds, that moral poetical & physical science have entirely withdrawn from poetry the attention of all whose attention is worth having, and that, the poetical reading public being composed of the mere dregs of the intellectual community, the most sufficing passport to their favor must rest on the mixture of a little easily intelligible fiction & mawkish sentiment with an absolute negation of reason and knowledge. These I take to be the prime and sole elements of Mr Barry Cornwall's madrigals.[87]

The tension Bourdieu describes between 'heteronomous' and 'autonomous' art is paradigmatically evident here. In fact, Peacock's own sense of the divide, pulled into sharp relief by the grating fact of Cornwall's celebrity, prompted him to write his polemical essay *The Four Ages of Poetry* (1820) in protest against the kind of low-status poetical effusions epitomized for him by Cornwall's 'drivelling doggerel'. In Peacock's eyes, Cornwall's popularity simply confirmed that *all* contemporary poetry had relinquished any relevance it might once have possessed in the ongoing project of societal improvement, an undertaking that Peacock insisted was now best left to the 'sciences of morals and of mind'.[88]

Shelley, self-exiled, smarting from the poor reception of his work in England ('enough to damp any man's enthusiasm'; *LPBS*, II, 245), agreed wholeheartedly with Peacock on the subject of Cornwall's merits, or singular lack of them. His animated reply to Peacock on 15 February 1821 culminates in a vehement sally against his fashionable contemporary (and Ollier bros stablemate):

> I have received ... your printed denunciations [Peacock's essay *The Four Ages of Poetry*] against general, and your written ones [Peacock's letter of 4 December 1820 denouncing Cornwall] against particular poetry; and I agree with you as decidedly in the latter as I differ in the former. The man whose critical gall is not stirred up by such *ottava rimas* as Barry Cornwall's, may safely be conjectured to possess no gall at all. The world is pale with the sickness of such stuff. At the same time, your anathemas against poetry itself excited me to a sacred rage ... of vindicating the insulted Muses. (*LPBS*, II, 261)

Shelley, however, registers a vital divergence of opinion over his friend's larger contention that *genuine* (Bourdieu's 'autonomous') poetry no longer had a role to play in the continued progress of civilization. His formal response to Peacock's letters and essay, *A Defence of Poetry* (1821), insists on the continued relevance and innate transformative value of poetry and poetic community. Cornwall isn't mentioned by name in Shelley's famous treatise; nevertheless, *A Defence of Poetry* – one of Romanticism's most urgent manifestos – owes its genesis in significant part to an exchange of letters between Shelley and his agent Peacock that focused on the problem of Cornwall's poetry, and which culminated in both men's horror-struck reaction to *Mirandola*'s triumphant Covent Garden staging in January 1821. Indeed, the news that Cornwall's play had taken London by storm was final confirmation for Shelley of the poverty of contemporary taste. Issues given new edge by Cornwall's popular hit, then, materially help to crystallize for Shelley his views on 'genuine' poetry, audience and public taste.[89]

Charles E. Robinson argues that Charles Ollier, the only publisher prepared to take on the scandalous tragedy *The Cenci*, 'served Shelley at least as well as he could, given the popular literary taste that preferred Procter's verses to Shelley's during this time' (p. 213). Even Ollier's willingness to elevate artistic concerns above financial considerations had its limits, however, and in the summer of 1820 he declined to print a second edition of the play. A recently rediscovered letter of 27 August 1820 reveals Shelley attempting, fruitlessly, to persuade Ollier that his notorious drama could still turn a profit: 'Prometheus ... is intended only for the esoteric readers of poetry, – but indeed the Cenci ought to sell'.[90] There's little doubt that Shelley's aversion toward Ollier's star writer is partially rooted in the circumstance that while Cornwall's poems were rushed into new editions (as little as five months separate the first and second editions of *A Sicilian Story*), Shelley's own work was effectively shelved by Ollier.[91] Such disparity of treatment led inevitably to strained relations. On 16 June 1821, writing to inquire whether Ollier would consider publishing John Taaffe's translation of *The Divine Comedy*, Shelley was unable to resist a snide aside: 'I know you will not take my opinion on Poetry; because I thought my own verses very good, & *you* find that the public declare them to be unreadable. Show it to Mr. Procter, who is far better qualified to judge than I am' (II, 303). *Prometheus Unbound* may not be 'unreadable', but it was unsaleable. As Robinson points out in his recent *DNB* entry for Ollier, when the brothers went bankrupt in 1822–23, selling the firm's complete inventory on 5–11 March 1823, 288 unsold copies of Shelley's poem remained in quires.[111]

Self-exiled in Pisa, Shelley focused his disappointment and frustration on Cornwall. Corresponding with Peacock on 21 March 1821, finding fault with the boxes of literary first-aid regularly sent out to him from England, Shelley carps that his well-meaning friends ought to read *The Four Ages of Poetry*: the worst thing about the consignments, Shelley grumbles, was that they always seemed to contain some or other of Cornwall's 'trashy' verses:

> I had much rather, for my private reading, receive political geological and moral treatises than this stuff in terza, ottava, & tremilesima rima, whose earthly baseness has attracted the lightning of your indiscriminating censure upon the temples of immortal song. – ... Procter's [Cornwall's] verses enrage me far more than those of Codrus did Juvenal: & with better reason ... my boxes are packed with this trash. (*LPBS*, II, 276)[93]

Put simply, Cornwall's success – Cornwall per se – rattled Shelley.

Shelley's opinion of the fashionable poet was categorically at variance with the view of most early nineteenth-century readers. Then again, Shelley was perhaps willfully out of touch with contemporary poetic taste: as he reported to Peacock on 8 November 1820, 'I have been reading nothing but Greek and Spanish. Plato and Calderon have been my gods' (*LPBS*, II, 245). Even though Shelley fantasized to Ollier about the possibility of soliciting a wider audience for *The Cenci*, elsewhere his jaundiced view of mass readership is clear. An earlier letter to his publisher in August 1818 confiding his high hopes for *Rosalind and Helen* (1819) sounds its own note of caution: 'I cannot expect that that prig the public will descend to desert its wines and drink a drop of dew so evanescent' (*LPBS*, I, 31).

For all Shelley's and Peacock's condescension, Cornwall's sensational 'verse dramas', embellished with gothic furniments and fashionably lurid inlay, flew off book-sellers' shelves. Eager audiences were also flocking to *Mirandola*. An animated review of the play in the *London Magazine* (in all probability biased due to Cornwall's links with the journal as a contributor), trumpeted that 'nothing possibly could be more complete than its success', adding that 'the house was crowded to overflow on the first night; and the piece still runs with the same effect'.[94] Eighteen months earlier in July 1819, Shelley had asked Peacock to procure a Covent Garden staging for *The Cenci* (*LPBS*, II, 102). Gallingly, if predictably enough given the play's subject matter – incest – Peacock's petition bore no fruit. News of Cornwall's dramatic triumph at Covent Garden of all places must have grated, notwithstanding the fact that Shelley told Ollier through gritted teeth in February 1821: 'I am delighted to hear of Procter's success, and hope that he will proceed gathering laurels' (*LPBS*, II, 270). Keats also failed to get his tragedy on a tenth-century Holy Roman Emperor, *Otho the Great*, performed at Covent Garden, having likewise envisaged Macready in the lead role. Cornwall was aware of the fervidity with which rival poets – including Ollier stablemates such as Shelley and Keats – were trying to break into the Covent Garden schedule. In his appraisal of Cornwall for the *Fortnightly Review*, published in 1876 shortly after the poet's death, George Simcox recalled a remark that Cornwall had made about *Mirandola*:

> 'Had I taken pains I could have made a much more sterling thing; but I wished for its representation, and there were so many authors struggling for the same object that I allowed the play to appear, while I was conscious of its many shortcomings'.[95]

Close to death in Rome at the beginning of 1821, Keats is unlikely to have heard about the play's more than respectable run; but he was certainly aware that Cornwall's tragedy was due to be staged. As I noted in my Introduction, jealousy towards Cornwall produced some vinegarish correspondence between Keats and his co-dramatist, Charles Brown. Brown was the author of a comic opera, *Narensky, or, The Road to Yaroslaf*, which had been produced at Drury Lane in January 1814. The piece had turned £300 in profits, raising Keats's hopes that his collaboration with Brown would be similarly lucrative. In the light of *Otho the Great's* failure to get off the starting blocks, we can, perhaps, forgive Brown's uncharitable pun on Mirandola as 'Mire and O la!' (*LJK*, II, 366); equally, for all Keats's generosity of spirit, it would be unreasonable to expect intelligence of Cornwall's latest coup to have been received with much pleasure. It's not going too far to suggest that *Mirandola* would have represented to Keats a final nail in the coffin of his contemporary ambition.

The hit Cornwall's tragedy scored with the public was registered by the *Gentleman's Magazine*. On 9 January, it reported that the play was 'well written' and 'very successful';[96] the *Literary Gazette* also informed readers in similar tones that the play was performed with an 'éclat' and was 'eminently successful'.[97] On 10 January 1821, *Mirandola* received a positive notice in *The Times*, which praised Cornwall's 'colloquial ease' and 'pure taste' in scattering poetic gems throughout his drama.[98] The critic did, however, detect an inherently overblown quality about Cornwall's work, a dramatic excess that extended into the performances themselves: while Charles Kemble's 'spirited' turn as Mirandola's son Guido is lauded, the reviewer notes that 'in the last scene [Macready] fell into the very unusual error with him of overacting his part' (p. 3). The critic for *The Times* was likewise unsettled by the all too rare presence in the dramatis personae of a strong female character in the shape of the Duke's scheming sister, Isabella: 'It is repugnant to our best feelings to present any being on the stage, in female shape, with attributes so truly diabolical' (p. 3). We perhaps warm to Cornwall for the offence his play offered to such chauvinistic sentiments. In addition to female diabolism, *The Times* also recoiled at the play's 'gratuitous' depiction of 'villainy'. No doubt *because* it boasted wicked women and gratuitous violence, the play went into three printed editions that year. Together with sales of individual copies priced at 4s 6d, before the play 'passed away into the region of the moths' (in George Simcox's phrase), copyright on *Mirandola* earned Cornwall the sum of £630, according to his own calculations in *An Autobiographical Fragment* (p. 44).[99]

6. *The Flood of Thessaly*: The Tide Turns

In part due to what Chris Rojek has called the 'peculiar fragility of celebrity', and in part to insuperable impediments presented by 'Cockney School' allegiances, Cornwall's success came to an abrupt halt in 1823 with *The Flood of Thessaly*.[100] Two years earlier, with the successful but 'slip-slop' *Mirandola*, Cornwall had first tasted the undiluted ire of *Blackwood's*, who accused him of being a 'poacher on the domains of tragedy'. 'Forty stripes save one' was considered 'infinitely too good' a punishment for such a crime.[101] A passing reference to *The Flood of Thessaly* in the same journal earlier in 1823 had presaged the bursting of the dam. There Wilson had denounced Cornwall's persistent 'affectations' of Hunt-derived diction and Cockney pretensions in general:

> There is something surely not a little absurd in the notion of a person under-taking the 'Flood', whom the slightest shower would drive under a balcony, or into a hackney-coach. I have no doubt that [Cornwall] would carry 'The Deluge' in his pocket to Colburn,[102] under an umbrella.[103]

In the full-length review of *The Flood of Thessaly* that followed on its heels, Wilson, plainly exasperated by Cornwall's refusal to renounce Hunt, dismissed the 'very dull' volume for its preposterous Cockney 'Greekish'. Perhaps the most notorious statement in the entire 'Cockney School of Poetry' controversy – 'A hottentot in top-boots is not more ridiculous than a classical Cockney' – is directed at Cornwall for his free, often erroneous use of classical mythology.[104] One could speculate about whether Cornwall's change of publisher from Blackwood's friend Ollier to Henry Colburn in 1823 had some bearing on the magazine's newly hostile stance. The problem according to Wilson, however, lay with the fact that Cornwall 'sympathize[d] too closely with the lieges of Leigh the First', producing some of the 'most exquisite trash that was ever attempted to be foisted down the throats of reasonable animals'. Cornwall's 'go' at Greek mythology is judged as bad as 'Rimini Hunt himself, translating Theocritus', or 'John Keats celebrating Diana of the Ephesians' (p. 534). Hunt's baleful influence, the implacable Wilson insists, had distorted beyond recognition Cornwall's original talent for investing scenes with 'human passion': 'Is there any new, or any powerful, or any pathetic exhibition of human nature in it? – No. – Is there any inter-esting or skilful combination of incidents? – No – no. – Is there any story? – No. – Any passion? – No. All is frigid.'

The political thrust of such attacks is drawn into sharp context by a blistering 33-page letter addressed to Wilson in 1850 by R. L. Borradaile, a clerk in the Bank of England cheque office. In a lengthy harangue, Borradaile upbraids Wilson for his 'impudence & spitefulness', also for the 'wearisome sameness', of his attacks on Keats, Shelley, Hunt and Cornwall. In Cornwall's case, as with other poets 'given the epithet Cockney', Borradaile contends, the 'chief cause' of Wilson's sustained assault was 'very obviously, that this poet was a liberal, & you yourself a conservative'.[105] Borradaile expands on his sense of injustice:

> I must [...] remark on your treatment of this poet; as you have perhaps been more indefatigable in your hatred of him (disguised under a veil of lightness [&] ridicule, as is, indeed, most of your malevolence) than of any other poet. – How, indeed, you could have persisted in your coarse ridicule & abuse of him, so late even as the year 1838, is indeed a marvel to me. – Why, I myself should be ashamed to exist if I were to annoy & persecute a writer, (as you annoyed & persecuted his edition of Jonson,) in the manner in which you did, – & all for no better reason than that he differed from myself in political thinking. (14th of 33 pages)

Borradaile presented Wilson as a 'melancholy example of the length to which political prejudices & bigotry, aided by a savage & impetuous temper' could run.

He was not the only member of the public roused to leap to Cornwall's defence. An equally perturbed contributor to the American journal the *Southern Literary Messenger*, signed 'J. F. O.', similarly protested at *Blackwood's* jaw-bone-of-an-ass attack on Cornwall's uneven edition of *The Works of Ben Jonson* (1838), memorably ridiculed in ornithic terms: 'BEN JONSON by Barry Cornwall! – An eagle heralded by a wren; or is it absolutely a tom-tit?'[106] 'J. F. O.' objected to the article's 'unmethodized, desultory, incoherent compilation of personal allusions, and flings', which formed yet 'another chapter in the long list of 'Quarrels of Authors'.[107] 'Personal motive', 'J. F. O.' insisted, together with Wilson's indignation at Cornwall's defence of Keats, had motivated *Blackwood's* ill-temper:

> Some few years have gone by, since Barry Cornwall wrote a biographical memoir of John Keats, in which he took occasion to allude in terms of becoming severity to the course that had been pursued towards that promising poet, by certain critics: among these, Blackwood's Magazine came in for its share ... From that time to this, Barry Cornwall has been a marked man.

By 1823, the celebrated poet's breathing art had petrified for readers, and Cornwall's literary reputation never fully recovered from the politically inflected drubbings meted out to the *Flood of Thessaly*. Other than publishing a book of short lyrics, *English Songs: And Other Small Poems*, in 1832 – which briefly refurbished his celebrity thanks to musical settings by the fashionable Austrian composer Sigismond von Neukomm (1778–1858) – for the next decade, Cornwall largely withdrew into legal practice, contributing occasional poems to journals or literary annuals such as *The Keepsake* and *Friendship's Offering*. In 1831, he accepted a post as Metropolitan Commissioner of Lunacy, and for the next 30 years undertook physically taxing tours of England and Wales as inspector of licensed mental institutions.[108] Even his closest allies began to view him as a figure of fun. An 1827 letter from Charles Lamb (the beneficiary of Cornwall's generous *Memoir* in 1866) to P. G. Patmore is astonishingly cruel: 'Procter has got a wen growing out at the nape of his neck, which his wife wants him to have cut off; but I think it rather an agreeable excrescence, – like his poetry, redundant.'[109] In similar vein, a letter to Mary Russell Mitford from 1830 finds Thomas Noon Talfourd referring to Cornwall as 'a good fellow despite his verse'.[110]

Reviewing *Marcian Colonna* in 1820, the *New Monthly Magazine* had assured readers of Cornwall's glorious future: 'The words he has uttered *will* live. May he long continue [to] advance in his noble career and pursue it rejoicingly.'[111] In fact, Cornwall's literary star proved almost as 'short lived and self-consuming' as Keats's own.[112]

Notes

1 Nicholas Roe, *Fiery Heart: The First Life of Leigh Hunt* (London: Pimlico, 2005); also see *Leigh Hunt: Life, Poetics, Politics*, ed. Nicholas Roe (London: Routledge, 2003).
2 Previous editions of Wu's anthology included Cornwall's 'A Dream' from *Dramatic Scenes* – Charles Lamb's favourite – and 'A Poet's Thought' from Cornwall's last collection of original work, *English Songs* (1832).
3 Susan J. Wolfson, 'Representing some Late Romantic-Era, Non-Canonical Male Poets: Thomas Hood, Winthrop Mackworth Praed, Thomas Lovell Beddoes', *Romanticism On the Net*, 19 (August 2000) <http://users.ox.ac.uk/~scat0385/19hood.html> [date of access: 9.4.5].
4 Carroll's crew of snark hunters have been linked to members of the Lunacy Commission. Carroll's maternal uncle, Robert Wilfred Skeffington Lutwidge, the Baker's uncle in *The Hunting of the Snark*, was also an inspector of lunatic asylums. He died in an assault in 1873 when a patient stabbed him in the temple with a large rusty nail. See E. Fuller Torrey and Judy Miller, *The Invisible Plague: The Rise of Insanity from 1750 to the Present* (Rutgers University Press, 2002), p. 89.
5 *Blackwood's Edinburgh Magazine*, 6 (1819), p. 246.
6 *New Monthly Magazine*, 14 (1820), pp. 76–77, at p. 76. 'Popular' is, of course, a relative term. We cannot talk of a popular book-buying (as opposed to book-reading) market

before the 1850s that doesn't overwhelmingly refer to the 'professional classes' of British society. One of Cornwall's 7s volumes would have cost a labourer the equivalent of a week's wages in 1820. As Simon Eliot points out, a study of *Bent's Monthly Literary Advertizer* reveals that medium- and high-priced books (3s 7d to over 10s) dominate the market in terms of percentage of titles until around 1855, when cheaper books began to take over. See *Literature in the Marketplace: Nineteenth-century British Publishing and Reading Practices*, ed. John O. Jordan and Robert L. Patten (Cambridge: Cambridge University Press, 1995), pp. 39–40.

7 *Eclectic Review*, 2nd series, 14 (1820), pp. 158–71, at p. 167.

8 *New Letters from Charles Brown to Joseph Severn*, ed. Grant F. Scott and Sue Brown, *Romantic Circles Electronic Edition* <http://www.rc.umd.edu/editions/brownsevern/> [date of access: 21.3.8].

9 *Asiatic Journal and Monthly Miscellany*, 11 (1821), p. 545.

10 See Tim Chilcott, *A Publisher and his Circle: The Life and Work of John Taylor, Keats's Publisher* (London: Routledge & Kegan Paul, 1972), pp. 48, 51. For Keats's posthumous sales figures, see also William St Clair, *The Reading Nation in the Romantic Period* (Cambridge: Cambridge University Press, 2004), p. 612. St Clair calculates Keats's total sales in the Romantic period at 1500 copies.

11 For information on the Olliers' business practice, see Charles E. Robinson, 'Percy Bysshe Shelley, Charles Ollier, and William Blackwood: The Contexts of Early Nineteenth-Century Publishing', in Kelvin Everest (ed.), *Shelley Revalued: Essays from the Gregynog Conference* (Leicester: Leicester University Press, 1983), especially p. 212; and John Barnard, 'First Fruits or "First Blights": A New Account of the Publishing History of Keats's *Poems* (1817)', *Romanticism*, 12.ii (2006), 71–101.

12 See Hyder Rollins, *Notes and Queries*, 198 (1953), p. 118. Rollins points out that in *Inesilla* (1824), Ollier made up for his attack of spleen by praising Keats's *The Eve of St Agnes* as 'one of the most enchanting gems of literature – the abstracted essence of love, poetry, and romance'.

13 John Hamilton Reynolds's term in a letter to Francis Jeffrey dated 13 July 1820, in which Reynolds discusses Keats's poor treatment in the *Quarterly Review* and *Blackwood's Edinburgh Magazine*. See *The Letters of John Hamilton Reynolds*, ed. Leonidas M. Jones (Lincoln, NE: University of Nebraska Press, 1973), p. 19.

14 *Edinburgh Review*, 34 (1820), pp. 449–60, at p. 450.

15 *Blackwood's Edinburgh Magazine*, 6 (1819), pp. 235–47, at p. 240.

16 *The Autobiography of William Jerdan*, III, 230, 254. In 1819, Jerdan, who was by then editor of the London *Literary Review*, also wrote to Blackwood in an effort to secure an early review of Cornwall's *A Sicilian Story*. The petition was successful and Jeffrey's appraisal of the volume appeared in the *Edinburgh Review* in January 1820. See St Clair, *The Reading Nation in the Romantic Period*, p. 574.

17 William Howitt, *Homes and Haunts of the Most Eminent English Poets*, 2 vols (London: Bentley, 1847), II, 687, 293.

18 An enthusiastic *Athenaeum* review of Hood's annual, *The Gem*, singles out Cornwall's poem on Titian for particular praise; *Athenaeum*, 51 (1828), pp. 800–02.

19 Thomas Hood, *The Gem, A Literary Annual*, 4 vols (London: Marshall, 1829). For more information on printed albums and annuals, see William St Clair, *The Reading Nation in the Romantic Period*, pp. 229–32. Also see Katherine Harris's hypertext of *The*

Forget-Me-Not, a fund of invaluable information on other albums: <http://www.orgs.
muohio.edu/anthologies/FMN/Index.htm> [date of access: 19.2.8].

20 Watts's album is not analysed in William St Clair's seminal 2004 statistical study of
reading histories, *The Reading Nation in the Romanic Period*.

21 By the time the volume appeared, Watts griped, some of the 'fugitive' pieces had 'crept'
into collections.

22 This figure is recorded by the editor's son. See Alaric Alfred Watts, *Alaric Watts: A
Narrative of his Life*, 2 vols (London: Bentley, 1884), I, 171. For more on the magazine's
sales figures, see Peter J. Manning's essay in *Literature in the Marketplace*, p. 44; and Lee
Erickson, *The Economy of Literary Form: English Literature and the Industrialization of
Publishing, 1800–1850* (London: Johns Hopkins, 1995), p. 29. By 1832, over 60 different
annuals were competing for book-buyers' attention.

23 See 'Monologue, or Soliloquy on the Annuals', *Blackwood's Edinburgh Magazine*, 26
(1829), pp. 948–76, at p. 955.

24 Watts to Blackwood, 1 September 1822; cited by Nicholas Roe, *John Keats and the
Culture of Dissent* (Oxford: Oxford University Press, 1997), pp. 274–75.

25 *The Autobiography of William Jerdan*, 4 vols (London: Arthur Hall, 1852–53), III, pp.
231–32.

26 Two of these poems (the sonnets on the Elgin Marbles) appeared simultaneously, or near
simultaneously, in three publications. Keats tended not to collect previously published
pieces, reprinting only 6 of the 14 poems in his three volumes.

27 *Blackwood's Edinburgh Magazine*, 6 (1819), p. 643.

28 *Edinburgh Monthly Review*, n.s. 84 (1819), p. 122.

29 *Salt-Bearer*, 1 (1821), p. 344.

30 *Edinburgh Review*, 33 (1820), pp. 144–55, at p. 147.

31 *Blackwood's Edinburgh Magazine*, 5 (1819), pp. 310–16, at p. 315.

32 *Blackwood's Edinburgh Magazine*, 6 (1819), pp. 235–47, at p. 240.

33 *Blackwood's Edinburgh Magazine*, 6 (1819), pp. 646–47.

34 See Benedict's introduction to *Making the Modern Reader: Cultural Mediation in Early
Modern Literary Anthologies* (Princeton, NJ: Princeton University Press, 1996).

35 *Eclectic Review*, 2nd series, 14 (1820), pp. 158–71, at p. 169.

36 See 'Percy Bysshe Shelley, Charles Ollier, and William Blackwood: The Contexts of
Early Nineteenth-Century Publishing', pp. 198–99.

37 *Blackwood's Edinburgh Magazine*, 13 (1823), pp. 532–41, at p. 534.

38 *Dramatic Scenes*, 2nd edn (London: C. and J. Ollier, 1820), p. vii. For Romantic philology,
see my book, *The Politics of Language in Romantic Literature* (London: Palgrave, 2002).

39 See 'The Field of Cultural Production', in *The Book History Reader*, ed. David Finkelstein
and Alistair McCleery (London: Routledge, 2002), p. 77.

40 Gittings suggests that Keats paid Cornwall an 'unconscious' compliment by mimicking
the style of *Dramatic Scenes*. See *John Keats* (Harmondsworth: Penguin, 1968), p. 477.

41 *Annals of Fine Arts*, 4 (1820), p. 640.

42 Jeffrey N. Cox notes the appearance of the sonnet next to Keats's poem, but without
further comment. See *Poetry and Politics in the Cockney School: Keats, Shelley, Hunt and
their Circle* (Cambridge: Cambridge University Press, 1998), p. 150.

43 Entitled 'To Michael Angelo' in the second edition of *Dramatic Scenes*, p. 168.

44 *New Monthly Magazine*, 14 (1820), p. 76. For its sales figures, see Nanora Sweet, 'The *New*

Monthly Magazine and the Liberalism of the 1820s', in *Romantic Periodicals and Print Culture* (London: Frank Cass, 2003), p. 147. After the death in 1821 of John Scott, editor of the *London Magazine*, in a duel with John Christie, agent of *Blackwood's Edinburgh Magazine*, Cornwall – who was a contributor to the *London Magazine* – joined Hazlitt, Lamb and Horrace Smith in writing for the *New Monthly*. The publication quickly achieved a circulation of over 5000 copies, short of the 12,000–13,000 regularly boasted by the *Quarterly Review* and *Edinburgh Review*, but respectable none the less.

45 *New Monthly Magazine*, 14 (1820), p. 76. The echo suggests that the *New Monthly's* reviewer not only registered the joint appearance of Keats's ode and Cornwall's sonnet in *Annals*, but also appreciated both poems' mutual preoccupation with the relationship between marbled stasis and breathing art.

46 *Edinburgh Review*, 38 (1823), pp. 177–208, at p. 206.

47 *Marcian Colonna* was a popular choice among women authors and editors for epigraphs – especially when setting the scene for dark tales. Lines from the poem appear, for example, at the head of the short story, 'The Widow's Nuptials' (Chapter 3), included in Marion and Margaret Corbett's *The Odd Volume* (Edinburgh: Lizars, 1826). This collection of stories was popular, as a letter from Owen Rees to James Ballantyne from 28 November 1826 indicates: 'We will thank you to reprint 750 of the "Odd Volume" in the same manner as the second edition; & 1250 of "Another odd volume" when the copy is put into your hands'; see the Longman Archives (Longman I, 102, no. 29B). For a brief recent mention of Corbett's anthology, see Hilary Brown, 'German Women Writers in English Short Story Anthologies of the 1820s', *Modern Language Review*, 97 (2002), pp. 620–31, at p. 624.

48 Occasionally Keats came off better from the comparison with his 'fellow pupil', as in the *Monthly Magazine*, 50 (1820), which insisted that Keats's 'boldness of fancy' and 'classical expression of language ... entitle him to stand equally high in the estimation of public opinion, as ... 'Barry Cornwall', and added that 'as long as fair originality shall be thought superior to good imitation, he will always be preferred' (p. 166).

49 See Richard Willard Armour, *Barry Cornwall: A Biography of Bryan Waller Procter* (Boston: Meador, 1935), pp. 48–49.

50 'Young Poets' is the label introduced by Hunt in the *Examiner*, 1 December 1816.

51 *Edinburgh Monthly Review*, n.s. 84 (1819), pp. 121–22.

52 *Edinburgh Review*, 33 (1820), pp. 144–55, at p. 146.

53 *Blackwood's Edinburgh Magazine*, 5 (1819), p. 311.

54 *Monthly Magazine*, 50 (1820), p. 166.

55 See *Autobiography of Benjamin Robert Haydon*, 3 vols (London: Longman, 1853), I, 253.

56 'Letters of Timothy Tickler, Esq. No. VIII', *Blackwood's Edinburgh Magazine*, 14 (1823), p. 227.

57 *The Literary Life and Correspondence of the Countess of Blessington*, ed. R. R. Madden, 3 vols (London: T. C. Newby, 1855), II, 125.

58 *The Story of Rimini*, pp. xv–xvi.

59 *The Making of English Reading Audiences, 1790–1832* (Madison, WI: University of Wisconsin Press, 1987), p. ii.

60 Letter dated 4 December 1820. See *The Letters of Thomas Love Peacock*, ed. Nicholas A. Joukovsky, 2 vols (Oxford: Clarendon Press, 2001), I, p. 174.

61 *The Making of English Reading Audiences, 1790–1832*, p. 133.

62 Ayumi Mizukoshi, *Keats, Hunt, and the Aesthetics of Pleasure* (London: Palgrave Macmillan, 2001), p. 80.

63 *New Monthly Magazine*, 14 (1820), p. 76.

64 *Monthly Review*, 92 (1820), pp. 310–18.

65 See Chapter 2, pp. 76–77.

66 See Armour, *Barry Cornwall*, pp. 152–56.

67 See John Barnard, *John Keats: The Complete Poems*, 3rd edn (Harmondsworth: Penguin, 1991), p. 676.

68 For an engaging discussion of arbitrariness in Byron's work, see William Keach's *Arbitrary Power* (Princeton, NJ: Princeton University Press, 2004).

69 *Edinburgh Review*, 33 (1820), p. 454.

70 As evidence of the taste for long narrative verse, Henry Hart Milman's epic of Saxon struggle, *Samor, Lord of the Bright City: An Heroic Poem* (1818), favourably reviewed by John Taylor Coleridge in the *Quarterly Review* in February 1819, achieved a second edition within a year of publication.

71 See *Keats, Narrative and Audience: The Posthumous Life of Writing* (Cambridge: Cambridge University Press, 1994), p. 23.

72 *Monthly Review*, 91 (1820), pp. 291–96 at p. 293.

73 Kurt Heinzelman, 'Self-Interest and the Politics of Composition in Keats's *Isabella*', *English Literary History*, 55 (1988), pp. 159–93, at p. 173.

74 *Edinburgh Magazine and Literary Miscellany*, 7 (1820), pp. 313–16, at p. 313.

75 For a perceptive recent essay on *Isabella* and money, see Porscha Fermanis, 'Isabella, Lamia, and "Merry Old England"', *Essays in Criticism*, 56 (2006).

76 Jeffrey C. Robinson has addressed the problem of how modern critics, used to finding a different kind of 'presence' in Romantic texts, are to read sentimental literature. See 'Romantic Passions: Passion and Romantic Poetics', *Romantic Circles* (April, 1998). Available online at: <http://www.rc.umd.edu/praxis/passions/robinson/rbsn.html> [date of access: 12.4.8].

77 *A Sicilian Story, with Diego de Montilla and Other Poems* (London: C. and J. Ollier, 1820), p. 15.

78 *Blackwood's Edinburgh Magazine*, 6 (1820), pp. 643–50, at p. 645.

79 Ralph Pite, 'The Watching Narrator in *Isabella*', *Essays in Criticism*, 40 (1990), pp. 287–302, at p. 302 (n. 12).

80 Hermann Fischer, *Romantic Verse Narrative: The History of a Genre*, trans. Sue Bollans (Cambridge: Cambridge University Press, 1991), p. 281 (n. 25).

81 *Edinburgh Review*, 33 (1820), pp. 144–55, at p. 145.

82 George Yost, 'Keats's Poignancy and the Fine Excess', *South Atlantic Bulletin*, 45 (1980), pp. 15–22, at p. 22n.

83 *Eclectic Review*, n.s. 14 (1820), pp. 323–33, at p. 323. The reviewer points out that both poets belong to the 'same school'.

84 *Monthly Review*, 92 (1820), pp. 310–18, at p. 308. In 1857, Cornwall published a new edition of *Dramatic Scenes* with other selected poems, illustrated by John Tenniel. *Blackwood's*, noting that Cornwall had unaccountably dropped his once-popular adaptation of Boccaccio, recalls that in its own day *A Sicilian Story* represented 'a worthy rival to Mr Keats's *Isabella*'. See *Blackwood's Edinburgh Magazine*, 81 (1857), pp. 356–65, at p. 360.

85 Jack Stillinger, 'Keats and Romance', *Studies in English Literature, 1500–1900*, 8 (1968),

pp. 593–605, at p. 593.

86 *Keats, Narrative and Audience: The Posthumous Life of Writing*, p. 85.

87 Letter dated 4 December 1820. *Letters of Thomas Love Peacock*, I, 174.

88 *Peacock's Four Ages of Poetry*, ed. H. F. B. Brett-Smith (Oxford: Blackwell, 1921), p. 9.

89 *The Four Ages of Poetry* was first printed in Ollier's short-lived *Literary Miscellany* (1820). *A Defence of Poetry* was scheduled to follow in the second issue. However, as Charles E. Robinson points out, the first number lost £100 and a second never appeared. See 'Percy Bysshe Shelley, Charles Ollier, and William Blackwood: The Contexts of Early Nineteenth-Century Publishing', p. 206. Shelley's formal response to Peacock was not published until 1840.

90 See Christopher Goulding, 'An Unpublished Shelley Letter', *The Review of English Studies*, 52 (2001), pp. 233–37, at p. 234. On 25 September 1821, Shelley asks Ollier, hopefully, 'Is there any chance of a second edition of the *Revolt of Islam*?' (*LPBS*, II, 354).

91 John Warren co-published the second edition of *A Sicilian Story* in 1820, publishing a third edition in 1821 on his own. Warren was also behind both editions of Cornwall's *Mirandola*.

92 See Charles E. Robinson, 'Ollier, Charles (1788–1859)', *Oxford Dictionary of National Biography*, Oxford University Press, September 2004; online edn, May 2006 <http://www.oxforddnb.com/view/article/20739> [date of access: 22.12.6].

93 Shelley was wary of revealing his true feelings about Cornwall to their mutual publisher, Ollier. In one of his letters, he specifically requests that Ollier include a copy of *Mirandola* (1821) in one of his literary boxes (later fulminating to Thomas Love Peacock about the volume's presence). In other correspondence, he maintains a strategic politeness when the topic of his rival's work crops up.

94 *London Magazine*, 3 (1821), pp. 211–15, at pp. 211, 215.

95 George Augustus Simcox, 'Barry Cornwall', *Fortnightly Review*, n.s. 20 (1876), pp. 708–18, at p. 715.

96 *Gentleman's Magazine*, 14 (1821), p. 81.

97 *Literary Gazette*, 13 January 1821, p. 17.

98 *The Times*, 10 January 1821, p. 3.

99 Also see Edwin P. Whipple, *Recollections of Eminent Men* (Boston: Ticknor, 1886), p. 317.

100 Chris Rojek, *Celebrity* (London: Reaktion, 2001), p. 16.

101 *Blackwood's Edinburgh Magazine*, 10 (1821), pp. 476–78, at p. 477.

102 Henry Colburn was Cornwall's main publisher after the Olliers' bankruptcy in 1822–23.

103 *Blackwood's Edinburgh Magazine*, 14 (1823), p. 431.

104 *Blackwood's Edinburgh Magazine*, 13 (1823), pp. 532–41, at p. 541.

105 Letter dated 13 October 1850 (13th of 33 pages). For an online facsimile see the "Leigh Hunt Digital Collection," *Iowa Digital Library*: <http://www.lib.uiowa.edu/spec-coll/leighhunt/index.html> [date of access: 14.12.7].

106 *Blackwood's* had added 'The most masculine of intellects *edited* by the most effeminate', *Blackwood's Edinburgh Magazine*, 45 (1839), pp. 145–169, at p. 145.

107 *Southern Literary Messenger*, 5 (1839), p. 268.

108 For an extensive account of this institution, see Andrew Roberts's excellent Middlesex University online resource, 'The Lunacy Commission: A Study of its Origin, Emergence

and Character': http://www.mdx.ac.uk/WWW/STUDY/01.h [date of access: 17.5.7].

109 *The Letters of Charles Lamb: To which are Added Those of His Sister Mary Lamb*, ed. E. V. Lucas, 3 vols (London: Dent, 1935), III, 106.

110 Quoted in A. C. Grayling, *The Quarrel of the Age: The Life and Times of William Hazlitt* (London: Phoenix Press, 2001), p. 339.

111 *New Monthly Magazine*, 14 (1820), p. 77.

112 The phrase is quoted by Cornwall in his generous *London Magazine* obituary of Keats, signed 'L', *London Magazine*, 3 (1821), pp. 426–27, at p. 426; attributed to Cornwall by Bertram Dobell, *Sidelights on Charles Lamb* (London: Dobell, 1903), p. 192.

2

'Slippery Steps of the Temple of Fame':
Cornwall and Keats's Reputation

In July 1820, Keats's career was in the doldrums. Having pinned all his hopes for 'living by the pen' on the delayed *Lamia* volume, he was dismayed when his new collection, despite boasting such tour-de-force performances as 'Ode to a Nightingale' and *The Eve of St Agnes*, appeared to mixed or hostile reviews. For most Romantic readers, Keats remained the jejune, sidelined author of one of 1818's biggest flops, *Endymion*. In August, however, a beacon light arrived in the form of an unattributed review in Constable's *Edinburgh Magazine and Literary Miscellany*, a second instalment following in October.[1]

1. Barry Cornwall and Keats's Reputation

Written by an 'outside contributor' with the 'avowed purpose of gaining Keats a larger readership', as Donald H. Reiman points out in his standard edition of Romantic reviews, the mysterious critique pronounced Keats a 'poet of high and undoubted powers' (p. 107). 'If this be not poetry', the reviewer declared, defiantly quoting excerpts of the vilified *Endymion*, while promising in the same breath a full-length review of *Lamia*, 'we do not know what is' (p. 110). The exercise in public relations was effective, marking the point at which the tide of negative reviews began to turn in Keats's favour.

Reiman believes that the finger of probability points towards John Hamilton Reynolds, Keats's close friend, for authorship of the timely defence.[2] To be sure, Reynolds had already published a partisan appraisal of *Poems* (1817) in the *Champion*, and some of his own lines, 'Dian and Endymion', appear at the foot of the October half of the review.[3] Leonidas M. Jones, on the other hand, states that Reynolds was not the author, 'though he must have welcomed its praise'.[4] The issue is cleared up by an unpublished letter to the editor of the *Edinburgh Magazine*, written in two goes in early August 1820. It refers to a recently submitted 'Critique on Keats', and seems to suggest that Keats's white knight was not the faithful Reynolds, but his most formidable poetic rival 'Barry Cornwall'.

The overlooked letter, part of the Carl H. Pforzheimer Collection of Shelley and His Circle, New York Public Library (Pforz MS, Misc 3729), not only provides the basis for a confident attribution of authorship to Cornwall but also opens a fascinating aperture on the complex, conflicted relationship between two fiercely competitive poets. This is the text of the letter in full:

> D^r. Sir,
>
> I return you the Critique on Keats as it stood – I have spoken I think quite well enough of his book – I was fearful when I sent it off that I had not. I send you some lines, which you can use or not as you please – pray use no ceremony with me.
>
> I shall leave town in a few days but shall return in less than a month when I will send you a section of something – not of poetry I think, for I should only write of that when I could wished [*sic*] to speak <u>very</u> favourably, which cannot often occur. I scribble to you in haste, as usual driving off every thing to the last moment –
>
> > Yours very truly,
> > B. W. Procter
> > 25 Store S^t.
> > Bedford Square
> > Tuesday

> 7 August – On my return to town this Evening I find that the people at the Coach-office would not take this in as a parcel – they said that it was too small – I have added therefore some news paper –
>
> > Rev^d. R. Morehead
> > Constable & Co.
> > Edinburgh[5]

The reverend Robert Morehead, Dean of Edinburgh, edited the *Edinburgh Magazine and Literary Miscellany* (a new series of Constable's *Scots Magazine*) between 1817 and 1826, together with Pringle and Cleghorn, refugees from the newly launched *Blackwood's Edinburgh Magazine*. The journal defined itself against the 'delinquencies' of *Blackwood's*, whose eviscerating *ad hominem* attacks on 'Cockney School of Poetry' authors Leigh Hunt, Keats – and in due course, Cornwall himself – Morehead abhorred.[6] A Whig in politics, the Dean counted among literary confrères and correspondents prominent figures such as Byron, Scott, Hogg and *éminence grise* of the *Edinburgh Review*, his cousin Francis Jeffrey.[7] Unusually for the period, the *Edinburgh Magazine* accepted unsolicited reviews; hence

Cornwall's reference to sending Morehead another 'section of something' on returning to town. Inspired by the magazine's spirit of idealism, most contributors were happy to offer copy 'gratis'.

The likely background to Cornwall's decision to send a review of Keats to Morehead is elucidated by a Reynolds letter. On 13 July 1820, Keats's friend wrote to Francis Jeffrey to discuss plans for an article on English drama to be co-authored by Cornwall: 'I have seen Mr. Procter since the receipt of your letter & have informed him on the question of the division of the article – so that we now understand that he is to take the Tragic and I the Comic Drama'.[8] In fact, no jointly written article ever appeared, although Cornwall's piece 'On Tragedy' was published in the *Edinburgh Review* in 1823.[9] In the next paragraph of his letter, Reynolds petitions Jeffrey to notice Keats, playing up his friend's youth – Reynolds reports Keats's age as '22 I should think', when in fact he was 24 years old – and appealing to Jeffrey's dislike of *Blackwood's* and the *Quarterly's* savage, politically motivated attacks.[10] Keats's 'politics are strong against the Quarterly Review', he assures the fair-minded Whig editor. The ruse was successful and Jeffrey's critique appeared in the *Edinburgh Review's* August 1820 issue.[11]

Given that Reynolds had recently been discussing the prospect of a collaborative article with Cornwall, he had probably also mentioned Keats's frustration at the failure of the *Lamia* volume to attract the attention of major reviewers (the two topics are, after all, broached back-to-back in his letter to Jeffrey). Since Cornwall's second volume *A Sicilian Story* (1820) had already been appraised by the *Edinburgh Review* in January that year, the idea that Reynolds should promote Keats's book to the journal's editor may even have been Cornwall's. But as the letter to Morehead now reveals, Cornwall also decided to act under his own steam; moreover, the first section of his two-part review of *Endymion* and *Lamia* beat Jeffrey's to the book stands.

Reynolds doesn't seem to have had an inkling of Cornwall's intention to write a review of Keats himself, and in his letter to Jeffrey he blithely sets about demolishing Cornwall's reputation: 'I agree with you quite about Procter's new Book [*Marcian Colonna*], with the exception of Amelia Wentworth, which [I] think is written with great simplicity and pathos. The rest of the Book bears marks of haste – and is therefore sketchy and indecisive' (p. 19).

To return to the letter to Morehead, Cornwall's allusion to sending back his essay 'as it stood' suggests that he was parcelling up unaltered proofs for the editor. Despite anxieties that his original manuscript hadn't been sufficiently positive about Keats when he first 'sent it off', Cornwall seems to have been pleased enough with his defence of the bruised poet once he'd seen it set up in type.[12]

Cornwall's own works had been well received under Morehead's conductorship of the *Edinburgh Magazine*. The journal's review of his dazzling début, *Dramatic Scenes* (1819), praised the 'agreeable' volume, although it was perturbed by Cornwall's Cockney penchant for 'breaking in upon the prevailing uses of language'.[13] A report on the *au courant* poet's third volume, *Marcian Colonna* (1820), a careening portrait of a violent sexual fantasist, balked at its occasional flimsiness and sensationalism, but judged the work 'extremely perfect within its own range'.[14] A more serious caveat, however, was the critic's sense that Cornwall was 'getting into the way of writing too much and too hurriedly', with the consequence that he could 'scarce avoid falling into the prevailing fashion, of whatever that might be' (p. 14).

What does Cornwall's letter to Morehead tell us about the contours of his relationship with Keats? To address that question, it is helpful to pull into relief Cornwall's current reputation as measured against his status in Romantic literary London. The comparison throws up some instructive, not to mention surprising, parallels between the poetic careers of Keats and Cornwall. Born eight years before Keats in 1787, Cornwall lived until 1874, ending up like 'Simon Lee' practically the 'sole survivor' of an age.[15] The son of a prosperous wine merchant, he attended Harrow with Robert Peel, and Byron was also an 'old schoolfellow'.[16] From 1816 to 1820, he practised as a London solicitor, renting rooms in fashionable Brunswick Avenue. For a spell, he juggled conveyancing with life as a city spark and pugilist, engaging former bare-knuckle boxing champion of England, Tom Cribb, as his instructor and sparring with celebrated slugger, the 'Game Chicken'. Standing like Keats at a smidgeon over five foot, 'timid' in character with a 'very white forehead', as Nathaniel Parker Willis recalled, he must have cut a curious figure opposite those slogging physiques.[17]

His first poems appeared in the *Literary Gazette* in late 1817. By February 1820, under Hunt's tutelage, the 'rising poet', in the words of the *Edinburgh Monthly Review*, had published three full volumes of verse.[18] His 'great popularity' was traced by the *Gazette* to an unerringly 'fine feeling for the pathetic'. Cornwall's theatrical portrait of an 'unsettled mind', *Marcian Colonna* (1820), even reminded its reviewer 'powerfully' of *Hamlet*.[19] Eighteen months later in June 1821, in the wake of the triumphant Covent Garden staging of Cornwall's tragedy, *Mirandola* (1821), the *Asiatic Journal and Monthly Miscellany* declared that if the age's most popular trio of authors, Byron, Scott and Moore, were measured against Cornwall for 'rich imagery', 'elegant diction' and 'delicacy of feelings', the newcomer would 'equal, if not surpass all the three!'[20]

Charles Lamb was a keen advocate, dedicating a sonnet to 'The Author of Poems Published under the Name of Barry Cornwall' that praised Cornwall's 'A Dream' for holding a 'glass' to the 'world's antique glories'.[21] Walter Savage Landor wrote in similar eulogistic terms that:

No other in these later times
Has bound me in so potent rhymes.[22]

Cornwall's reputation as a leading poetic light extended beyond England. His first volume, *Dramatic Scenes*, inspired two musical settings by Mikhail Glinka, and individual poems served as forerunners to Alexander Pushkin's *Little Tragedies*. Macabrely, the last thing Pushkin wrote before tending to his fatal duel with d'Anthes was a hurried note to Alexandra Ishimova on the subject of translating Cornwall into Russian.[23]

On the up in literary London, Cornwall was fully immersed in commodity culture. His perfectly confected, à la mode 'dramatic scenes' chimed closely with late-Romantic taste. According to figures published in the *Theatrical Inquisitor*, *Marcian Colonna* – whose publication marked the apex of Cornwall's popularity – sold 700 copies in a single day, prompting the novelist Mary Russell Mitford to exclaim: 'Every body is talking of Barry Cornwall'.[24] In the estimation of the *London Magazine*, even though 'the gloomy thunder of Lord Byron's popularity was at its loudest', Cornwall had become the most 'observed of all observers'.[25] For a less anecdotal perspective on Cornwall's popular standing, William Hazlitt's suppressed anthology, *Select British Poets* (1824), allocated the solicitor nine complete pages, the same number as Keats, and more than Southey, Lamb or Shelley.[26]

Reviewers of all stripes found much to admire in Cornwall. This is actually surprising, since Cornwall's literary touchstones were unmistakably 'Cockney'. He stuck to his principles: in essays contributed to the *Edinburgh Review* in the 1820s, 'On English Tragedy' and 'On English Poetry', Cornwall argued that Charles II's Restoration had been fatal to English poetry, since the event allowed the rise of 'French' taste in Britain.[27] Rejecting the artificiality of Pope and Dryden, Cornwall's critical work strongly echoes the sentiments of Hunt's preface to *Rimini*. Nevertheless, even the crotchety John Wilson at *Blackwood's Edinburgh Magazine* lauded Cornwall's 'originality and genius', at the same time as encouraging his right-hand man J. G. Lockhart ('Z.') to cast a succession of calumnies on his Cockney counterpart, 'Johnny Keats'.[28] Despite his affiliations with Hunt, as Philip Flynn has recently calculated, Cornwall was one of the most regularly reviewed authors in Maga: 'Byron and Scott – the contemporary colossi who bestrode *Blackwood's* literary world – received the most attention. Wordsworth and Thomas Moore were close thirds, followed by Shelley, Leigh Hunt, Barry Cornwall, James Hogg, and the now almost-forgotten Henry Hart Milman.'[29] The *Edinburgh Monthly Review* declared that Cornwall's poetry evinced 'truth, delicacy, and sometimes profundity of feeling'. In 1821, Gold's *London Magazine* declared that in terms of 'tenderness and delicacy', even Shelley was 'surpassed very far indeed' by Cornwall.[30]

Few modern scholars agree. Cornwall's achievement is usually ascribed to the vagaries of taste. To be sure, these days critics are unlikely to demur from André Henri Koszul's censorious judgement in 1922 that Barry Cornwall was a 'deservedly obscure' poet, or from Edmund Blunden's in 1930 that the once à la mode poet was little more than an 'elegant but watery imitator' of Percy Shelley and Keats.[31] Keats, on the other hand, is probably the writer whose name is most often invoked first after Shakespeare's in popular pantheons of literary genius. Clive James put it well recently in the *TLS* when he suggested that 'every modern poet is obliged to have a view on Keats, as if he were part of the living competition.'[32] Isn't it perverse that the work of a man who was an *actual* living competitor of Keats, moreover, a writer who decisively outmanoeuvered his opponent in the public's affections, should so profoundly fail to interest us?

Cornwall composed on similar themes to Keats, but garnered all the plaudits. With scant regard to quality control, he churned out a series of chattily Cockneyfied volumes that were racy without (quite) breaching decorum, and wore their erudition lightly. What is more, Cornwall was shrewd enough to encourage, rather than dismiss petulantly like Keats, an increasingly flush constituency of female book buyers. Tactically sophis-ticated, Cornwall addressed the 'crimsoning beauty' of *A Sicilian Story* – a pouting verse romance based like Keats's darker-cornered *Isabella* on Boccaccio's grisly pot of basil tale from the fifth day of the *Decameron* – to 'sweet ladies'. In 1911, Cornwall's first critical biographer, Franz Becker, judged fairly of Cornwall's version that 'Im einzelnen kann es einen Vergleich mit Keats's *Isabel* [sic] aushalten' [individual details stand comparison with Keats's *Isabella*].[33] There are no prizes for guessing which of the two poems proved most popular among early nineteenth-century female reading audiences, however. As the *London Magazine* confirmed, Cornwall quickly established himself as 'one of Woman's distinguished favourites.'[34]

Orthodox critical narratives dismiss the idea of meaningful interaction between Cornwall and Keats as fanciful. None the less, the pivots, cogs and levers of the poets' acquaintance are more intricate than is generally acknowledged. Cornwall and Keats were both protégés of Leigh Hunt, and active within his political and literary coterie. They published poems in the *Examiner*, as well as in Hunt's subtly subversive forerunner to the Filofax, the *Literary Pocket-Book*, which Wilson described approvingly as a 'sort of almanack ... quite dressy-looking with its scarlet coat'.[35] In 1819, both men joined Percy Shelley in couching protest at the Peterloo massacre in seasonal poetic allegories on Autumn. They also appeared alongside each other in albums and literary magazines – in January 1820, 'Ode on a Grecian Urn' was printed on a facing page to Cornwall's sonnet 'To Michel Agnolo', which also mused, if rather more one-dimensionally, on the immortality of stony-faced art. Moreover, in the early stages of their careers they were both associated with the same publishing house.[36] When the Ollier brothers dropped Keats, or as John Barnard suggests were dropped by him following the failure of *Poems* (1817), they enthusiastically added Cornwall to their lists.[37] In 1820, the poets also competed to stage a tragedy at Covent Garden. Unsurprisingly, given Cornwall's superior commercial nous, it was *Miran-dola*, a dizzying tale of patrifilial fracas that ends spectacularly with the execution of the Duke's son Guido on his cuckolded father's behest, that secured a lucrative run of 16 nights in January 1821, Kemble and Macready playing the leads, with music by Henry Rowley Bishop. In his last letter to Keats, Charles Brown, co-author of the rejected *Otho the Great*, puns cattily on how bad Cornwall's play was likely to be:[38] 'Oh! Barry C: has a tragedy coming forth at the Theatre, christened Mirandola, – Mire and O la!' (*LJK*, II, 366).

Today, Cornwall is discounted as humdrum, irredeemably adrift of signif-icant movements within literature of the period. He's a mere 'Romantic versifier' in W. J. Bate's opinion; 'melodious but trite', according to James Sambrook, author of Cornwall's revised entry in the new edition of *Dictionary Of National Biography*, terminally 'bland' in Marilyn Butler's view; 'trivial' according to his facsimile editor, Donald H. Reiman; and 'content to cater for the "mawkish" taste' in the estimation of Ayumi Mizukoshi, who picks her words carefully to incorporate Keats's own signifier of poetic failure.[39] There's a prejudice against the poet's name itself, admittedly difficult to say without performing an audible moue. (Even in Cornwall's day, the *Edinburgh Monthly Review* referred to it as a 'pretty cognomen'.)[40] Gill Gregory suggests, intriguingly, that the awkward moniker possibly even registers Cornwall's own sense of his creative limits, signalling his realization that he was destined to bump up against 'land's end' in his writing.[41]

What little attention Cornwall still commands is due to candid *aperçus* into the characters of more illustrious figures such as Keats, Coleridge and Wordsworth, as well as those difficult, disputatious characters, Hazlitt and Hunt, that liberally salt his posthumously published *An Autobiographical Fragment* (1877). His generous *Charles Lamb: A Memoir* (1866) has also been mined for quotable gobbets. Cornwall claims footnote space, too, for his brief courtship of the recently widowed Mary Shelley. In journal entries from September 1824, she recalls in astonishingly frank terms how Cornwall reminded her of her dead husband: '[His] voice, laden with sentiment, passed as Shelley's'. Mary adds that Cornwall 'read with the same deep feeling as he'. When Cornwall abruptly broke off contact to marry his fiancée, Anne Skepper, Mary remarked wryly: 'So much for my powers of attraction'.[42]

We tend to regard Cornwall as something of a Jack Vettriano figure, undeniably popular, but not to be taken all that seriously. Just as the art establishment winces at Vettriano's un-ironic butlers and faux-noirish semi-nudes, we reject Cornwall for not offering the layered complexities, which our long admiration for Keats's aesthetic has conditioned us to expect in Romantic poetry. Yet Cornwall's poems are more than just a cornucopia of fine phrase-making, and in fact form a vital context to Keats's own poetic evolution and reception. Early drafts show that Keats was seduced on various occasions by Cornwall's commercial style, and Cornwall himself needs to be recognized as an axial, structuring presence in Keats's career. To be certain, Keats is most canonically 'Keatsian' at moments of strategic retreat from his rival's populist aesthetic; by the same token, Cornwall achieves his most durable success, seen through a modern lens, when he eschews voguish cliché to reproduce the hallmarks of Keats's poetry, poetry lived at a pitch.

Notwithstanding his wide acclaim, Cornwall's feelings towards a writer whose friendship he seems to have been more anxious to secure than vice versa were mixed – especially when the issue of originality was at stake. Cornwall's advocates were charmed by his trademark blend of the spirit of English and Italian Renaissance writers with a modern sensibility, which they credited with rejuvenating contemporary poetics; in a review of Hunt's translation of Tasso's *Amyntas, A Tale of the Woods* (1820), the *Edinburgh Magazine* thanked Cornwall for helping to create the vogue for medievalizing poems with Italianate settings that was referenced by Keats's own work:

> We are happy to observe, that the success of Mr Cornwall has induced other writers to recur to the same source from which so much may yet be drawn. Mr Keats has been versifying Italian tales; and we have now to make some remarks

on a translation of Tasso's Aminta by Mr Leigh Hunt, who has already made an admirable use of his knowledge of Italian literature in his Story of Rimini.[43]

Nevertheless, several of the age's *soi-disant* arbiters of taste regarded Cornwall as a fraudulent imitator who sponged off more distinguished precursors. Sheer speed of composition, they opined, had led him to mimic Massinger, Beaumont and Fletcher, Spenser and Boccaccio, rather than carefully distilling their spirit.[44] Question marks also hung over his debt to living authors, especially Keats.

Cornwall was not as thick-skinned as we might suppose, his 'Critique on Keats' for Morehead revealing his anxiety on this subject. Let's look again at the point where he seeks to clarify the chronologies of the pair's cognate adaptations from the *Decameron*: "'Isabella; or The Pot of Basil," is a story from Boccaccio, and is the same as was given to the public some time ago, by Mr Barry Cornwall, under the title of "*A Sicilian Story*"'. 'Some time ago' does no less than record a factual sequence of publication, but it doesn't tell the whole story, either. It was the imprimatur of Hazlitt's recommendation as far back as February 1818 that sent both Keats and Cornwall to Boccaccio's basil pot in the first place. Lecturing on the English poets at the 'Surry' in February 1817, Hazlitt paused to reflect on current trends in the poetry trade: 'I should think that a translation of some of the ... serious tales in Boccaccio and Chaucer, as that of Isabella, the Falcon, of Constance, the Prioress's Tale, and others ... could not fail to succeed in the present day'.[45] Seated among the fashionables, Dissenters and Quakers in the colonnaded auditorium, eager for insights into the sort of poetry that was selling, or likely to sell, were Cornwall and Keats. Cornwall's future wife, Anne Skepper – dedicatee of both Milnes's 1848 *Life of Keats* and Sidney Colvin's 1887 edition of Keats's letters – was there, too, and long afterwards recalled the unusual shape of Keats's face, noting that it 'had not the squareness of a man's, but more like some women's face I have seen (particularly one in the Looking Glass)'.[46] We can only conjecture whether Cornwall also saw Keats in his wife's visage.

The aspiring poets began composing their respective versions in early 1819. But where Cornwall's strategically soft-focused re-imagining reached reviewers' hands in December that year, publication of the grisly *Isabella*, with its loamy, putrefying secrets, was delayed until 1 July 1820, when the *Lamia* volume appeared in an edition of 500 copies priced 7s 6d. By the time Keats's poem made it onto the book stands, a second edition of Cornwall's poem, which the *Examiner* had been advertising since 21 May, had already beaten it to press. Even *Marcian Colonna*, punctuated by groans and lunatic wails, published in the third or fourth week of June and laurelled with an advance review on 10 June in the *Literary Gazette*, pipped *Isabella* to the book stands by about a week, deflecting still more interest away from the frustrated Keats.[47] It was hardly a propitious context of reception. When the 'eminently beautiful' *Isabella* (as Cornwall put it in his review) finally appeared, potential pundits were too familiar with the tale, as re-told by a significantly more popular poet.

Critics today unfairly dismiss Cornwall's re-imagining of Boccaccio as poetic confectionary alongside Keats's *Isabella*. Even Hermann Fischer, whose summarizing paragraph on Cornwall in *Romantic Verse Narrative: The History of a Genre* notes the poet's 'adoption of the most important characteristics of the Cockney School', scoffs that *A Sicilian Story* 'can hardly be considered a rival to Keats's *Isabella*'.[48] As we will see in Chapter 5, there were actually very good reasons why Romantic readers so emphatically preferred Cornwall's poem.

2. 'A Little Sketch of Mine'

Although he had deprived Keats of the popular vote, presenting work that was similarly themed and styled, but ideologically less challenging, more accessible, Cornwall seemed to sense that the critical wind would soon blow from a different direction. As Gill Gregory suggests, Cornwall was 'clearly disturbed by his status as a "minor" and perhaps in the future an anonymous poet' (p. 53). In 1930, collector of rare manuscripts F. L. Pleadwell transcribed a Cornwall letter to Ollier for *Notes and Queries*. It appeared with virtually no commentary and was not subsequently collected in R. W. Armour's 1935 critical biography of Cornwall.[49] This letter, too, shows that Cornwall was pricklish on the topic of Keats and plagiarism and makes for interesting reading alongside the earlier correspondence with Morehead:

25 Store S^t.[50]
Bedford Square
Tuesday

Dear Sir,

I send you Coleridge's Wallenstein & his earlier poems (some of which you will perceive have been incorporated with the Sybilline Leaves.)

I send you a little sketch of mine (Peleus & Thetis), written & <u>printed</u> before Endymion came out, & to which, more especially to the last part, the Hymn to Diana bears a stronger resemblance in point of Style than to the hymn to Pan. I do this in order to exonerate myself from plagiarism. In Truth tho my Hymn was sketched before I ever read the address to Pan.⁵¹ I have added something ~~to my Hymn~~ you will see.

If when I have improved it a little you like it, it is of course at ~~yourself~~ Service – but I would rather that you should print it without my name, as I was nearly losing a Client sometime since because it was conjectured I had been guilty of the Sin of Poetry⁵² – This is all very silly but unfortunately <u>for the present</u> I must be an 'Anonny mouse' as the author of Highgate Tunnel says.

Yours truly,
B. W. Procter

The 3 lines against which I have placed an X were added by a friend.

– Remember <u>half past five</u>!
of Course I <u>can</u> have no other objection to
appear in good Company than what I
have mentioned.

Cornwall is eager to clarify that his 'Hymn to Diana' – set 'upon the Latmos hill' and focused on the goddess's 'own pale boy, Endymion' – published in Leigh Hunt's *Literary Pocket-Book* for 1819, printed by Ollier, owes a debt 'in point of style' not to Keats's epic, but to his own poem, 'The Marriage of Peleus and Thetis', which he emphasizes was 'written and <u>printed</u> before Endymion came out'. Of course, Cornwall is also claiming, 'in Truth tho', that he was 'doing' Endymion *before* Keats.

Despite Wilson's assurance in his review of the *Literary Pocket-Book* that Cornwall's 'Hymn to Diana' was worth two of Hunts' and Keats's 'Cockney' offerings, the poem was not subsequently collected by Cornwall, possibly due to Cornwall's squeamishness on the issue of precedence. Hunt's volume is now rare – one of the few remaining copies may be consulted in Duke Humphrey's Library, Oxford University – and has not been scanned as part of the Google Books Library Project. Indeed, other than in embedded form in the *Blackwood's* review of Hunt (which has been digitally scanned), the poem is to all extents unavailable, a circumstance that warrants printing it here:

'Hymn to Diana'

Dian! – We seek thee in this tranquil hour;
We call thee by thy names of power;
Lucina! first – (that tender name divine,
Which young and travail'd dames adore and fear;)
Child of the dark-brow'd Proserpine!
Star-crowned Dian! Daughter of Jove

Olympian! Mother of blind Love!
Fair Cynthia! Towered Cybele!
Lady of stainless chastity!

Bend low thy listening ear,
And smile upon us, now the long day's toil,
Beautiful queen! is done,
And from the withering sun
Save thou and bless the perch'd and fainting soil;
So may thy silver shafts ne'er miss their aim,
But strike the heart of every bounding fawn;
And not a nymph of thine e'er lose her fame
By loitering in the beechen glades;
Or standing, with her mantle half undrawn,
Like hearkening Silence, near the skirting shades
Of forests, where the cloven satyrs lie
Sleeping with upward face, or piping musically.

Oh! smile upon us Dian! smile as thou
Art wont, 'tis said, at times to look upon
Thy own pale boy, Endymion,
When calm he slumbers on the mountain's brow:
And may no doubt, not care,
When thou shalt wish, on nights serene and still
To stay thy car upon the Latmos hill,
Touch with a clouded hand thy look of light;
Nor elemental blight
Mar the rich beauties of thy hyacinthine hair.

Queen of the tumbling floods! oh lend thine ear
To us who seek and praise thee here –
– Fright not the Halcyon from her watery nest,
When on the scarcely-moving waves she sits
Listening – sore distrest
Lest that the winds, in sullen fits,
Should come, and lift the curling seas on high: –
– Yet if the storm *must* come – then Dian! then
Scatter the billows from the Delphic shore,
And bid the monsters of the deep go roar
In those far foreign caves
Sicilian, where the ocean raves
For ever, (dug, 'tis said, by giant men
Beneath Pelorus' rugged promontory.)

On thy white altar we
Lavish in fond idolatry.
Herbs and sweet flowers such as the summer uses:
Some that in wheaten fields
Lift their red bells amidst the golden grain: –
Some that the moist earth yields,
Beneath the shadows of those pine trees high,
Which, branching, shield the far Thessalian plains
from the fierce anger of Apollo's eye –
And some that Dephic swains
Pluck by the silver springs of Castaly –
(Yet, there – thus it is said – the wanton Muses,
Their dark and tangled locks adorning,
Lie stretch'd on green slopes 'neath the laurel boughs
Or weave sad garlands for their brows;
And tho' they shun *thee* thro' the livelong night,
Bend their blue eyes before the God of morning,
And hail with shouts his first return of light. –)

Now and for ever hail, great Dian! Thou,
Before whose moony brow,
The rolling planets die, or lose their fires,
And all the bravery of Heaven retires —
– There, Saturn dimly turns within his ring,
And Jove looks pale upon his burning throne;
There, the great hunter-king
Orion, mourns with watery glare,
The tarnish'd lustre of his blazing zone –
Thou only through the blue and starry air,
In unabated beauty rid'st along,
Companion'd by our song —
Turn hither, then, thy clear and stedfast smile,
To grace our humble welcoming,
And free the poet's brain
From all but that so famous pain,
Which sometimes, at the still midnight,
Stirs his creative fancyings, while,
(Charm'd by thy silvery light)
He strives, not vainly then, his sweetest song to sing.

This early poem is itself sing-song in places ('sing'/'song' are unfortu-
nate line endings in such close proximity), and it is marred by Cornwall's
maddening penchant for parenthetical clauses. It also contains a particularly

egregious specimen of 'Cockney' rhyme ('upon/Endymion'); and we find several phrases of the kind that had earned Hunt imprecations from 'Z.' and Wilson, such as 'watery glare' and 'moony brow'. None the less, there are more sonorous moments, such as the images of harvest echoing Marvell's 'The Garden' (as well as anticipating Cornwall's sonnet on 'Autumn', published in the *Literary Pocket-Book* for 1820; see Chapter 3): 'Herbs and sweet flowers such as the summer uses/ Some that in wheaten fields/ Lift their red bells amidst the golden grain: –/ Some that the moist earth yields'.[53] Similarly, Cornwall's commercial eye for titillating scenes is already apparent in the salacious comment on the reputation of 'loitering' nymphs with 'mantle half undrawn' in the second verse paragraph.

Cornwall was possibly justified in bristling when the subject of *Endymion* came up, since elsewhere the issue of plagiarism between the rival poets isn't as clear-cut as we might assume. I'd like to pause to weigh a suggestive episode of creative exchange involving two 'Bright Star' sonnets – one famous, the other obscure; one composed between October and December 1819 but not published until 1838, the other published in June 1820.

First Keats's celebrated lines:

Bright star! would I were stedfast as thou art –
Not in lone splendour hung aloft the night
And watching, with eternal lids apart,
Like nature's patient, sleepless Eremite,
The moving waters at their priestlike task
Of pure ablution round earth's human shores,
Or gazing on the new soft-fallen mask
Of snow upon the mountains and the moors –
No – yet still stedfast, still unchangeable,
Pillowed upon my fair love's ripening breast,
To feel for ever its soft swell and fall,
Awake for ever in a sweet unrest,
Still, still to hear her tender-taken breath,
And so live ever – or else swoon to death.

This sonnet was traditionally regarded as the poet's last, composed during the wretched voyage to Italy aboard the 130-ton cargo brig *Maria Crowther* in September 1820. Keats laboriously inscribed the lines into Joseph Severn's copy of Shakespeare's poems. The discovery of an earlier version in the form of an 1819 transcript made by Keats's friend Charles Brown (the Crewe House Quarto, known as T²), obliged scholars to reconsider the sonnet's date. Credible alternatives are July 1819, favoured by Aileen Ward; or – generally considered more likely – October–November 1819. Bate pushes the envelope forward slightly to December 1819. The sonnet was not published in Keats's lifetime, and first appeared in *Plymouth and Devonport Weekly Journal* on 27 September 1838, where it was sent by Charles Brown. It was also included shortly afterwards in Richard Monckton Milnes's seminal publication in the history of Keats's posthumous fame, the two-volume *Life and Letters of John Keats* (1848).

In June 1820, six months after *A Sicilian Story*, and only a year after the appearance of *Dramatic Scenes* (1819), the prolific Cornwall published a third collection, *Marcian Colonna*. Now obscure, the volume's experimental title piece, a pullulating study in hereditary madness, violence and emotional instability, influenced Robert Browning's 'Porphyria's Lover' and anticipated *Maud*, Tennyson's own stark étude in violent psychological interiority. The last item in the collection is a 'miscellaneous' sonnet:

> Perhaps the lady of my love is now
> Looking upon the skies. A single star
> Is rising in the East, and from afar
> Sheds a most tremulous lustre: Silent Night
> Doth wear it like a jewel on her brow:
> But see, it motions, with its lovely light,
> Onwards and onwards thro' those depths of blue,
> To its appointed course stedfast and true.
> So dearest, would I fain be unto thee,
> Stedfast for ever, – like yon planet fair;
> And yet more like art *thou* a jewel rare.
> Oh! brighter than the brightest star, to me,
> Come hither, my young love; and I will wear
> Thy beauty on my breast delightedly.

Objections to Cornwall inevitably centre on the unevenness of his poetry, and the above lines do not count among his most felicitous. My primary concern at this point, however, is not with issues of literary 'value' but rather with the matter of Cornwall's complex interactions with Keats. Any study that seeks to rehabilitate Cornwall faces a keen heuristic challenge: his work has become radically unfamiliar to us in so far as it has been overtaken by our preference for Keats's aesthetic. Although the process is now largely concealed to us, we define what we like about Keats precisely in terms of what we don't like (what we no longer respond to) in writers like Cornwall. The result is that Cornwall begins to appear as 'trivial', adrift from the most important trends in Romantic political and literary culture. One means of countering this 'double alienation' effect is to show that Cornwall may actually have been close enough to Keats to enjoy access to his work in manuscript form.

While my larger argument for the importance of a writer like Barry Cornwall to an understanding of late-Romantic literary culture does not depend on establishing direct influence, or plagiarism, between Cornwall and Keats, the correspondences between Cornwall's published sonnet and Keats's unpublished 'Bright Star' are striking. Not only do similar words and phrases occur in each, but a remarkably similar subjunctive conceit is also in play:

> Keats: 'would I were stedfast as thou art'
> Cornwall: 'would I fain be unto thee/ Stedfast for ever'
>
> Keats: 'Bright Star!'
> Cornwall: 'brighter than the brightest star'
>
> Keats: 'love's ripening breast'
> Cornwall: 'thy beauty on my breast'

In addition, the sonnets share key words: 'love', 'fair', 'forever' and – as we'd expect in a poem about stars – 'night'. Each poem begins by contemplating a star in the night sky, and ends with, or rather on, a breast: the 'ripening' breast of Keats's lover (Keats is boyishly rocked to sleep on his love's pillowing breast), and via a star/jewel conceit, the delighted breast of his close bosom-friend, Cornwall. Keats has the North Star in mind, while Cornwall chooses Venus, the evening star. Similarly, while Keats's boyish sonnet self-centredly muses on his wish to be constant as the polar star, Cornwall – as one *ought* in a love sonnet – shifts attention to his 'young love', his watcher of the skies, flattering her that *she* is the real jewel in the firmament, brighter than the brightest star.

Both poets, of course, are utilizing a common trope. There's a whole tradition of 'bright star' sonnets – including Shakespeare's sonnet 116, which Garrod thought had inflected Keats's poem, and sonnet 27, which J.-C. Sallé believed to have contributed Keats's 'eternal lids' image[54] – several of which can be sampled on the Chadwyck-Healey *Literature Online* database; as well as a plenitude of eighteenth- and early nineteenth-century examples. For instance, we find one by a poet born in the same year as Keats, Jeremiah Joseph Callanan (1795–1829):

> When each bright star is clouded that illumin'd our way,
> And darkly through the bleak night of life we stray,
> What joy then is left us, but alone to weep
> O'er the cold dreary pillow where loved ones sleep?'[55]

Wordsworth, too, wrote a 'Fair Star' sonnet in 1802, which Nicholas Roe suggests is one of the contexts for reading Keats's sonnet as a meditation on political steadfastness.[56] Cornwall even included an apostrophe 'Oh! Thou bright Star' in a short piece, 'To a Star', published in *A Sicilian Story*. However, none of these contain the crucial concatenation of bright stars, steadfastness and breasts that occurs in the two poems under discussion.

The parallels are too singular to be safely ascribed to coincidence. The question is, whose poem has impressed itself on whose? Perhaps the first thing to say is that whoever saw the other's poem first, it must have been in manuscript. Keats's sonnet wasn't published until 1838; similarly, Cornwall's sonnet didn't appear in print until after the latest date suggested for the composition of Keats's poem. It would be a tantalizing prospect to imagine that Keats read Cornwall's poem first (the chronological window of opportunity just allows it). But weighing against this explanation is a letter composed during Keats's walking tour of the Lake District. On 25 June 1818, Keats described for his brother Tom two views of Lake Windermere that refined his 'sensual vision into a sort of north star which can never cease to be open lidded and stedfast over the wonders of the great Power' (*LJK*, I, 299). The alignment of stars, open-liddedness, and steadfastness in both letter and sonnet indicates that the storehouse of imagery supplying 'Bright Star' existed long before Keats could have seen Cornwall's poem.[57] (There is little doubt that Keats read Cornwall's 'Bright Star' at some point, though: in June 1820, Cornwall gave Keats a copy of his third volume, as recorded in his only surviving letter to Keats.)[58]

Whichever way the issue is turned – whether we accept a scenario in which Keats 'plagiarizes' Cornwall's sonnet, or the more likely scenario in which Cornwall sees Keats's unpublished poem in manuscript form before writing his own – the association between the two poets, and Cornwall's part in the circulations of Cockney School political and literary culture, is evidently more complex than suggested by conventional Romantic studies narratives, in which Cornwall meets Keats only after the latter's tuberculosis is advanced and illness prevents any meaningful creative interaction. It is not unthinkable that Cornwall might have had access to a draft of Keats's poem, if not shown to him by Keats himself then by Hunt or a member of his group.

Keats's 'Bright Star' sonnet to his fiancée possesses a special resonance for Keats lovers: the poet's copying of the improved version of T^2 into the flyleaf of Severn's Shakespeare from his sweat-soaked sickbed fuelling the myth that it was his last poetic effusion. The sonnet's title has – inevitably,

perhaps – been used as the title for Jane Campion's big-screen treatment of
Keats's and Fanny Brawne's ill-fated relationship, *Bright Star* (2009). Given
the poignant centrality of the sonnet to the Keats story, then, it's fascinating
to note how the presence of Barry Cornwall's own love poem may, in some
sense, be felt in this most intimate of poetic addresses.

To return to the Cornwall letter that was printed in *Notes and Queries* in
1930, it was William Jerdan who first published Cornwall's 'little sketch', the
epyllion 'The Marriage of Peleus and Thetis' on 4 April 1818 in the *Literary
Gazette* (signed 'B'). It was reprinted by Alaric Watts, 'father of the literary
album', in his 1828 anthology, the *Poetical Album*.[59] The volume was ready
for press in 1824 and printed in 1825 (its appearance was delayed by four
years due to a series of copyright disputes). In the light of the touchy letter
to Ollier, it would seem obvious that caginess over likely comparisons with
Keats was responsible for Cornwall's decision not to collect another of his
more accomplished early poems in any of his full volumes.

'The Marriage of Pelleus and Thetis' delivers an erotic frisson that plainly
appealed to readers, climaxing with this pillowy passage:

And midnight came, and all the gods departed,
And nymphs – and left the lovers to repose
On pillows of the fresh-blown rose;
The winds were silent, and the waters played
No more – lest that they should the sea-green maid
Disturb (no longer pale and broken-hearted).
Love only on the couch was hovering,
A couch that gods had deigned to bless,
Where each had given some gift of happiness;
Love only staid, he kissed each forehead fair,
And flung narcotic odours from his wing
(Sweet beyond man's imagining);
Then took his flight upon the morning air:
Yet every night returned and blessed that happy pair!
        ('The Marriage of Peleus and Thetis')

Other sections in the poem might easily be confused with Keats's own
early idiom, which heard against Cornwall's early work seems less distinctive
somehow:

                    ... yet as day declined
They came – then first was heard Favonius's sigh,
Wild whispering through the blossoms, as he pined
Away, in notes of fragrant melody –

And Cupid, who till then had fluttered far,
Blushing, and fretful on the varying wing,
And wept to see the Nereids fear,
Came wheeling round and round – near and more near –
(As doves come homeward in their narrowing ring)
And loitering Dian sent her vesper star
To tell her coming, and to say, that night
She nearer to the Earth would bend her head,
And rest a moment on old Pelion's height,
And kiss pale Thetis on her bridal bed.

Cornwall was right to worry about how his relation to Keats, especially *Endymion*, was perceived by outsiders, however. In its review of *A Sicilian Story* in June 1820, the *Monthly Magazine* wagged a censorious finger: 'In a few passages we observe rather too strong a resemblance to the Endymion of Mr. Keates [*sic*], who is the precursor of Mr C in the mythological and classical style of poetry, engrafted on that of the present age'.[60] Pooh-poohing the idea of debt in his dispatch to Ollier, Cornwall nevertheless appears – doubtless parapractically – to pick up in his phrase 'stronger resemblance' the *Monthly Magazine*'s own rhetoric ('too strong a resemblance').

Targeting his books at the same audience as Keats, all the while anxious to disperse the lingering whiff of plagiarism, Cornwall had enough reasons to be content to watch his contemporary's volumes sink without trace. Fortunately for the better poet, however, Cornwall had a generous spirit. In spite of conflicted emotions he was able to acknowledge, and it seems take genuine delight in, his rival's genius (later in life, Cornwall acknowledged Keats as 'by nature the most essentially a poet in the present century').[61] What the letter to Morehead now allows us to appreciate is that Cornwall, when it mattered most, was also prepared to evangelize on his luckless competitor's behalf.

Perhaps the fashionable writer felt guilty that his often flimsy verse had so entirely displaced Keats's poetry in the public's imagination. Contributing one of the earliest obituaries of Keats in Baldwin's *London Magazine* in April 1821, shortly after news of the poet's death reached England, Cornwall tries to set the record straight. In doing so, he alludes to *The Fall of Hyperion*, Keats's extended meditation on the pain of usurpation: '[Keats] has been suffered to rise and pass away almost without a notice; the laurel has been awarded (for the present) to other brows: the bolder aspirants have been allowed to take their station on the slippery steps of the temple of fame'.[62] It's a fascinating circumstance, and one that invites us to revise our prejudices about Cornwall's importance to Romantic literary culture, that as well as performing a crucial service to Keats's posthumous reputation with his

obituary, Cornwall also did his best for Keats's reputation during the poet's
own lifetime.

3. Coda: Letting the Reader Judge

Romanticists often catch themselves wondering whether they would have
been equal to the task of recognizing Keats's masterpieces when they first
appeared. Cornwall faced precisely this 'test', we now know, in his 'Critique
on Keats' in the *Edinburgh Magazine and Literary Miscellany*. Mastery of the
market hadn't vulgarized his taste; on the contrary, he was one of the first
readers to proclaim the genius of 'Ode to a Nightingale':[63]

> Among the minor poems we prefer the 'Ode to a Nightingale.' Indeed, we are
> inclined to prefer it beyond every other poem in the book; but let the reader
> judge. The third and seventh stanzas have a charm for us which we should find
> it difficult to explain. We have read this ode over and over again, and every time
> with increased delight. (p. 315)

Keats told Reynolds that Cornwall's poems, composed on 'the Seasons,
the Leaves, the Moon &c.', teased him and he portrayed his arch rival's irresistible appeal as no more than a knack for ringing 'triple bob majors' on fashionable topics (*LJK*, II, 268). Still, Keats had the judgement to see that Cornwall
'likes poetry for its own sake, not his'. This selflessness comes through strongly
in Cornwall's defence of his floundering Cockney stablemate.

In Cornwall, Keats found his worst imaginable competitor, someone
who on the face of it sounded just like him, but who managed to market
himself as the acceptable face of 'Cockney' poetry. And yet, in the genial
solicitor Keats might also have found his best reader. Without Cornwall's
altruistic act of sending Morehead what was almost certainly an unsolicited
review of an unpopular author, Keats's reputation may have taken longer
to recover after the debacle of *Endymion*. Aside from a reasonably favourable appraisal in the *Monthly Review* in July, and an obviously partisan
review by Cornwall's friend, Charles Lamb, in the *New Times* on 19 July
1820, reprinted by Hunt in the *Examiner* on 30 July – hardly the kind of
endorsement Keats needed – initial reviews of *Lamia* were dispiriting. On
29 July, the *Literary Chronicle* professed to feeling let down, having 'augured
better things' from the young poet; and on 6 August 1820, one day before
Cornwall's 'return' to town, the anti-radical *Guardian* dismissed *Lamia* as a
'nose-gay of enigmas'.[64] With characteristic good timing, then, Cornwall got
his review out at a vital juncture. The first instalment challenged the critical

consensus on *Endymion*, and laid the ground for serious reconsideration of Keats's talents. It seemed to do the trick, for at this point Keats's fortunes began to improve. With the exception of *Blackwood's* dogged ill-will, other literary journals followed the *Edinburgh Magazine's* authoritative lead and at last began to tune in to the frequencies of Keats's achievement. In September 1820, the *New Monthly Magazine* noted the poet's astonishing improvement; in the same month a glowing report appeared in Baldwin's *London Magazine*. Shortly after, the *Monthly Magazine* trumpeted that Keats was entitled to stand 'equally high in the estimation of public opinion, as ... he of the Dramatic Scenes [Cornwall]'.[65] By the time the second half of Cornwall's critique was published in October, it capped a run of favourable reviews.

Keats, it seems, was and remained unaware of Cornwall's guiding hand in repairing his fortunes, and I think it unlikely that any of his circle, including Reynolds, knew about it either. If they had been cognizant of Cornwall's behind-the-scenes activities they might have reimbursed the voguish poet with a less condescending attitude towards his work. In 1824, Cornwall went on to perform another service to Romantic poetry, helping to arrange the bankrolling of Mary Shelley's edition of her recently drowned husband's poems (Percy, too, had sneered at Cornwall behind his back). The hitherto unsuspected role of Cornwall in talking up Keats in his own day, however, should attract new attention to this colourful and unfairly forgotten figure's conflicted relationship with the greatest lyrical poet of his generation.

Notes

1 See *Edinburgh Magazine and Literary Miscellany*, 7 (1820), pp. 107–10, 313–16.
2 Donald H. Reiman (ed.), *The Romantics Reviewed: Contemporary Reviews of British Romantic Writers*, 9 vols (New York: Garland, 1972), C, II, 828.
3 Poem signed 'I. R.'. Reynolds is cited as its author on the online database, *English Poetry 1579–1830: Spenser and the Tradition*: <http://198.82.142.160/spenser/CommentRecord.php?&action=GET&cmmtid=8089> [date of access: 12.6.8].
4 Leonidas M. Jones, *The Life of John Hamilton Reynolds* (London: University Press of New England, 1984), p. 147; for Reynolds's connections with Constable's new magazine, see pp. 161, 181–82.
5 I am grateful to the Carl H. Pforzheimer Collection of Shelley and His Circle, The New York Public Library, Astor, Lenox and Tilden Foundations for permission to quote in full from the manuscripts of the Cornwall letters in this chapter. I am also indebted to Elizabeth C. Denlinger for her generous assistance.
6 In 1818, Morehead wrote to Wilson and Lockhart, protesting at *Blackwood's* 'delinquencies'. Letter quoted in Mary Gordon, *'Christopher North': A Memoir of John Wilson* (New York: Widdleton, 1863), p. 193.

7   See Charles Morehead, *Memorials of the Life and Writings of the Rev. Robert Morehead, D.D.* (Edinburgh: Edmonstone and Douglas, 1875).

8   Leonidas M. Jones (ed.), *The Letters of John Hamilton Reynolds* (Lincoln, NE: University of Nebraska Press, 1973), p. 19.

9   See *Edinburgh Review*, 37 (1823), pp. 177–208. As Jones points out, no section on comic drama ever appeared.

10 On 4 July, Reynolds had written to Taylor complaining that Jerdan's 'damn'd' *Literary Gazette* had only devoted a single line of commentary along with a few quotations to the just-published *Lamia* volume. See *The Letters of John Hamilton Reynolds*, p. 18.

11 See *Edinburgh Review*, 34 (1820), pp. 203–13. Although Jeffrey's sympathetic appraisal was printed in the August issue of the *Edinburgh Review*, it wouldn't have reached readers until September, Leonidas M. Jones notes, due to the editor's notorious tardiness in getting the journal out for distribution (p. 198).

12 A further clue to Cornwall's penmanship of the review is provided by the high incidence of 'fingerprint' parenthetical clauses. Bracketed asides are a signature of Cornwall's poetry, a stylistic tic carried over into his prose works.

13 *Edinburgh Magazine and Literary Miscellany*, 5 (1819), pp. 121–25, at p. 121.

14 *Edinburgh Magazine and Literary Miscellany*, 7 (1820), pp. 7–14, at p. 7.

15 Keats's nurse on the voyage to Italy, the painter Joseph Severn (1793–1879), lived for even longer.

16 Cornwall made light of this 'honour'. In an unpublished autograph letter from 1820, sent with a copy of *A Sicilian Story* to J. W. Broughton, Cornwall remarks: 'I was the school fellow at least of a great poet. I don't know whether this goes for anything in the Estimate of myself. I am afraid not'. Manuscript in Carl H. Pforzheimer Collection of Shelley and His Circle, New York Public Library (Pforz MS, Misc 1610).

17 Willis visited Cornwall in 1832. See *Pencillings by the Way: Written During Some Years of Residence and Travel in Europe*, 3rd edn (Auben: Alden, Beardsley & Co., 1853), p. 491.

18 *Edinburgh Monthly Review*, 4 (1820), pp. 176–77.

19 *Literary Gazette*, 10 June 1820, pp. 369–70. A performance of *Hamlet*, judged indifferent by the *Literary Gazette*, had recently run at Drury Lane (reviewed on p. 238).

20 *Asiatic Journal and Monthly Miscellany*, 11 (1821), p. 545. Eight years later the journal changed its mind, arguing that only due to 'corrupt taste' had Cornwall been 'dignified with the prostituted title of poet'; *Asiatic Journal and Monthly Miscellany*, 28 (1829), p. 513.

21 Charles Lamb, *Works: Including His Most Interesting Letters*, ed. Thomas Noon Talfourd, new edn (London: Bell and Daldy, 1852), p. 156.

22 Walter Savage Landor, 'To Barry Cornwall', from *Poems, Dialogues in Verse and Epigrams* (1892).

23 In a brief note to the author Alexandra Osipovna Ishimova, Pushkin apologizes for being unable to attend an appointment that afternoon to discuss the projected translations, promising to send along instead a copy of *The Poetical Works of Milman, Bowles, Wilson and Cornwall*, with five of his favourite dramatic scenes marked in pencil. Ishimova published the translations in *The Contemporary*. See Richard Willard Armour, *Barry Cornwall: A Biography of Bryan Waller Procter* (Boston: Meador, 1935), pp. 103–04. Also see Serena Vitale, *Pushkin's Button*, trans. Ann Goldstein and Jon Rothschild (Chicago: University of Chicago Press, 2000), pp. 233–34.

24 *Theatrical Inquisitor*, 1 (1820), p. 53; Mary Russell Mitford to Sir William Elford, letter dated 5 July 1820; See A. G. L'Estrange, *Life of Mary Russell Mitford*, 3 vols(London: Bentley, 1870), I, 340.

25 *London Magazine*, 7 (1823), pp. 669–72, at p. 669.

26 William *Hazlitt, Select British Poets; or, New Elegant Extracts from Chaucer to the Present Time* (London: Hall, 1824). The volume was suppressed due to pressure from other publishers that inclusion of 'their' living authors might harm their sales. For an excellent discussion of Hazlitt's anthology, see William St. Clair, *The Reading Nation in the Romantic Period*, pp. 222–23. A year later, a shorter version of Hazlitt's selection appeared without living or recent writers as *Select Poets of Great Britain* (London: Tegg, 1825). The original 1824 prefatory material and table of contents is available online, edited by Laura Mandell, at: <http://www.orgs.muohio.edu/anthologies/haz1.htm> [date of access: 10.9.5].

27 These essays, along with the poet's own 'A Defence of Poetry', were collected in Cornwall's *Essays and Tales in Prose* (Boston: Ticknor, Read and Fields, 1853).

28 *Blackwood's Edinburgh Magazine*, 5 (1819), pp. 310–16, at p. 311.

29 Philip Flynn, 'Beginning *Blackwood's*': The First Hundred Numbers (April 1817–May 1825)'. Available online at: <http://www.english.udel.edu/Profiles/flynn_blackwood.htm> [date of access: 1.5.8]. Also see Flynn's related essay (which does not include any references to Cornwall), 'Beginning *Blackwood's*: The Right Mix of Dulce and Utile', *Victorian Periodicals Review*, 39 (2006), pp. 136–57.

30 *London Magazine* (Gold's), 3 (1821), pp. 278–80, at p. 278.

31 Mary Wollstonecraft Shelley, *Proserpine and Midas*, ed. André Henri Koszul (London: Milford, 1922), p. xxxi; Edmund Blunden, *Leigh Hunt: A Biography* (repr. Archon, 1970), p. 138.

32 Clive James, 'Cultural Amnesia', *Times Literary Supplement*, 19 May 2007, p. 19.

33 Franz Becker, *Bryan Waller Procter (Barry Cornwall)* (Wien: Baumüller, 1911), p. 74.

34 *London Magazine*, 7 (1823), p. 669.

35 *Blackwood's Edinburgh Magazine*, 6 (1819), pp. 235–47, at p. 236. The series was published by the Olliers.

36 Keats's and Cornwall's fathers both made their money in alcohol. In 1802, Thomas Keats took over the management of the Swan and Hoop on 24 Pavement Row (now Finsbury Pavement, in Moorgate). Cornwall's father dealt in wine and brandy; between 1799 and 1804 his operations were based less than 3 miles away from the Swan and Hoop at 241 Piccadilly.

37 See John Barnard, 'First Fruits or "First Blights": A New Account of the Publishing History of Keats's *Poems* (1817)', *Romanticism*, 12.2 (2006), pp. 71–101.

38 In this letter, Brown also shares with Keats some 'interesting small talk' about Cornwall's engagement to 'Miss Montague' (Anne Skepper).

39 Marilyn Butler, *Romantics, Rebels and Reactionaries: English Literature and its Background, 1760–1830* (Oxford: Oxford University Press, 1981), p. 173; Donald S. Reiman (ed.) *Brian Waller Procter: A Sicilian Story and Mirandola* (London: Garland, 1977), p. viii; Ayumi Mizukoshi, *Keats, Hunt and the Aesthetics of Pleasure* (London: Palgrave, 2001), p. 136.

40 *Edinburgh Monthly Review*, 4 (1820), p. 176.

41 Gill Gregory, *The Life and Work of Adelaide Anne Procter: Poetry, Feminism and Fathers* (Aldershot: Ashgate, 1998), p. 53.

42 *The Journals of Mary Shelley, 1814–1844*, 2 vols, ed. Paula R. Feldman and Diana Scott-Kilvert (Oxford: Clarendon Press, 1987), II, pp. 481–82.

43 *Edinburgh Magazine and Literary Miscellany*, 7 (1820), pp. 214-18, at pp. 215-16.

44 The otherwise supportive *Edinburgh Monthly Review* thought similarly. It labelled *Marcian Colonna* a 'hasty performance', and accused Cornwall of 'indulging in a culpable measure of carelessness and speed'; *Edinburgh Monthly Review*, 4 (1820), pp. 176–86, at pp. 178–79.

45 William Hazlitt, *Lectures on the English Poets, Delivered at the Surrey Institution* (London: Taylor and Hessey, 1818), p. 162.

46 See Hyder Edward Rollins (ed.), *The Keats Circle: Letters and Papers, 1816–1878*, 2 vols (Cambridge, MA: Harvard University Press, 1948), II, p. 158. Cornwall's wife, Anne Procter, née Skepper (1799–1888), related this suggestive description to Richard Monckton Milnes in a letter of 14 May 1846. Milnes was gathering materials for his watershed *Life, Letters, and Literary Remains of John Keats* (1848). She doesn't mention an obvious feature about Keats: his stature. Her husband stood at about the same height – Keats was just under, Cornwall just over, five feet one inch. Milnes, without providing details, believes that Keats became 'intimate with Mr. Basil Montague and his distinguished family'; see Richard Monckton Milnes, *Life, Letters and Literary Remains of John Keats* (New York: Putnam, 1848), p. 26 (one-volume edition).

47 *Literary Gazette*, 10 June 1820, pp. 369–71. The journal's circulation figures numbered a respectable 1000 copies or so. For circulation figures of other literary journals and magazines see John O. Hayden, *The Romantic Reviewers, 1802–1824* (London: Routledge, 1969). For more on the chronology of *Marcian Colonna*'s publication, see G. H. Ford, 'Keats and Procter: A Misdated Acquaintance', *Modern Language Notes*, 66 (1951), pp. 532–36 at p. 533 (and note).

48 Hermann Fischer, *Romantic Verse Narrative: The History of a Genre*, trans. Sue Bollans (Cambridge: Cambridge University Press, 1991), p. 281 (n. 25). Fischer also brands Cornwall's *Diego de Montilla* and *Gyges* 'feeble imitations' of Byron's *Beppo*.

49 Oddly enough, since just a year later in March 1931, Armour appealed to *N&Q* readers to alert him to the existence of unknown Cornwall letters.

50 Cornwall married Anne Skepper in 1824; the following year, he moved with her to her stepfather Basil Montagu's residence at 25 Bedford Square. Before that, Cornwall lived at 25 Store Street, an impressive crescent terrace just around the corner from Bedford Square and the British Museum. Today, it's home to a design consultancy, flanked on either side by computer software firms.

51 Cornwall's 'Hymn to Diana' was published in Hunt's *Literary Pocket-Book* for 1819. The letter must therefore date from between the publication of *Endymion* in May 1818 and the end of that year.

52 Cornwall was anxious to keep his poetical and legal interests separate. Although Procter's identity as 'Barry Cornwall' was well-known within literary circles by the end of 1820, having been exposed by the *Edinburgh Monthly Review*, it wasn't common knowledge for a further year or two. (In March 1823, Hazlitt's confederate in the Sarah Walker conspiracy, the dastardly 'Mr F.', doesn't seem to realize that Procter and Cornwall were the same person; see my discussion in chapter 5.)

53 While we might also expect Cornwall's 'Hymn to Diana' to engage Ben Jonson's own poem of that name, there does not, in fact, appear to be any interaction.

54 *Notes and Queries*, n.s. 14 (1967), p. 24.

55 Pillows – in the form of breasts – also feature in Keats's sonnet.
56 See Nicholas Roe, '"Bright Star, Sweet Unrest": Image and Consolation in Wordsworth, Shelley, and Keats' in *History and Myth: Essays on English Romantic Literature*, ed. Stephen C. Behrendt (Detroit, MI: Wayne State University Press, 1990), pp. 130–48. Wordsworth's poem – the first of 26 'Sonnets Dedicated to Liberty' published in *Poems in Two Volumes* (1807) – also contains breast imagery: Wordsworth's 'bright star' seems to stoop to 'sink / On England's bosom' (ll. 3–4).
57 On the other hand, the fact that Cornwall's sonnet was not published until June 1820 doesn't mean that it didn't exist in draft before then.
58 See 'Keats and Procter: A Misdated Acquaintance', p. 532.
59 Cornwall also contributed poems to Watts's *Literary Souvenir*. A surviving letter from Cornwall to the editor, written between 1828 and 1832 (the period during which Watts lived at 58 Torrington Square), was published without commentary in *Notes and Queries* in 1931. In it, Cornwall comments: 'I have been trying one or two things for you – I scarcely know which I can make most fit for your souvenir'; *Notes and Queries*, 160 (1931), p. 340.
60 *Monthly Magazine*, 49 (1820), p. 447.
61 Barry Cornwall, *Charles Lamb: A Memoir* (London: Moxon, 1866), p. 85.
62 Cornwall writes as 'L'. See *London Magazine*, 3 (1821), p. 426. For attribution of authorship, see Joanne Shattock (ed.), *The Cambridge Bibliography of English Literature*, 3rd edn (Cambridge: Cambridge University Press, 1999), IV, p. 388; and Olive M. Taylor, 'John Taylor, Author and Publisher', *London Mercury*, 13 (1925), p. 260.
63 Given what we now know about Cornwall's authorship of the two-part critique of Keats in the *Edinburgh Magazine*, it may bolster McGillivray's identification of Cornwall as the author of an 1828 tribute to Keats in *The Olio* that the poems picked out there for praise – *The Eve of St Agnes*, *Isabella* and the odes – correlate with those lauded in Cornwall's review. By the same token, uncertainty about *Hyperion* is voiced in both the review and *The Olio*. Years later in a letter to John Forster, Cornwall was still bothered by *Hyperion*, which he judged '*not* one of Keats's best things', adding that the 'smaller pieces, The Eve of St. Agnes, and the Ode to the Nightingale', were 'so good' by contrast. For the letter to Forster, see Armour, pp. 69–70.
64 *Literary Chronicle*, 29 July, 1820, p. 484.
65 *Monthly Magazine*, 50 (1820), p. 166.

Bright Stars and Close Bosom-Friends:
Keats, Cornwall and 'Cockney' Politics

Jeffrey N. Cox's study of a 'Cockney' community of writers gathered around Leigh Hunt dismantles tenacious myths about Romantic isolation. Second-generation Romantic poets, Cox argues, should be seen in the context of a rich network of writers, editors, dilettantes and friends who published, read and reviewed each other's work.[1] This 'community' included Keats, Percy Shelley, John Hamilton Reynolds, Cornelius Webb, P. G. Patmore, Charles Cowden Clarke, Hazlitt, the Ollier brothers, Charles Lamb and Barry Cornwall. As long ago as 1951, G. H. Ford suggested that Keats must have known Cornwall to some degree from an early stage: 'Both moving in the same circles during 1818 and 1819, it would have been remarkable if they had not been acquainted'.[2] However, apart from noting an exchange of books between the two men – in June 1820, Keats gave Cornwall an inscribed copy of *Lamia* (1820); and before that Cornwall had sent Keats his *Dramatic Scenes* (1819) and *A Sicilian Story* (1820), both of which Keats received by 27 February 1820[3] – recent scholarship has found little to connect Cornwall to Keats in the 'Cockney' culture of literary production. Indicative of his wider neglect is the fact that Cornwall's presence in Cox's otherwise excellent book is largely confined to lists of names associated peripherally with Hunt.

What little interest Cornwall attracts today is primarily directed towards the question of how he managed to garner plaudits that should have gone to Keats. This chapter addresses political points of contact between the two poets – more numerous, more significant than scholars have granted – which culminated in a jeopardous association during the marching season of Autumn 1819. Keats may not appear to have cared greatly for Cornwall's work. As he remarked in a letter to John Hamilton Reynolds, Cornwall had an annoying habit of ringing 'triple bob majors' on any and everything. It certainly seems that when it came to cultivating friendship, Cornwall was the more assiduous of the two. Nevertheless, I believe that interfriction between the pair was more thorough-going, politically and poetically, than hitherto acknowledged.

1. 'Forced Amongst One's Antipathies'

On the face of things, it's difficult to ascertain Cornwall's political leanings. Hunt told Mary Shelley that Cornwall's response to her husband's poetry had been positive, 'albeit' that he had been 'bred up in different notions'.[4] S. R. Townshend Mayer remembered Cornwall telling him he had 'no politics';[5] and in the preface to *Dramatic Scenes* (1819), Cornwall claims (facetiously, I'll argue) to have 'touched neither on politics or polemics' (p. viii). In a letter to Francis Jeffrey dated 2 May 1820, Hazlitt thought that his friend Cornwall was probably 'a tory, as far as he is anything in politics'.[6] Jeffrey's review of *A Sicilian Story* a few months earlier had presented the volume as a refreshing retreat from the 'fever of party spirit' and 'moral and political animosities', and declared 'it is delightful to turn from them awhile, to the unalloyed sweets of such poetry as Mr. Cornwall's.'[7]

It is also true that in 1824, Cornwall married a tory in the figure of socialite Anne Skepper (Mrs Montagu's daughter by her first marriage; the actress Fanny Kemble described her as 'like a fresh lemon – golden, fragrant, firm and wholesome'[8]), at which point he more or less abandoned poetry for the steadier income provided by conveyancing. Yet Cornwall was by no means innocent of politics. Far from it. Gill Gregory draws attention to fascinating correspondence between the poet and James T. Fields from 1861, in which Cornwall declares his abolitionist views and exhorts Americans to 'stand up at once (and finally) against the slave trade'.[9] But much earlier, in a letter of 3 March 1824 to John Bowring, editor of the *Westminister Review*, Cornwall explains how certain political realities, such as the Greek War of Independence, had broken in on his 'private, comfortable' existence: 'I hate politics it is true – But in the case of Greece – and of Spain also – one is forced amongst one's antipathies.'[10]

Indeed, in his poetry from this period Cornwall frequently finds himself forced among his antipathies, and his work is often sharply and openly critical of various forms of injustice. *Gyges*, a jaunty ottava rima from *A Sicilian Story*, ends by celebrating the death of the 'silly' king Candaules. Moreover, Cornwall declines to defuse his poem's political charge with a puerilizing 'moral' commensurate with the witty form. Furnishing an example of Cornwall's best writing, *Gyges* draws poignant attention to the ignominious treatment suffered by the poor:

> I saw a pauper once, when I was young,
>   Borne to his shallow grave: the bearers trod
> Smiling to where the death-bell heavily rung,

And soon his bones were laid beneath the sod:
On the rough boards the earth was gaily flung:
    Methought the prayer which gave him to his God
Was coldly said: – then all, passing away,
Left the scarce-coffin'd wretch to quick decay.

It was an autumn evening, and the rain
    Had ceased awhile, but the loud winds did shriek
And call'd the deluging tempest back again,
    The flag-staff on the church-yard tow'r did creak,
And thro' the black clouds ran a lightning vein,
    And then the flapping raven came to seek
Its home: its flight was heavy, and its wing
Seem'd weary with a long day's wandering.
        (*Gyges*, p. 59)

These stanzas are quieter, distinct in tone and diction from the Cockneyfied passages elsewhere in *Gyges*, and were recognized as exceptional by reviewers of the day.[11] They strike a note of 'social realism' two decades before Dickens and others inhabit the mode more fully. In their light, Keats's suggestion to Reynolds that his stylish rival composed only on 'amiable' topics (*LJK*, II, 268) seems a little unfair. There's a political substance to Cornwall's work that at certain junctures reveals itself more legibly than the often submerged or concealed radical consciousness of Keats's own poetic.

In 1831, Cornwall became a Metropolitan Commissioner for Lunacy, a job which entailed undertaking taxing tours of England and Wales to inspect the often-appalling conditions found in licensed mental institutions. The Lunacy Commission, as Armour points out, was a 'political office'. Armour suggests that Cornwall was 'enough aligned with the Whigs' that with their return to power in 1830, Lord Brougham could appoint him as one of the commissioners (p. 95). With his instinctive hatred of injustice, the diligent Cornwall found the experience of inspecting asylums emotionally gruelling. In 1843, more than a decade into his job, Cornwall wrote to Thomas Carlyle deploring the management of pauper lunatics in Wales:

I do not like Wales. It is a mean country, notwithstanding its high places. There are many hundred lunatics in Wales, who (many of them as helpless as children) are boarded out at various rates, (ranging from *one shilling* to three!) *per week*. The gentry will not conspire to build an asylum – and the parish people will not pay enough to keep the poor creatures in decency.[12]

In the same letter, Cornwall alludes to the Rebecca Riots against tollgates. After beginning in a droll fashion, Cornwall's mood suddenly changes into one of political seriousness:

> I hear you have been coquetting with Rebecca. She is an ill-used woman and bites and scratches vigorously. Tell me, – is she handsome? Is the night air pleasant in the Welsh Vallies? – And is it fatiguing to saw down a gate? It is not the first time that that unholy Trinity (the Lawyer, the Parson, and the Justice of the Peace) has trod upon the corn or corns of the poor, but it is the first time that the poor have especially given them a kick in return.

Even Cornwall's political disclaimer in the preface to his first volume is freighted with irony, as the final clause makes clear: 'If an occasional sentence should seem to bear upon either of those subjects [politics or polemics], it is contrary to my wish, and I disclaim the inference' (p. viii). It's worth calling to mind the store Cornwall set by prefaces when we read his own in *Dramatic Scenes*. James Baldwin remembered Cornwall's 'pertinent' advice, discovered among the poet's posthumous papers: 'Always read the preface to a book. It places you on vantage ground ... You frequently discover the character of the author ... and see his aims.'[13]

There's no disguising either the political content or the 'aims' of his next collection, *A Sicilian Story* – and Cornwall makes little attempt to do so. At any rate, the spikiness of *Gyges* speaks for itself. But the volume also contains a less obviously conspiratorial set of sonnets on the seasons, first printed in Leigh Hunt's *Literary Pocket-Book* for 1820, a publication that is imbued with political irony and subversiveness. It seems to me highly unlikely that the recently jailed Hunt would have invested so much energy in mentoring a political 'cuckoo' who harboured Tory sympathies, have puffed his work in the *Examiner* or invited him to his famous mutton and potato dinners, if the two men hadn't shared a similar outlook and values. The friendship, moreover, was enduring; in 1855, Hunt dedicated his volume of dramatic extracts, *Beaumont and Fletcher*, to Cornwall – having to fight the publisher Bohn hard on the issue (the rest of Bohn's publications appeared without dedications).[14] In the following sections, I look closely at Cornwall's contributions to the *Literary Pocket-Book*, especially the sonnet 'Autumn', alongside Keats's ode 'To Autumn'. I contend that these poems – huddled together tightly in the dangerous immediate aftermath of the Peterloo Massacre on 16 August 1819 – share a distinctive political valency. On top of which, I show, their conspiratorial dialogue forms part of wider 'Cockney' resistance to Liverpool's government in which protest was figured as seasonal imagery.

2. Hunt's Literary Pocket-Book: Political Coterie and Peterloo

Although Shelley regarded Cornwall's popular and popularist idiom as an odious concession to a degraded readership, the fashionable poet's saleability, his immersion in commodity culture, doesn't appear to have excluded his close participation in Cockney School politics. Indeed, political subversiveness may even have added a *frisson* that increased his appeal to reading audiences. At several points in Cornwall's work we encounter allusions to political tumult, at times committed to astonishingly transparent language. As we have seen, the narrator in *Gyges* speaks openly of 'kill[ing] the king' (p. 60);[15] concluding the indecorous tale of King Candaules, his perfidious queen Lais and her young lover *Gyges*, the mischievous speaker quips seditiously:

> How the frail pair lived on I know not: I
> Have but subdued Candaules to my strain.
> It was enough for me that he should die,
> And having kill'd the king, why – that's the main.
>   (*Gyges*, p. 60)

I'd like to turn to a more discreet political engagement and intriguing example of intertextual play between Keats's and Cornwall's work. In November or early December 1819, Leigh Hunt published his *Literary Pocket-Book* for 1820.[16] The volume, the second of a series that ran from 1819 to 1823, included Hunt's 'Calendar of Observers', a politically nuanced description of the seasons, and Charles Cowden Clarke's 'Walks Round London', which pointed out where one could go to find the spot where the 'conspirators' in James the First's reign used to meet.[17] Clarke's 'conspirators' are, of course, Guy Fawkes and his co-plotters; although on the 'wrong' side, so to speak, they are the archetypal autumn conspirators. Also included in the volume for 1820 are various items of 'Original Poetry' by living authors, including a sequence of sonnets by Barry Cornwall. The sequence as a whole is obliquely political. I'm particularly interested in two of Cornwall's sonnets, 'Spring' and 'Autumn':

Spring

It is not that sweet herbs and flowers alone
   Start up, like spirits that have lain asleep
   In their great mother's iced bosom deep
For months; or that the birds, more joyous grown,
Catch once again their silver summer tone,
   And they who late from bough to bough did creep,

Now trim their plumes upon some sunny steep,
And seem to sing of Winter overthrown:
No – with an equal march the immortal mind,
As tho' it never could be left behind,   10
   Keeps pace with every movement of the year,
     And (for high truths are born in happiness)
   As the warm heart expands, the eye grows clear,
     And sees beyond the slave's or bigot's guess.

Autumn

There is a fearful spirit busy now.
   Already have the elements unfurled
   Their banners: the great sea-wave is upcurled:
The cloud comes: the fierce winds begin to blow
About, and blindly on their errands go;
   And quickly will the pale red leaves be hurled
   From their dry boughs, and all the forest world
Stripped of its pride, be like a desert show.
I love that moaning music which I hear
   In the bleak gusts of Autumn, for the soul   10
Seems gathering tidings from another sphere,
   And, in sublime mysterious sympathy,
   Man's bouncing spirit ebbs, and swells more high,
Accordant to the billow's loftier roll.

To begin with, there are clear stylistic echoes of Keats (and Hunt) in evidence: 'upcurled' in line 3 of 'Autumn' recalls Keats's penchant for using prepositions to coin compound words; similarly 'for high truths are born in happiness' in line 12 of 'Spring' has a Keatsian ring to it. But there are more startling, mutually illuminating interactions between these two poems and Keats's more famous ode 'To Autumn' (which was composed at some point around 19 September 1819, but not published until July 1820 – that is, until *after* Cornwall's sonnets were printed – when it appeared in the *Lamia* volume). Since I will be making extensive reference to Keats's ode, I reprint it here in its entirety:

To Autumn

I
Season of mists and mellow fruitfulness,
   Close bosom-friend of the maturing sun,
Conspiring with him how to load and bless
   With fruit the vines that round the thatch-eves run;

To bend with apples the mossed cottage-trees,
    And fill all fruit with ripeness to the core;
        To swell the gourd, and plump the hazel shells
    With a sweet kernel; to set budding more,
And still more, later flowers for the bees,
Until they think warm days will never cease,   10
    For summer has o'er-brimmed their clammy cells.

2

Who hath not seen thee oft amid thy store?
    Sometimes whoever seeks abroad may find
Thee sitting careless on a granary floor,
    Thy hair soft-lifted by the winnowing wind;
Or on a half-reaped furrow sound asleep,
    Drowsed with the fume of poppies, while thy hook
        Spares the next swath and all its twinèd flowers;
And sometimes like a gleaner thou dost keep
    Steady thy laden head across a brook;   20
    Or by a cider-press, with patient look,
        Thou watchest the last oozings hours by hours.

3

Where are the songs of Spring? Ay, where are they?
    Think not of them, thou hast thy music too –
While barrèd clouds bloom the soft-dying day,
    And touch the stubble-plains with rosy hue:
Then in a wailful choir the small gnats mourn
    Among the river sallows, borne aloft
        Or sinking as the light wind lives or dies;
And full-grown lambs loud bleat from hilly bourn;   30
    Hedge-crickets sing; and now with treble soft
    The red-breast whistles from a garden-croft;
        And gathering swallows twitter in the skies.

The first interchange I'd like to draw attention to centres on the 'songs of spring'. In response to Keats's wistful question 'Where are the songs of spring? Ay, where are they?' (l. 23), Cornwall provides the birds who 'seem to sing of winter overthrown' ('Spring', l. 8). To Keats's injunction to Autumn to 'Think not of them [the songs of spring], thou hast thy music too' (l. 24), Cornwall concurs 'I love that moaning music which I hear / In the bleak gusts of Autumn' (ll. 9–10). And Cornwall's 'moaning music' perhaps echoes the *mournful* music of the 'small gnats' in Keats's ode. Yet as striking as these verbal and thematic reverberations may be, the depth of dialogue in which Keats's and Cornwall's poems engage becomes apparent only when all three pieces are read in the context of the political unrest that spread through England in the spring preceding Peterloo, and in the autumn that followed it.

Seen within the frame of watchful protest and general paranoia that set in after the brutal dispersal of workers and radicals who converged on St Peter's Field in August 1819, individual words and phrases in Keats's ode sound in 'unusual and intriguing ways'.[18] For instance, as Nicholas Roe has shown, 'close bosom-friend' (l. 2) acquires overtones of 'close' conspiracy not just intimacy, and the 'clammy cells' (l. 11) and 'barrèd clouds' (l. 25) hint at incarceration, rather than simply describing 'o'er-brimm[ing]' honey-combs and an autumn sky. Similarly, the 'stubble-plains' touched with 'rosy hue' (l. 26) begin to appear, not only as harvested fields lit by a red sun, but also as the bloody fields where reformers were cut down by the sabres of the Manchester Yeomanry; and the 'wailful choir' (l. 27) of gnats that hover around stanza three seem to mourn not the departing year, but the murdered at Peterloo. I would argue that Cornwall's sonnet sequence is equally, and as knowingly, attuned to political circumstances as Keats's ode; indeed, I suggest that the political events of 1819 are mapped by Cornwall onto a series of seasonal vignettes.[19] This, despite the judgement of Donald Reiman, facsimile editor of Cornwall's *A Sicilian Story* (the volume in which the sonnets were reprinted in 1820),[20] that Cornwall's poetry is 'futile' and 'trivial'.[21] What's more, Cornwall's sonnets and Keats's ode share a common vocabulary for articulating fugitive political sentiments.

We are invited to 'listen' for political overtones from the outset of Cornwall's sonnet, 'Spring'. In line 1, the 'sweet herbs and flowers' invoke the last lines of Marvell's 'The Garden', a poem that famously debates the relative merits of political withdrawal or involvement: 'How could such sweet and wholesome hours / Be reckoned but with herbs and flowers!' (ll. 71–72).[22] But where Marvell's poem remains equivocal on the subject of political engagement or retreat, Cornwall's is more confident. The herbs and flowers of the sonnet 'start up like spirits that have lain asleep' after an icy winter (l. 2) – a clear call to action to those who have undergone a period of inactivity or who have been forced to keep a low profile in dangerous times?

Cornwall is by no means oblivious to the potential consequences of polit-ical involvement. These were, after all, uncertain times when – as recently, and in Britain – the inviolability of Habeas Corpus could no longer be taken for granted (it had been suspended for the second time in living memory between 4 March 1817 and 1 July 1818). Indeed, 'Spring' records a

pervasive atmosphere of jeopardy: in line 6, for instance, we discover birds
'who late from bough to bough did creep' (avoiding prosecution under the
Seditious Meetings Act, in force from the end of February 1817 until 24
July 1818). But Cornwall's birds remain conspiratorial and 'seem to sing of
winter overthrown' (l. 8). The reference to 'overthrowing' changes the line
from a seasonal cliché to a possible allusion to the toppling of an unpopular
government. We could go further: the plumes trimmed by the birds at line
7 might be interpreted, literally, as the trimmed quills of pens, conjuring the
untiring efforts of radical editors and essayists to assail Liverpool's regime
from pamphlets and the pages of publications like the *Black Dwarf*, the
Cap of Liberty, and of course Hunt's *Literary Pocket-Book*. Furthermore, the
reference to the 'equal march' of the 'immortal mind' (ll. 9–10) also sounds
like an allusion to the huge marches and rallies held across major manufac-
turing towns between 1816 and 1819.

The tone of Cornwall's 'Spring', then, is wary but optimistic. Hopes for
reform have not yet been crushed at Peterloo. 'Summer', the second sonnet
in the sequence, is also marked by defiant tones, similarly couched in a
seasonal register. At lines 6–7, Cornwall proclaims that June's 'green crown
shall wither, and the tune / That ushered in his birth be silent soon'. This
is possibly intended to be understood by the *Literary Pocket-Book*'s politically aware readership as a contestation of the monarchy's authority, which
renders the lines almost openly seditious. Oddly enough, even arch-conser-
vative reviewers like John Wilson in *Blackwood's Edinburgh Magazine* appear
to have missed the political charge of words like 'overthrow'. In fact, while
Wilson's review of the *Literary Pocket-Book* as a whole is far from favourable
and registers the general spirit of subversion – the volume is described as a
'very clever and cunning contrivance' – sections of Hunt's volume are singled
out for praise.[23] Indeed, Cornwall's sonnets, which Wilson considers (using
a perverse choice of words in the circumstances) 'perfect in their beauty and
majesty', and are printed in full.[24]

By 'Autumn', however, Cornwall's optimism has changed, as we might
expect following events in Manchester. The sonnet begins with a reference
to a 'fearful spirit' that is 'busy' in autumn, then makes explicit allusion to
the marches for reform that had characterized the political landscape in the
high summer of 1819, and which culminated in the rally at St Peter's Field:
'Already have the elements unfurled / Their banners' (ll. 2–3). These 'banners'
could be read as referring to those held aloft on 16 August by liberals, radicals
and workers demanding 'reform', the right to political organization, and an
extension of the franchise. The description of the 'fierce winds' in line 4,

which '*blindly* on their errands go' (my emphasis), creating havoc and devastation, leaving only 'dry boughs, and all the forest world / Stripped of its pride' (ll. 7–8), correspondingly serves for the yeomanry that rode through the rally, slashing and trampling indiscriminately. It was a fierce wind indeed that blew around St Peter's Field on 16 August. After this desperate scene, Cornwall's claim to 'love that moaning music which I hear / In the bleak gusts of Autumn' (ll. 9–10) might seem incongruous. It is, however, explained in the ensuing lines: 'for the soul / Seems gathering tidings from another sphere, / And, in sublime mysterious sympathy, / Man's bouncing spirit ebbs, and swells more high, / Accordant to the billow's loftier roll' (ll. 10–14).[25] That is, Cornwall rejoices because he believes national outrage at the numbers of dead and wounded at Peterloo will ultimately help the reformers' cause, resulting in the undying radical spirit swelling even higher than it did before. Indeed, the governing conceit of 'Spring' lays emphasis on the fact that it is not the 'sweet herbs and flowers' *alone* that seem dead but return to life in spring, but also the 'immortal mind' that keeps pace with the seasons – that is, the radical visionary consciousness that 'never could be left behind' (l. 10).

Keats and Cornwall are not alone in using such seasonal allegories or 'codes' to communicate dissent. Percy Shelley's 'Ode to the West Wind', composed according to Mary Shelley on an Autumn day in 1819, and published with *Prometheus Unbound* in 1820, utilizes a similar set of radical conventions. Shelley imagines the wind, the 'breath of Autumn's being' (l. 1), driving forth 'pestilence-stricken multitudes' of dead, 'hectic red' leaves (ll. 4–5). This resonates interestingly with lines 6–7 from Cornwall's 'Autumn': 'And quickly will the pale red leaves be hurled / From their dry boughs'. Both poets' emphasis on the redness of the leaves, while on the one hand entirely what we might expect from a description of autumn leaves, has another significance. As we see from contemporary illustrations depicting the scenes across St Peter's Field, many of the banners carried by the protesters proclaiming 'Reform' were red in colour.[26] Pale red, to be precise, as we can judge from an illustration entitled 'The Field of Peterloo', published by S. W. Fores on 25 January 1820. The print shows five blue-jacketed members of the Manchester Yeomanry on horseback trampling members of the crowd and slashing them with sabres. Two large flags are visible in the centre and right of the illustration, both red in colour, bearing the inscription 'M.Y.C.' and 'REFORM', respectively. At the top of one of the flagpoles hangs a red liberty cap. Shelley's phrase 'hectic red' conflates the falling flags with the confused attempts of the crowd to flee the scene of massacre, while

Cornwall's depiction of the 'pale red leaves' hurled from their 'dry boughs' perfectly captures the yeomanry's efforts to tear the protesters' flags and banners from their wooden poles. There is little doubt that the yeomanry made a concerted effort to secure the protesters' flags at any cost. John Tyas's eyewitness report, partly written in the New Bayley prison, appeared in *The Times* on 19 August 1819 and records that 'a cry was made by the cavalry, "Have at their flags", and [...] the riders immediately dashed not only at the flags which were in the wagon [carrying Henry 'Orator' Hunt], but those which were posted among the crowd, cutting most indiscriminately to the right and to the left in order to get at them. This set the people running in all directions' (Walmsley, 1969, p. 218).

Indeed, Cornwall's and Shelley's descriptions of wind-strewn leaves and 'dry boughs' also echo the account given by the 'weaver-poet', Samuel Bamford, of the scene at St Peter's Field after the crowd had been dispersed: 'The hustings remained, with a few broken and hewed flag-staves erect, and a torn and gashed banner or two drooping; whilst over the whole field, were strewed caps, bonnets, hats, shawls and shoes, and other parts of male and female dress; trampled, torn, and bloody' (Walmsley, 1969, p. 230). Another onlooker, a Reverend Stanley, also records the yeomanry's endeavours to 'capture' the protesters' banners: 'I saw nothing that gave me an idea of resistance, except in one or two spots where they [the crowd] showed some disinclination to abandon the banners; these impulses, however, were but momentary, and banner after banner fell into the hands of the military power' (Walmsley, 1969, p. 222).

Cornwall's and Shelley's poems share other points of interfriction. Like Cornwall, Shelley, too, uses a seasonal discourse to underline his conviction that although the reform movement had suffered a setback it would return stronger than ever: the 'wingèd seeds' borne by the dead leaves in 'Ode to the West Wind' will only 'lie cold and low, / Each like a corpse in its grave', until 'Thine azure sister of the Spring shall blow / Her clarion o'er the dreaming earth' ('Ode to the West Wind', ll. 7–8, 9–10). That is, like Cornwall, Shelley uses what at first appears to be a seasonal cliché to emphasize the immortal nature of the radical, reforming spirit, at the same time as calling this dormant spirit to renewed action. The use of seasonal tropes to convey subversive sentiments and inflect seemingly innocent passages with political valence had already been established by Leigh Hunt's January entry in the 'Calendar of Nature' in the *Literary Pocket-Book* for 1819, a year before Cornwall's sonnets appeared: 'Under the apparent coldness of the snow, the herbaceous plants, which die down to the root in autumn, lie nourishing their roots for spring' (p. 5). Hunt's image hints at gagged and restrained reformers lying low to gather strength for renewed effort in more fortuitous times; the icy political climate, Hunt insists, only *seems* to destroy the will for reform, which emerges again in 'finer weather' (p. 6).

The seasonal code utilized by Keats, Cornwall, and Shelley had been ratified by none other than Thomas Paine, whose 1791 tract, *The Rights of Man*, concluded with a passage that made explicit links between the world of natural rhythms and the political seasons:

> It is now towards the middle of February. Were I to take a turn into the country, the trees would present a leafless, wintery appearance. As people are apt to pluck twigs as they go along, I perhaps might do the same, and by chance might observe that a *single bud* on that twig had begun to swell. I should reason very unnaturally, or rather not reason at all, to suppose *this* was the *only* bud in England which had this appearance. Instead of deciding thus, I should instantly conclude that the same appearance was beginning or about to begin everywhere; and though the vegetable sleep will continue longer on some trees and plants than on others, and though some of them may not *blossom* for two or three years, all will be in leaf by summer, except those which are *rotten*. What pace the political summer may keep with the natural, no human foresight can determine. It is, however, not difficult to perceive that the spring is begun.[27]

Echoes between this passage and Cornwall's 'Spring' are unmistakable. If Paine is uncertain as to 'what pace the political summer may keep with the natural', Cornwall replies confidently: 'with an equal march the immortal mind, / As though it never could be left behind, / *Keeps pace* with every movement of the year' (ll. 9–11; my emphasis). It becomes clear, then, that Cornwall's richly allusive 'Spring' not only engages Keats's 'To Autumn' in dialogue over Peterloo, but also involves itself with debates rehearsed in Marvell's 'The Garden', Shelley's 'Ode to the West Wind', and Paine's *Rights of Man*. Cornwall, a figure neglected by modern scholarship, deserves to be located within the context of political dissent, and more specifically within the frame of Cockney School politics associated with Hunt.

That the political inflections of Hunt's 'Calendar of Nature', later serialized in the *Examiner* and, in expanded form, in *The Months* (1821), were recognized by Romantic writers has been demonstrated in Nicholas Roe's outstanding study, *Keats and the Culture of Dissent*. Roe argues that 'To Autumn', for example, finds a ready store of imagery in the September entry in 'The Calendar of Nature', which appeared in the *Examiner* on 5 September 1819: 'details such as [...] migrating birds, cider-making, swallows and insects, warm days, and even the chill and fog', all elements of Hunt's calendar journal, 'all reappear in Keats's poem'.[28] From the point of view of liberal and radical writers, the expediency of hiding subversion in seasonal tropes and metaphors is clear: the fact that even John Wilson in *Blackwood's* seems oblivious to the seditious nature (pun intended) of Cornwall's verse suggests that reformers had successfully developed a discourse of resistance that was intelligible to other 'right-minded' thinkers, but which dissolved into mere seasonal images before unknowing eyes. If more evidence of the sonnets' subversive undertones and post-Peterloo frame were needed, all four poems were reprinted in 1820 in the *New Annual Register* – a journal with a long history of opposition – for the year 1819.[29] In their preface, the editors clarified that the new volume 'endeavoured to give a faithful picture of the state of Britain in 1819, particularly of the dreadful meeting at Manchester' (p. iii).

The range of echoes, specific allusions and dialogues between Keats's ode and Cornwall's sonnets indicates a level of interaction that might have arisen in one of three ways. In the first 'scenario', Cornwall sees Keats's 'To Autumn' at some point before it was published in July 1820. This would not necessarily have been contingent on close friendship between the poets, since a draft version of the ode was in circulation. On 22 September 1819, a couple of days after composing the poem, Keats copied out the ode for Richard Woodhouse (*LJK*, II, 170–71). Perhaps Cornwall got to see the letter shortly after it was sent.[30] A second, more radical explanation is that Keats was familiar with Cornwall's sonnets on the seasons before writing 'To Autumn'. To be sure, in correspondence with Reynolds (28 February 1820) and with Dilke (4 March 1820), Keats claims not to have seen Cornwall's published volumes until late in February 1820. However, should we necessarily infer that he hadn't seen draft copies of single poems, perhaps given to him by Hunt?

The likely chronology of the sonnets' and ode's compositions by no means excludes the possibility that Keats had been privy to Cornwall's work in manuscript form. The Peterloo Massacre took place on 16 August 1819. If, as I have suggested, Cornwall's 'Autumn' alludes to this event, then we have an outside earliest date for composition. The other parameter is set by the poem's appearance with 'Spring' in the second volume of Hunt's *Literary Pocket-Book*, which had been 'just published' when it was noticed by Wilson in *Blackwood's* in December 1819. (The sonnet, along with the other three on the seasons, also appeared in Cornwall's *A Sicilian Story*, dated 1820, but published like the *Literary Pocket-Book* at the end of 1819.) Given the fact that Hunt would have been collating the contents of the *Literary Pocket-Book* in the weeks and months leading up to its publication, it is entirely feasible in respect of chronology that Cornwall's sonnets were drafted before Keats's ode. If we add to this the likelihood, or even probability, that Hunt would have been discussing prospective contributors' poems informally with Keats, who after all had strong links with Hunt's project, having already supplied poems for the previous volume (for 1819, published at the end of 1818), then a scenario in which Keats encounters Cornwall's sonnets before writing his ode begins to appear as an intriguing possibility.

A third way of accounting for the specific nature and number of the links between the poems I have been discussing, one that doesn't depend on third-party interventions, is to entertain the possibility that Keats and Cornwall did in fact know each other before 1820, as Ford moots – moreover, well enough to have exchanged manuscripts in the coterie manner described by Cox.[31] Although Cornwall claimed in his literary remembrances to have 'little to record' about Keats,[32] as fellow contributors to Hunt's *Literary Pocket-Book*, and fellow aspiring writers on the London literary 'scene', attending lectures together and meeting the same people, whose work was often reviewed alongside each other, it would, as Ford says, indeed be remarkable if they had not shown some degree of interest in each other, and equally, in each other's poetry.[33]

This explanation would also throw light on other parallels between Keats and Cornwall, such as those we discover in Keats's description of Thea in *Hyperion* (written in late 1818, published in 1820) and Moneta in *The Fall of Hyperion* (written in Summer 1819, published posthumously in 1856), and Cornwall's description of Athena in 'A Vision' (published by December 1819 in *A Sicilian Story*). Cornwall's Athena speaks in 'tones cathedral organs ... never gave' (ll. 16–17); while Thea speaks 'in solemn tenor and deep organ tune' (*Hyperion*, I, 48). Similarly, the vision of Athena 'spoke / Cheering, and as it spoke, the air became / Painfully sweet' with 'such odours as the rose / Wastes on the summer air, or such as rise / from beds of hyacinths, or from jasmine flowers' (ll. 7–11); when Moneta speaks for the first time, 'incense from all flowers ... fills the air with so much health', and 'spread[s] around / Forgetfulness of everything but bliss' (I, 99–104). The 'cheering', 'healthy' speech of both Athena and Moneta, then, is associated with the incense of flowers; and both deities' discourse is compared with the 'tones' or 'tunes' of 'organs'.

The difficulty in deciding whether these echoes are merely coincidental, or whether they indicate some deeper communion between Keats and Cornwall, is bound up with the whole issue of how poems talk to each other.

Put another way, it is a problem of determining how poems align themselves to each other along a series of axes. These 'alignments' include conscious and unconscious borrowing,[34] plagiarism, imitation, parody, emulation, the use of common sources, taking cues from enabling or inspiring words and phrases, employing what is 'in the air', and adhering to the tenets of a shared literary project, such as that outlined in the preface to Hunt's *The Story of Rimini* (1816), a poetic 'manifesto' that inspired both Keats and Cornwall (Cornwall's use of 'upcurled' could be ascribed to the philological influence of Hunt as much as to conscious emulation of Keats). When we address questions of influence, we necessarily confront the troubled limits of the text. We are obliged to explore the boundaries and teasing overlaps between texts, to search out the interstices. The problem is compounded by historical distance. Rarely, if ever, can the nuances of influence be settled beyond dispute, and poetic creativity instinctively resists being reduced to line and rule. None the less, I hope this discussion has demonstrated that Cornwall's relationship to Keats, as well as to other prominent Romantic figures such as Percy Shelley, who, seen through the modern scholarly and critical lens, appear to have been indescribably more important than Cornwall in their own day, cannot be explained simply by branding Cornwall a servile imitator of his poetic betters, who produced 'trivial' works that simply had the good fortune to chime with prevailing taste. Cornwall's poems *were* important in the literary and political culture of the early nineteenth century; and from them Keats's poems derive a portion of their own significance.

To conclude, Cornwall's 'Spring' and 'Autumn', Keats's 'To Autumn', and Shelley's 'Ode to the West Wind' emerge out of a wider community of lyrical resistance. Drawing on a mutually comprehended seasonal code, these texts protest the excesses of Liverpool's government. Poems on the seasons, particularly those that allude to Spring and Autumn, were a well-established means of voicing dissent from a position of relative safety. The practice had been established for Romantic authors by Paine in 1791, and more recently by Hunt's 'Calendar of Nature'; indeed, the 'ruse' is in evidence throughout the *Literary Pocket-Book* for 1820. Despite Wilson's belief that the idea behind the *Literary Pocket-Book* was 'good and ingenuous', the volume is full of *dis*ingenuous moments where writers either employ the code utilized by Hunt's 'Calendar', or follow Charles Cowden Clarke's related practice, exemplified in 'Walks Round London', of using an otherwise mundane passage – literally pedestrian in Clarke's case – to carry a subversive parcel.[35] Cox is right to suggest that the interaction of literary and political figures grouped around Hunt was more thorough-going than has hitherto been acknowledged. The *Literary Pocket-Book* for 1820, a composite document charting and protesting myriad abuses leading up to and following Peterloo, clearly demonstrates this. To centrepieces in Hunt's volume such as Clarke's 'Walks Round London', Hunt's own 'Calendar of Observers' and Cornwall's sonnets, we could add 'satellite' pieces that appeared elsewhere, such as Keats's 'To Autumn' and Shelley's 'Ode to the West Wind' – works that are involved in a mutually illuminating dialogue with specific items in the *Literary Pocket-Book*. Cornwall's sonnets may only represent one layer of conversation in a dialogue that includes better-known – and perhaps simply *better* – literary interventions into the vexed politics of 1819. But to dismiss Cornwall's work as 'futile', or to confine Cornwall to footnotes on the Hunt Circle, is to lose an important insight into the nature of that Circle's inter-actions, and the natural figurations of protest it employed.

Notes

1 See Jeffrey N. Cox, *Poetry and Politics in the Cockney School: Keats, Shelley, Hunt and their Circle* (Cambridge: Cambridge University Press, 1998).

2 G. H. Ford, 'Keats and Procter: A Misdated Acquaintance', *Modern Language Notes*, 66 (1951), pp. 532–36, at p. 535.

3 A date of late February – conjectured as the 27th by Rollins – is established by a letter mentioning the exchange, which Keats sent to Fanny Brawne (*LJK*, II, 266). Keats received Cornwall's second volume of poetry, *A Sicilian Story* (1820), before *Dramatic Scenes* (1819). This reversed order is due to the fact that Cornwall gave a copy of his first collection to Hunt to convey to Keats, but Hunt neglected to do this (see Keats's letter to Dilke, 4 March 1820; *LJK*, II, 271). We cannot be exactly sure when Keats received *A Sicilian Story*, but it must have been some time before 27 February because on that day he informed Fanny that 'another Book' had arrived from Cornwall – identified in a letter to Reynolds the following day as *Dramatic Scenes* (*LJK*, II, 267–68). In a letter dated 'March 1820', Hunt wrote to Cornwall: 'You will be very pleased to hear that Keats admires some passages of your work very much'. See *Leigh Hunt: A Life in Letters*, ed. Eleanor M. Gates (Essex, CT: Falls River, 1998), p. 103.

4 Letter dated 9 March 1819. See *The Correspondence of Leigh Hunt*, ed. Thornton Hunt, 2 vols (London: Smith, Elder and Co., 1862), I, p. 128.

5 S. R. Townshend Mayer, *Gentleman's Magazine*, 237 (1874), pp. 555–68, at p. 568.

6 *The Letters of William Hazlitt*, ed. Herschel Moreland Sikes (London: Macmillan, 1979), p. 200.

7 *Edinburgh Review*, 33 (1820), pp. 144–55, at pp. 146–47.

8 Frances Kemble, *Records of a Girlhood* (1878; New York, NY: Cosimo, 2007), p. 353. Kemble became acquainted with the Cornwall household in the early 1830s.

9 Quoted in Gill Gregory, *The Life and Work of Adelaide Anne Procter: Poetry, Feminism and Fathers* (Aldershot: Ashgate, 1998), p. 95. The manuscript of this letter is held by the University of Iowa Libraries.

10 Gregory, p. 95.

11 For example, in his appraisal of *A Sicilian Story* in January 1820, Francis Jeffrey singled out the passage; *Edinburgh Review*, 33 (1820), p. 151.

12 Letter dated 20 September 1843. See Armour, *Barry Cornwall*, pp. 218–19.

13 James Baldwin, *The Book-Lover: A Guide to the Best Reading* (London: Putnam, 1893), p. 51.

14 See Hunt's letter to John Forster from 31 July 1855 in *The Correspondence of Leigh Hunt*, II, p. 177.

15 Edward Bulwer Lytton was to include a poetic version of the story of 'Gyges and Candaules' in his *Chronicles and Characters* (1868). Perhaps in homage to Cornwall's version of the 'silly king' (l. 217), Lytton also cast his tale of the 'silly-smiling king' (l. 194) in ottava rima.

16 In a review of December 1819, John Wilson referred to the *Literary Pocket-Book* for 1820 as having been 'just published'; *Blackwood's Edinburgh Magazine*, 6 (1819), pp. 235–47, at p. 241. As G. E. Bentley points out, the volumes 'must have been on sale by December, because the "long calendar of the months" begins with January of the new year', 'Leigh Hunt's "Literary Pocket-Book" 1818–22: A Romantic Source Book', *Victorian Periodicals Newsletter*, 8 (1975), pp. 125–28, at p. 125.

17 Leigh Hunt, *The Literary Pocket-Book; or, Companion for the Lover of Nature and Art* (London: C. and J. Ollier, 1819), p. 143.

18 Nicholas Roe's phrase from *John Keats and the Culture of Dissent* (Oxford: Clarendon Press, 1997), p. 254.

19 Significantly, in *A Sicilian Story* (1820), Cornwall chose not repeat his claim in the preface to *Dramatic Scenes* (1819) that he had 'touched on neither politics nor polemics'. Perhaps the sonnets' presence in the volume influenced this decision.

20 In fact, as Armour notes, although *A Sicilian Story* bears the date of 1820, it was 'in the hands of reviewers early in December 1819', as evinced by a review of the volume in the *Literary Gazette*, 4 December 1819), pp. 771–72. See *Barry Cornwall: A Biography of Bryan Waller Procter* (Boston: Meador, 1935), p. 62n. The sonnets, then, appeared in the *Literary Pocket-Book* and *A Sicilian Story* almost simultaneously. Hunt reprinted 'Spring', along with three other Cornwall sonnets, in his posthumously published anthology *The Book of the Sonnet*, ed. Leigh Hunt and S. Adams Lee, 2 vols (London: Sampson Low, Son, and Marsten, 1867), I, p. 301. Hunt also included ten of Keats's sonnets in this volume.

21 'The poems of "Barry Cornwall" are, perhaps, the best example we possess of the futility of a poet with neither philosophic depth nor extraordinary command of poetic language trying to follow in the footsteps of the great poets', Donald H. Reiman (ed.), *Brian Waller Procter: A Sicilian Story and Mirandola* (London: Garland, 1977), p. viii.

22 All references to Marvell's poetry are to *Andrew Marvell*, ed. by Frank Kermode and Keith Walker (Oxford: Oxford University Press, 1990).

23 *Blackwood's Edinburgh Magazine*, 6 (1819), pp. 235–47, at p. 236.

24 At the end of his review of the *Literary Pocket-Book*, Wilson even commented that 'the idea is good and ingenuous, and the execution is, on the whole, excellent', *Blackwood's Edinburgh Magazine*, 6 (1819), p. 246. In one sense, of course, the volume is thoroughly disingenuous.

25 Possibly, 'gathering' here links to the 'gathering swallows' in line 33 of Keats's 'To Autumn'. Although in Keats's ode the swallows are poised for (political) flight, significantly they

have not yet left; indeed, 'gathering' suggests that they are growing in numbers and strength. If this is a gesture of post-Peterloo defiance, it can be related to Cornwall's faith in the 'swelling' of 'Man's bouncing spirit' (ll. 13–14) after the setback in Manchester.

26 By no means all the flags and banners were red; eyewitness accounts mention green, blue, black and white flags. But many were red, as John Tyas, writer for *The Times*, records: 'The latter [i.e. the females of Royton] bore two red flags, the one inscribed *Let us die like men, and not be sold like slaves*; the other *Annual Parliaments and Universal Suffrage*'. See Robert Walmsley, *Peterloo: The Case Reopened* (Manchester: Manchester University Press, 1969), p. 152.

27 *Paine: Political Writings*, ed. Bruce Kuklick (Cambridge: Cambridge University Press, 1989), pp. 202–03. The emphases are Paine's.

28 *John Keats and the Culture of Dissent*, p. 260.

29 *New Annual Register* (London: McLean, 1820), pp. 146–47.

30 Cornwall was certainly friendly with Woodhouse by the end of 1820: both were part of a group of literary figures associated with Baldwin's *London Magazine* (other members of the group included Thomas Noon Talfourd, Charles Lamb, and Thomas De Quincey). Perhaps Cornwall knew Woodhouse – the most important transcriber of Keats's work – prior to this date.

31 We can be fairly certain, however, that the two poets weren't intimately acquainted. In a letter to Keats of 1820, Cornwall has to request that Keats set the example by leaving away the formal 'sir' at the beginning of their letters. See Ford, *Modern Language Notes*, 66 (1951), p. 535.

32 Barry Cornwall, *An Autobiographical Fragment and Biographical Notes: With Personal Sketches of Contemporaries, Unpublished Lyrics, and Letters of Literary Friends*, ed. Coventry Patmore (London: George Bell, 1877), p. 201.

33 The *Monthly Review*'s appraisal of Keats's *Lamia* volume (1820) was directly followed by a review of Cornwall's *Marcian Colonna* (1820), the two reviews sharing page 310 of the literary journal; see *Monthly Review*, 92 (1820), pp. 310–18. In particular, conservative critics liked to play Cornwall off against Keats, cautioning the former to avoid the political pitfalls that had waylaid the latter.

34 Cornwall was certainly capable of conscious and skilful imitation of Keats. For many years an anonymous poem entitled 'A Voice', which appeared in the *Indicator* in January 1820, signed 'XXX' but in fact written by Cornwall, was considered to be a passage of *Endymion* that Keats rejected at the last moment. It was frequently included in notes to subsequent editions of Keats's poem. See Armour, *Barry Cornwall*, p. 153.

35 *Blackwood's Edinburgh Magazine*, 6 (1819), p. 246.

4

The Scent of Strong-Smelling Phrases: Cornwall's Popular Eroticism

Leaving aside for the moment our own estimation of the respective merits of Keats and 'Barry Cornwall', popular Romantic taste preferred the latter's slant on medieval Italian verse and his Elizabethan-styled dramatic 'scenes' – self-contained verse dramas – to the former's own Hunt-inflected corpus. In this chapter, I return to one of this book's central conundrums – why did Cornwall appeal so decisively to early nineteenth-century audiences in a way that Keats emphatically didn't? – to suggest that a significant part of Cornwall's fascination lay in his frank skill with narratives of love.

To locate Cornwall's popularity in his success at supplying the appetite for risqué verse is not to tell the whole story, however. To be sure, Cornwall was garlanded for his erotic verse: in *The Retrospective Review*, Thomas Noon Talfourd singled him out as 'the most genuine poet of love, who has, for a long period, appeared among us'.[1] But Keats was also known as a 'sensual' writer, and yet far from achieving saleable status he was roundly condemned for his 'emasculated prurience'. Indeed, for many commentators a sea of vulgarity lapped at the edges of Keats's work, nauseating conservative reviewers.[2] 'Z.' (John Gibson Lockhart) publicly insulted Keats in *Blackwood's Edinburgh Magazine*, labelling him a 'boy of pretty abilities' and couching criticism of an early paean, 'To Mary Frogley', in a barely concealed discourse of teenage onanism: 'Johnny's affections are not entirely confined to the ethereal', Lockhart sniped insinuatingly, warning readers away from the young poet's 'prurient and vulgar lines'.[3] My aim, then, is to explore this vital disparity in Keats's and Cornwall's receptions, further elucidating what John Whale has recently referred to as the 'precariousness of taste, particularly in relation to romance and its representation of sexuality'.[4] As we shall see, Cornwall's love narratives offer a focal, though neglected, context for understanding Keats's relation to the literary marketplace. In the following discussions, I want to isolate the conditions of Cornwall's contemporary popularity in what can be envisaged as a poetics of erotic containment – work that skirts the boundaries of indecorum, generating excitement without transgressing far enough to exclude sections of his readership, notably women. Read alongside Keats's would-be 'masculine' romance, a sexual aesthetic perceived by conservative reviewers as onanistically self-referential, Cornwall's love poetry throws additional light on his less successful rival's fraught reception.

1. White Breasts and Voluptuous Limes

Early nineteenth-century readers were delighted at Cornwall's willingness to titillate. His amorous 'dramatic scenes' are laden with innuendo, often turning on characters' – and, of course, the audience's – implied sexual knowledge. While Cornwall's texts are not 'pornographic' in that tradition of transgressive publication surveyed by Julia Peakman in *Mighty Lewd Books: The Development of Pornography in Eighteenth-Century England* (2003), they participate in a long-established custom of erotic writing whose wide, gender-straddling readership Peakman's informative book elucidates. Often, this daring register was welcomed by critics. The *New Monthly Magazine*, for instance, referred coyly to *A Sicilian Story*'s 'rich love-scenes', lamenting their absence from Keats's *Isabella* when it appeared six months later.[5] Shelley, however, thought Cornwall had attempted to engage in an 'out-Hunting of Hunt and out-Byroning of Byron', resulting in 'indecencies ... against sexual nature'. He denounced Cornwall for literary conspurcation, labelling his work in uncompromising terms as 'filthy' (*LPBS*, II, 240). In a strikingly aromatic passage, the scandalized *Honeycomb* magazine (punning on, or possibly merely garbling, an old adage from Sir Edward Coke's *Reports*), accused Cornwall of always 'follow[ing] the scent of strong-smelling phrases'.[6] Even Cornwall's poetic mentor, Hunt, worried that his pupil's work was 'too wilful and sensual'. As the author of the 'odious and incestuous' tale of adulterous love,[7] *The Story of Rimini* – 1816's *Lady Chatterley's Lover* – Hunt could comment with some justification that 'We are no prudes, Heaven knows ...'. None the less, he added, Cornwall's work 'conspire[d] with unfeelingness itself to reduce ... sexual intercourse to selfishness in all its shapes, legitimate as well as illegitimate'.[8]

It is not difficult to see what Hunt is driving at. Cornwall's work is suffused with an atmosphere of casual sexuality, often displaced, in true 'Cockney' mode, onto descriptions of nature or the seasons. Consider the following riotous account of Summer in *Marcian Colonna*, published in June 1820:[9]

> Many a star
> Shone out above upon the silent hours ...
> The red rose was in blossom, and the fair
> And bending lily to the wanton air
> Bared her white breast, and the voluptuous lime
> Cast out his perfumes, and the wilding thyme
> Mingled his mountain sweets, transplanted low
> 'Midst all the flowers that in those regions blow.
> (*Marcian Colonna*, pp. 35-36)

With its mingled scents, stars, roses and sweets, the passage recalls stanza 36 of Keats's *The Eve of St Agnes*, published in *Lamia ... and Other Poems* in July that year.

> he arose,
> Ethereal, flushed, and like a throbbing star
> Seen mid the sapphire heaven's deep repose;
> Into her dream he melted, as the rose
> Blendeth its odour with the violet –
> Solution sweet.
> (*The Eve of St Agnes*, ll. 317-22)

In his wilder, revised manuscript of September 1819, Keats briefly substituted 'mingled' for 'melted', further mingling the two poets' aesthetics:[10]

> With her wild dream he mingled, as a rose
> Marrieth its odour to a violet.
> (*The Eve of St Agnes*, ll. 320-21, revised manuscript)

Whereas many critics praised Cornwall's taste and feeling in matters of love – in *The Romance of Biography; or, Memoirs of Women Loved and Celebrated by Poets*, Anna Brownwell Jameson argued that the 'pure stream' of Cornwall's sentiment flowed 'unmingled and untainted' – some commentators were perturbed by what they saw as his lack of 'expurgatory judgement'.[11] Such attacks became more common after the disastrous reception of *The Flood of Thessaly*, by which time Cornwall had been 'outed' as a Cockney writer. The *Monthly Review* was especially perturbed by Cornwall's X-rated asterisks at the climactic conclusion of one of the volume's miscellaneous pieces, *The Girl of Provence*. In this poem, the heroine Eva has been reading lurid romances, which Cornwall suggests (referencing anxieties about the effects of consuming the wrong kind of literature), have turned her brain. Deluded, gazing devotedly on a naked statue of Apollo in a Paris museum, Eva persuades herself that the divinity has descended to carry her off in his 'radiant arms'. After a long, impressionistically sensual description of paired flight, the poem ends in what the *Monthly Review* plaintively recognized as a description of physical orgasm, at which point language and narrative break down altogether:

37.
O girl! whose curling limbs
A god has breathed on till they sting the brain
With beauty – Look! how in her eye there swims
Intolerable joy – *   *   *   *
*   *   *   *   *   *
*   *   *   *   *   *
*   *   *   *   *   *

The *Monthly* opined, skittishly:

> In the exercise of his poetical licence, Mr. Barry Cornwall seems inclined in one or two instances to be rather licentious in his poetry. The decent compositor, however, has discretely omitted three lines and a half in stanza xxxvii, and has wisely inserted a competent quantity of stars: but if the same expurgatory judgment had been exercised on some other parts of the poem, it would have redounded more to Mr. C's credit. (p. 54)

Cornwall's 'licentious' poetics is put down to an imprudent devotion to Byron's 'voluptuous verses'. A whiff of eroticism still seems to linger around Cornwall's racy works. A 'hit' for the 1978 Garland edition of *Marcian Colonna* on Amazon.com calls up the following links: 'Sponsored Links: (What's this?) Extremely Sexy & Seductive Lingerie Save Up to 35%, Discreet Shipping'.[12] What's this, indeed.

While both poets were recognized as 'sensual' writers, Cornwall – for the most part, at least – successfully negotiated a crucial distinction between sanctioned levels of indecorum and out-and-out vulgarity. Cornwall's lime and wilding thyme promiscuously cast out their odours; but importantly they do not 'mingle' with the flowers of the region in quite so obvious a fashion as Keats's blatant coupleting of rose and violet. Cornwall's 'mingle', grammatically tied to the indistinct 'midst' rather than the bawdily conjunctive 'with', possesses a reflexive, intransitive timbre, and merely hints at consorting. In the revised version of *The Eve of St Agnes*, by contrast, 'mingle' is scandalously transitive.

Simply deploying the verb 'mingle' was to invoke a *frisson*, the word having incorporated unregeneratedly carnal connotations since Coverdale's Bible had castigated men and their sons for having 'mengled them selues with the

daughters' of alien peoples.[13] The presence of both 'mingle' and 'voluptuous'
in Cornwall's lines may even have reminded some readers uncomfortably of
William Fulbecke's *Pandectes of the Law of Nations* (1602), which alludes
to the people of Sodom and Gomorra 'voluptuously mingling themselues
with the women of the Moabites'.[14] On the whole, though, Cornwall's pulse-
raising verse delighted rather than disgusted readers and critics. The fact
that Cornwall – sensibly, from a commercial point of view – refrains from
commuting his playfully insinuating 'mountain sweets' into the poetically
more elegant, but near-pornographic, 'solution sweet' provides another
insight into the markedly different characters of Keats's and Cornwall's
reception. Keats, on – or, as some reviewers saw things, in – the other hand,
is unable to hold back 'solution sweet', revealing what hostile reviewers would
denounce as his morbidly prurient fantasy.[15] Keats, crucially, goes a step too
far, incurring not one but two levels of damaging critical opprobrium: his
cloying euphemisms identify him not only as unhealthily fixated on the
sexual act, but also as immaturely fixated. Where Cornwall purposefully
self-fashioned himself as an experienced, worldly writer, Keats remained a
'petulant boy' whose work could be set aside, as in the *Guardian*'s despairing
appraisal of the *Lamia* volume, as mere 'juvenile industry'.[16]

An overwhelming motivation for Keats's move in 1819 towards what John
Whale calls a 'more robust, masculinized version of romance',[17] was his determination to ward off charges of effeminacy in the face of Cornwall's popular
and popularly unabashed verse. It was this sort of resolve which prompted
Keats to make his notorious changes to stanza 36 of *The Eve of St Agnes*:

> See, while she speaks his arms encroaching slow,
> Have zoned her, heart to heart, – loud, loud the dark winds blow!
>
> For on the midnight came a tempest fell;
> More sooth, for that his quick rejoinder flows
> Into her burning ear: and still the spell
> Unbroken guards her in serene repose.
> With her wild dream he mingled, as a rose
> Marrieth its odour to a violet.
> Still, still she dreams, louder the frost wind blows ...
>   (*The Eve of St Agnes*, ll. 314-22 of the revised manuscript)

Keats's publisher, John Taylor, was convinced the new passages would
exclude women readers and refused to print the poem unless the original
text was restored. Keats's notorious 'rhodomontade' reply to Richard
Woodhouse, acting as Taylor's legal advisor, announced bravado indifference to the idea of a female readership. As Woodhouse reported to the

exasperated publisher: 'He says he does not want ladies to read his poetry: that he writes for men' (*LJK*, II, 163). It seems probable that both Keats and Taylor underestimated the reading habits of 'ladies'. For his part, Keats may not have realized the scale of women's involvement in the book trade, both as readers and writers. If his intention was genuinely to write exclusively for men, he was being short-sighted, to say the least. As Stuart Curran notes, by the 1780s and 1790s 'women had moved to the forefront of the publishing world'; they had also moved to the front of the book-buying world.[18] Similarly, Taylor may not have known, although as a publisher he *should* have known, that – as Peakman's study of pornography clarifies – women had been reading, and what is more writing and printing, bawdy and legally 'obscene' literature for at least a century.[19]

Supremely cognizant of women's purchasing power in the poetic marketplace, Cornwall was more than willing to capitalize on the fact that they were as equally fascinated as their male counterparts by erotic verse.[20] His aim to captivate this constituency appears to have been successful: in 1823, the *London Magazine* commented that Barry Cornwall had 'delighted most readers – but most of all those readers in whose hearts young poets are best pleased to be welcomed ... Women'.[21] A recollection of Cornwall's ability to charm women readers in Anna Brownwell Jameson's book, *The Romance of Biography; or, Memoirs of Women Loved and Celebrated by Poets*, underscores the *London Magazine*'s evaluation. In the final chapter, 'Heroines of Modern Poetry', Jameson comments: 'It is not without reason that Barry Cornwall has been styled the "Poet of Women", *par excellence*. It enhances the value, it adds to the charm of every tender and beautiful passage addressed to us, that we know them to be sincere and heartfelt.'[22]

If the 'gentle' Cornwall enjoyed a reputation as the 'poet of women' in Jameson's phrase, there was also a distinctly more buccaneering side to his character. We catch something of this roguish streak in two uncollected letters, the first to Helen Goldsmid – a family friend about to be married – dated 21 July 1855; and the second to Helen's sister Emma, from 14 August 1864. Full of whispered asides and parenthetically knowing allusions ('amongst other things', indeed!), they reveal a jaunty, worldly wise aspect to Cornwall in the 'presence' of women at odds with his often noted shyness among men:

> As I am not entitled to send you my blessing, I shall drink your health in pure wine ... on Wednesday next. If a wife who has (amongst other things) a charming temper can make a man happy, I need not send any wishes to Mr. Lucas. But tell him, in a whisper, that if ever I should become a widower & should be bold

enough to marry again I shall look out for just such a good-tempered girl as
Helen.

and:

> We think of you when ever the day is bright. We think of you when we see the
> bright young flowers. But I see how it is. You have heard of my admiration for
> your sister Helen (& I must even now confess to that) – That is true; but, being
> a lawyer, I may tell you that the late acts of Parliament allow gentlemen to like
> more than one lady at a time. This is a great relief to us.[23]

Cornwall's smooth operations, still evident in his late seventies, offer
an insight into his attraction for women such as Mary Shelley and Anne
Skepper. A phrase from *Gyges* on the protagonist's charm also seems apt,
applied to Cornwall: 'he pleased the women well' (p. 128).

Cornwall's genius lay in his ability to produce writing that was less
obviously objectionable than, say, Byron's licentious braggadocio,[24] but
which remained unimpeachably 'manly' with its allusions to sexual experience, and yet could still be addressed to a female constituency:

> A story (still believed through Sicily,)
> Is told of one young girl who chose to die
> For love. Sweet ladies, listen and believe,
> If that ye can believe so strange a story,
> That ever woman could ever so deeply grieve.
>   (*A Sicilian Story*, p. 7)

By skirting the borders of decorum without encroaching on the dangerous,
generically grey, zones between romance and pornographic registers,
Cornwall was able to invite both sexes to feast on his risqué flourishes, on
such crimsoning, self-betraying lines as:

>   ... and on his neck
> Her round arm hung, while half as in command
> And half entreaty did his swimming eye
> Speak of forbearance, 'till from her pouting lip
> He snatched the honey-dews that lovers sip,
> And then, in crimsoning beauty, playfully
> She frowned, and wore that self-betraying air
> Which women loved and flattered love to wear.
>   (*A Sicilian Story*, p. 13)

This knowing passage gets along swimmingly. Nowadays, Cornwall's poetry
is regarded as third-rate, 'sloppy' in G. M. Matthews's estimation.[25] In a sense,

though a good sense, the above extract *is* sloppy, and bravely so. Moreover, its sloppiness is exactly what readers responded to so warmly.

For additional evidence of Cornwall's enthusiastic female readership, in 1820 the *New Monthly Magazine* printed a eulogy to Cornwall by one of its readers, Ellen Janet, entitled 'Hail! Star of promise', which praised Cornwall's 'wondrous genius'.[26] Indeed, we need look no further for evidence of Cornwall's enthusiastic female audience, not to mention its fervent interest in his true identity, than Isabella Jones. Keats had formed an intense attachment to this well-read woman after meeting her in Hastings in 1818, although it remains uncertain whether the relationship progressed beyond flirtation.[27] She was later to develop a similarly ambiguous rapport with Keats's publisher John Taylor. In a letter sent on 31 May 1819, framed in a conspiratorial register, Jones makes an interesting reference to Cornwall, which draws parallels between his style and Keats's:

> ... moreover tell me who Barry Cornwall is and rely upon my secresy and discretion tho' a woman – *Lysander and Ione* [included in *Dramatic Scenes*] reminded me very often of *our* favourite *Endymion* and I fancy I discern Mr. Taylor in the well selected mottos to each poem – the *Magdalen* and *Woman* are my favourites among the smaller poems.[28]

Cornwall becomes caught up in an intriguing *ménage a trois* comprising Keats, Isabella Jones and Taylor. Most fascinatingly of all, Jones may even be implying that the pseudonymous 'Barry Cornwall' *was* Keats. At any rate, she correctly guesses that Cornwall was thick with the Keats–Taylor circle.

2. 'Sheathing the Sword': Cornwall's Bawdy

While indubitably market-savvy, Cornwall did not hit the right tone unfailingly. *Gyges*, part of Cornwall's second volume, *A Sicilian Story* (1820), incorporated a bedroom scene of such Byronic excess that many critics recoiled in embarrassment. As late as 1857, a reviewer for *Blackwood's Edinburgh Magazine*, noting the absence of *Gyges* from a new edition of Cornwall's work, observed with relief that the notorious poem had 'subsided, like a preposterous snapping-turtle, into the mud of oblivion'.[29]

Intriguingly, in a publication already linked to Keats's *Lamia* volume through its Boccaccio adaptation, *Gyges* sets itself up in illuminating contextual relationship to Keats's now, but not then, better-known *The Eve of St Agnes*, sharing with it a strikingly similar episode of voyeurism. Although long disregarded, *Gyges* makes for interesting parallel reading, rubbing up instructively against the limits of the popular appeal of racy verse, disclosing what John Whale identifies as the 'precariousness of taste' in relation to eroticized verse in the Romantic period.[30] Like its ottava rima bedfellow, *Diego de Montilla* – which Diego Saglia shows is a 'selective rewriting of the first canto of [Byron's] *Don Juan*' – *Gyges* adopts the form as well as the jaunty tone and colloquial register popularized by Byron's *Beppo* (1818).[31] Oddly enough, in *Don Juan* Byron portrayed Cornwall, his Harrow schoolmate, as 'a sort of moral me' (dismissing Keats in the same poem as an immature, 'fiery particle' that had allowed itself to be 'snuffed out by an article'.[32] His identification of Cornwall as a kind of 'moral' doppelgänger is curious, since *Gyges* is striking precisely for its morally unfiltered depiction of wanton sexual exchange. At any rate, Marilyn Butler surely over-simplifies things when, in passing (the condition of most recent commentaries on Cornwall), she lumps Cornwall's 'closet-dramas' with other Romantic-period works that 'opposed good to evil in unexceptionable, stylized terms'.[33] There are no unambiguously 'good' or 'evil' characters in *Gyges*, a text fascinated by its protagonists' desire to gratify their sexual urges, rather than detained by any sense of obligation to demonstrate clearly defined morals. Indeed, after concluding the poem with a mischievously qualified claim to have 'shewn the moral "in a way"', Cornwall announces that the only 'lesson' worth salvaging from his licentious tale is that 'women of the present day / Are not so bad, nor half, as those of old' (*Gyges*, stanza 39).

In some respects, *Gyges* encapsulates what Shelley labelled as Cornwall's 'indecencies ... against sexual nature'. The poem's frank depictions of physical desire unsettled reviewers eager to claim Cornwall as the uncontentious face of an emerging brand of freer, more colloquial poetry, whose 'dark side' was represented by the immoral excesses of Hunt, Keats and the 'Cockney School'. For instance, while the *New Monthly Magazine* was pleased to discover that *Gyges* lacked the 'frigid, demoralizing tone' of *Don Juan*, the reviewer adds nervously that 'here and there an allusion might be spared without diminishing the humour of the descriptions or weakening the effect of the poetry'.[34] Like *The Eve of St Agnes*, the story of *Gyges* narrates a highly eroticized scene of voyeuristic consumption within a lady's 'chamber'.[35] Cornwall's plot, inspired by Herodotus, relates the tale of the arrogant king of Lydia, Candaules.[36] The king's beguiling young wife, Lais, possesses a birthmark in the shape of a 'purple flower' on her 'swan-like breast' (stanza 23), news of which feature the 'broad and boastful' Candaules cannot resist divulging to his boyish, blushful – and distinctly Keatsian – confidante, Gyges, who burns to see the king's naked wife, 'tho' but for once':

25.
He blush'd and listen'd – panted like a fawn
That's just escaped the fraudful hunters' range,
And his eyes sparkled like approaching morn,
And on his cheek he felt the colour change
Until he trembled – and the blush was gone:
His brain was stagger'd with a notion strange:
He sighed to see, tho' but for once, the flower;
The monarch laughed ...

In an analogue of the Gyges story in Book 2 of Plato's *Republic*, the youthful
hero finds a ring of invisibility, gaining ingress to the queen's bedroom
through the agency of this magical token.[37] Cornwall, however, plumps for
Herodotus's version, since it involves the king in his own downfall (a politically resonant decision in 1819, as I will argue). The 'silly king' conveys Gyges
to a suitable vantage point where he can gaze on the undressed Lais:

28.
Candaules (shame upon the silly king!)
Vowed that the curious boy this mark should see.
He saw – (In faith 'twould be a pretty thing
If even kings could take this liberty)
He saw her in her beauty, fluttering
From pleasure as she glanc'd her smiling eye
On the broad mirror which displayed a breast
Unlaced, where Jove himself might sigh to rest.

29.
The boy came (guided by the king) to where,
In the most deep and silent hour of night,
Stood Lais: quite unloos'd,[38] her golden hair
Went streaming all about like lines of light,
And, thro' the lattice leaves gusts of soft air
Sighed like perfume, and touched her shoulders white,
And o'er her tresses and her bosom played,
Seeming to love each place o'er which they strayed.

30.
Then sank she on her couch and drew aside
The silken curtains and let in the moon,
Which trembling ran around the chamber wide,
Kissing and flooding the rich flowers which June
Had fann'd to life, and which in summer-pride
'Rose like a queen's companions. Lais soon,

Touch'd by the scene, look'd as she had forgot
The world: the boy stood rooted to the spot.

Just as Keats's schoolboyish joke on tumescence in *The Eve of St Agnes* is figured around acts of rising – '[Porphyro] arose, / Ethereal, flushed, and like a throbbing star' (ll. 317–18) – Cornwall jests bawdily on the chamber flowers, which, kissed by the moon, synecdochially 'rose like a queen's companions' (stanza 30).[39]

Gyges observes Lais as she reclines in an erotic reverie – she 'look'd as she had forgot / The world' (stanza 30); however, without warning she rouses herself, angrily confronting the reddening scoptophile:

> ... she asked him how –
> How a young gentleman like him who prided
> Himself upon his modesty could call
> At such an hour: he blush'd, and told her all.
>   (*Gyges*, p. 134)

Whereas Porphyro is rewarded for his juvenile act of peeping with Madeline's love, Lais is altogether less sanguine – at first, at least – about having been the object of voyeuristic consumption. Yet her anger is not directed at Gyges for long, falling instead upon her husband, the king. Forming an amorous union with the incursive youth, whom she 'fancied from that day', Lais arranges for Candaules to be slowly poisoned for his extravagant act of betrayal. (The inclusion of strong female personalities such as Lais in Cornwall's poetry is, perhaps, another reason for why women readers enjoyed his work.) The draught is administered by none other than the king's perfidious confidante:

> ... 'twas said his wine grew mighty strong,
> And that 'twas handed by this curious lad,
> (Gyges), whom Lais fancied from that day,
> And made Lord of herself and Lydia.
>   (*Gyges*, p. 134)

Gyges may have disturbed reviewers for other reasons than its titillating focus. The poem's anti-monarchical message would have confirmed to many their suspicions of close links between liberal morality and liberal politics, particularly given the circumstance that *A Sicilian Story* – in reviewers' hands by December 1819 – was published just four months after the political turmoil that culminated in the Peterloo massacre. While Cornwall is not usually thought of as a political writer, I don't believe it's fanciful to suggest that his audience would have readily discerned a contemporary political dimension in a tale about the usurpation and killing of a king by his subjects (particularly those who had first seen Cornwall's sonnets on the seasons, reprinted in *A Sicilian Story*, in Hunt's *Literary Pocket-Book* for 1820.) A fantasy of regicide was dangerous at any time, coming from a known associate of the *Examiner*'s obdurate editor, Leigh Hunt; but doubly so in 1819, the year of widespread dissatisfaction, workers' rallies and – in E. P. Thompson's opinion – near revolution.

Whether or not he was attempting to 'out-do' Hunt or Byron, Cornwall undoubtedly had a tendency to go too far in his depiction of sexual attraction. In September 1822, poet and future founding editor of the *Literary Souvenir*, Alaric Watts, tut-tutted to William Blackwood about the moral and sexual profligacy of a new breed of writer. Watts reserved the greater part of his opprobrium for Hunt, denouncing the 'villainous depravity of this creature's mind with respect to women'; but he also roped in Cornwall for disapprobation, sniping that the publisher 'Chas Ollier' and his star writer 'Procter' (Cornwall) belonged with Hunt to an undesirable 'class of persons'.[40] It's not difficult to imagine how Watts must have felt on encountering in *Dramatic Scenes* an astonishingly forthright pun on sexual coupling. In 'The Return of Mark Anthony', Cleopatra endeavours to pacify her enraged lover:

> *Anthony*. Oh! that you were
> A man – a soldier – fifty – with the souls
> Of a hundred swart Aegyptians. By my sword!
> *Cleopatra*. You'd sheath it.

The poem contains other ribald interludes, including a bawdy exchange in which Cleopatra demands to know from a Roman soldier how Italian and Egyptian women measure up in bed. Mark Anthony has to step in to curtail the risqué dialogue:

> *Cleopatra*. Now, can you boast
> Of Roman hearts like ours?
> *Domitius*. No, madam, no.
> They make us run to catch 'em. Here the women
> Are kinder: much.
> *Cleop*. I knew it.
> *Dom*. Aye; they'll give
> More than we want at times.
> *Anthony*. No more. No more.
>   ('The Return of Mark Anthony', p. 106)

In *Diego de Montilla* – Cornwall's second Byronic *ottava rima* outing in *A Sicilian Story* (1820) – we come across a similarly brazen stanza that describes the lustful thoughts of Spanish maidens for husbands:

They look'd and sigh'd, as girls can look and sigh
When they want husbands, or when gossips tell
That they shall have a husband six feet high,
(Tho' five feet nine or ten might do as well)
With curly hair, Greek nose, and sweet black eye,
And other things on which I cannot dwell ...
        (*Diego de Montilla*, p. 162)

Shelley may also have had such barely self-censoring passages as these
in mind when he labelled Cornwall's work a ludicrous attempt at an
'out-Byroning of Byroning'. Or he might have been thinking of Cornwall's
darkly claustrophobic take in *Dramatic Scenes* on the Don Juan theme. In
Cornwall's own 'Juan', the villainously unhinged anti-hero lies in wait for
his wife Olympia, accosting her as she emerges from midnight prayers.
Convinced of her infidelity, Juan draws his dagger with the words:

                        I who have
Rioted upon that bosom will at least
Take care that none beside shall sleep there.
        (*Dramatic Scenes*, p. 50)

The passage itself – and presumably the Romantic reader – riots on the
frisson generated by Cornwall's sexual candour.

As a final example, Cornwall's third volume, *Marcian Colonna*, contains
a sophisticated psychosexual drama, 'Amelia Wentworth'. The poem was
singled out by John Hamilton Reynolds in a letter to the reviewer Francis
Jeffrey for displaying 'great simplicity and pathos', and judged the high-point
of a volume otherwise bearing the 'marks of haste'.[41] Unusually for Cockney
School productions, Cornwall's astonishingly frank portrait of a failing
marriage is set in the present day, rather than in an idealized medieval or
classical past. The poem's eponymous heroine agrees to marry a rich, elderly
suitor at the behest of her dissolute father. The ill-matched couple then
adopt a young man, Amelia's junior by only a few years. The relationship
between Amelia and her new charge rapidly veers into dangerously erotic
territory, whose appeal to its readers can be gauged through such sparky
exchanges as the following:

Amelia. Give me the rose.
Charles. But where shall it be placed?
Amel. Why in my hand – my hair. Look! how it blushes,
To see us both so idle. Give it me.
Where? where do ladies hide their favourite flowers,

But in their bosoms, foolish youth. Away –
'Tis I must do it.
          ('Amelia Wentworth', pp. 127–28)

3. 'Lucent Syrops, Tinct with Cinnamon': Keats's Bawdy

In 1992, Christopher Lawrence insisted that it was a 'hopeless' task to find
contemporary medical reference frames in the poems of Keats, arguing that
the 'meaning of his images needs to be understood by reference to dramatic
traditions and circles, not medical ones.'[42] Studies by William Hale-White,
Hillas Smith, Donald C. Goellnicht, Hermione De Almeida and Nicholas
Roe have put beyond issue the specific and thoroughgoing ways in which
Keats's medical expertise inflects his poetic imagination.[43] Nonetheless, their
commentaries overlook a particularly disclosing instance of fecund literary–
medical interchange. I'd like to return to stanza 30 of *The Eve of St Agnes*,
where Porphyro prepares a sumptuous spread for the somnolent Madeline, a
childish buffet, as Marjorie Levinson points out, that is indigestibly sugary,
all creamy curds and jellies, a 'supper-not-for-eating'.[44] I think Levinson
is right – paradoxically, the comestibles aren't meant to be eaten, as such.
Equally, though, I would contend that they *are* intended for ingestion. Once
seen in a medical light, phrases such as 'syrops, tinct with cinnamon' begin
to resonate in fascinating ways. Indeed, from this perspective the entire feast
appears to have been assembled from a medical lexicon, or pharmacopoeia:

> ... forth from the closet brought a heap
> Of candied apple, quince, and plum, and gourd;
> With jellies soother than the creamy curd,
> And lucent syrops, tinct with cinnamon;
> Manna and dates, in argosy transferr'd
> From Fez; and spiced dainties, every one,
> From silken Samarcand to cedar'd Lebanon.
>   (*The Eve of St Agnes*, ll. 264–70)

In her excellent study of medical frames to Keats's poems, De Almeida
has drawn attention to a physician's context to Porphyro's 'magical and
tinctured feast' (p. 11). As she points out, the phrase 'lucent syrops' recalls
the medical term 'drowsy syrop'; and there are certainly interesting questions
to be pondered concerning the exact purpose of Porphyro's 'love-philtre' (p.
156). By the same token, there is more that we could say in scrutinizing the
precise ingredients of what she terms Porphyro's 'ambiguous' repast. The

syrupy mixture described by De Almeida as 'colored and perfumed with cinnamon', which she terms an 'exotic and magical' mixture or 'potion', doesn't just 'take on all the ambiguous characteristics of the *pharmakon* as a drug, a poison, a dye, and a perfume' (pp. 155–56). It actually reads like part of a *specific* medical recipe, one that would not have been in the slightest bit 'exotic' to the apothecaries of Guy's Hospital. Cinnamon was widely used as an ingredient in remedies for venereal infections, especially gonorrhoea. Like quince, it was added to the viscous medium of preparations deployed to treat gonorrhoea-related strictures of the urethra, such as the painful condition 'gleets'. William Houlston's *Pharmacopoeia Chirurgica; or, Formulæ for the Use of Surgeons* (1794), for example, includes a recipe for 'Mistura Copaibæ Cum Olibano'. Olibanum and copaiba are mixed to a syrupy base of honey and mucilage, to which is added 'cinnamon water': a dose of 'two or three table-spoonfuls, twice or thrice a day ... will be found of considerable service in gleets, and in the latter stage of gonorrhoea'.[45]

In a very particular manner, the ingredients of Porphyro's feast recall – or possibly mischievously allude to – recipes from the pharmacopoeia used in teaching hospitals such as Guy's. Keats, who was examined in his ability to translate from the Latin *Pharmacopoeia Londinensis*, was more than *au fait* with such preparations as Houlston adumbrates in his popular English translation. Viewed in this light, Porphyro's buffet is even less 'wholesome' than De Almeida imagines (p. 156).

Houlston's *Pharmacopoeia Chirurgica* also recommends 'Injectio Calomelanos' for treating the 'inflammatory stage of gonorrhoea', a preparation that combines 'mucilage of quince' with 'acquæ amoniæ' (p. 63). When not one but two key components of Porphyro's erotic feast turn up in contemporary cures for clap, I think we are justified in suggesting Keats's medical imagination borders on another guy's, or Guy's, joke, one that informs a characteristically Keatsian brand of bawdy. If we bear in mind that Porphyro's sole purpose is to have sex with Madeline, an aspiration that notoriously culminates in 'solution sweet' – a sexual euphemism itself couched in the apothecary's vernacular of a botanical compounding of roses and violets – then the hint of gonorrhoea lurking in the echoes of medical ingredients and professional terminology suddenly appears supremely knowing. Whether or not Keats himself ever contracted venereal disease, a debate given fresh impetus by Robert Gittings in the late 1960s, it is safe to say that Porphyro's archly assembled meal is, in one sense, at least, far removed from the infantilized and infantilizing registers of Levinson's 'childish' spread.

As Goellnicht comments, 'exactly why Keats had begun to treat himself with a "little Mercury" [*LJK*, I, 171] from as early as October 1817 is a highly debatable topic' (p. 201). Mercury may have been prescribed for venereal disease or possibly to combat a respiratory ailment. I find Gittings's arguments for the former scenario persuasive. At any rate, Gittings alerts us to the fact that early nineteenth-century medical practice limited the highly toxic substance for use in venereal complaints; moreover, doctors were especially wary about prescribing mercury preparations to tuberculosis sufferers, whose systems were already constitutionally weakened. Small amounts continued to be prescribed for gonorrhoea, however, with larger doses being adminis-tered in cases of syphilis. Solomon Sawrey, author of *An Inquiry into Some of the Effects of the Venereal Poison* (1802), helped popularize the erroneous belief that unsuccessfully treated gonorrhoea could develop into syphilis. It was probably Sawrey who attended Keats in 1817, and he who recom-mended mercury.[46] Gittings speculates that Sawrey significantly increased the dosage in the summer of 1818, by which time Keats was plagued by sore throats. Keats was also complaining of nervousness and toothache at this time, both of which can be symptoms of mercury poisoning. An increased dosage suggests that Sawrey believed Keats's gonorrhoea had 'progressed' to syphilis.

While Gittings interprets Keats's sore throats as a secondary symptom of venereal disease, other critics have associated them with tuberculosis. A third view, offered by Hale-White and Hillas Smith, both doctors themselves, rejects a diagnosis of either tuberculosis-related illness or venereal disease.[47] Goellnicht, reasonably enough perhaps, concludes that 'we cannot be certain why Keats was taking mercury during 1817 and 1818' (p. 202), echoing C. T. Andrews's recommendation that 'judgment on this issue be suspended unless and until new facts emerge' (p. 202).

One thing is certain, though: it is pertinent to ask what *Keats* thought had precipitated his complaint. In other words, what did Keats think he was taking mercury for? An interesting sidelight is thrown on the subject – equally on the subject of sweet solutions – by the *Pharmacopoeia Chirur-gica; or, A Manual of Chirurgical Pharmacy*, 3rd edition (1814), compiled by surgeon and long-standing Guy's assistant apothecary, James Wilson, and recommended in the 'strongest manner' by the *Edinburgh Medical and Surgical Journal*.[48] Moreover, this publication doesn't appear to have been taken into account in discussions of Keats and mercury. Wilson outlines current practice at Guy's, exemplified, as he explains, by Keats's surgical instructor Sir Astley Cooper and Richard Stocker, the translator of

Pharmacopoeia Officinalis Britannica (1810; 2nd edition 1816), a volume used by Guy's students.[49] Wilson reports that a preparation based on mercury in the form of 'hydrargyri oxymuriatis', and mixed with 'syrupus papaveris' (an opium-laced syrup), was 'first administered at Guy's hospital, by Mr. Stocker, apothecary to that institution, to a patient labouring under an inveterate venereal sore throat'.[50] He describes how a 'table-spoonful, twice a day, or oftener' of the syrupy mercury preparation worked 'the greatest possible alteration' in the health of the venereal patient, who was rapidly cured and discharged. Interestingly, Wilson's account of the preparation brings (sweet) syrups and solution into suggestively 'intimate' apposition: 'The oxymuriate of mercury should be intimately triturated with a small portion of the syrup, and the remainder should be added; taking care that the solution be complete' (p. 144). Whether or not Keats had consulted Wilson's *Pharmacopoeia Chirurgica* (there are no records of Guy's Physical Society Library ever having owned a copy), as a conscientious, high-flying surgeon's dresser at Guy's he would doubtless have been aware of Stocker's innovation at this time in treating symptoms of venereal diseases such as sore throats with mercury-laden syrups.[51] In addition to any light that Wilson's handbook possibly sheds on the 'little Mercury' Keats was self-adminis-tering for his own sore throat in October 1817, the ambiguous nature of the 'lucent syrops' in *The Eve of St Agnes* is rendered even more unstable, doubly so in the context of the routine use of quince and cinnamon in the treatment of gonorrhoea. We might say that Stocker's sweet solution of hydrargyri oxymuriatis and syrupus papaveris provides a tonic for diseases contracted in the service of 'solution sweet'.

The supremely manipulative Porphyro, then, has left nothing to chance. Having inveigled his way into his enemies' stronghold, persuaded Old Angela to betray her charge, picked a suitably concealed spot from which to watch Madeline undress, sung a love song into her sleeping ear at exactly the right moment for the St Agnes Eve dream, made sure he's the first man she sees after she wakes, and then had sex with her, he is able to present Madeline with a feast that is, in fact, nothing less than a cure for the clap.

Only readers versed in materia medica could be expected to 'get' the bawdy joke in Porphyro's feast (a banquet predicated precisely on 'taking care that the solution be complete'). By the same token, without necessarily appreciating the specific medical framework behind Porphyro's concoctions, Romantic readers and reviewers undoubtedly picked up on the general insalubriousness of the conceit, finding the poem's erotics as cloying as the sticky feast itself. If Keats hoped to deploy his cutting-edge knowledge of medical ingredients to spice up a racy romance that was explicitly designed to compete in the literary marketplace with productions such as Cornwall's, the manoeuvre back-fired. Where readers found themselves able to enjoy Cornwall's bawdy, which remained for the most part within sanctioned parameters, Keats's overheated erotics took them into itchier regions, and was rejected as perverse.

4. Heart to Heart

Remaining for the moment with *The Eve of St Agnes*, Richard Woodhouse was appalled by alterations Keats made to the poem in September 1819. For a start, the physical intimacy between the young lovers – a touchy subject, at best – had been rendered in a far less ambiguous manner. Hot under the collar, Woodhouse wrote to Taylor requesting that the publisher turn to the relevant passage to see for himself:

> As the poem was orig[inal]ly written, *we* innocent ones (ladies & myself) might very well have supposed that Porphyro, when acquainted with Madeline's love for him, & when "he arose, Etherial flushd &c. &c. (turn to it) set himself at once to persuade her to go off with him … to be married in right honest chaste & sober wise. But, as it is now altered, as soon as M[adeline] has confessed her love, P[orphyro] winds by degrees his arm round her, presses breast to breast, and acts all the acts of a bonâ fide husband, while she fancies she is only playing the part of a Wife in a dream. (*LJK*, II, 162–63)

Woodhouse's primary objection was prompted by the fact that the changes left Madeline in 'serene repose' while Porphyro 'acts all the acts of a bona fide husband' – 'turn[s] to it', so to speak. As Woodhouse clarifies for Taylor, Porphyro knows he is having sex 'for real', while Madeline merely dreams she is making love. These unequal degrees of knowing raised significant questions about volition and violation.

Subterranean anxieties are also in operation here, however, which may owe very little to genuine concern about Madeline's predicament. Consider more closely how Woodhouse voices his protest: 'She fancies she is only playing the part of a Wife in a dream'. Woodhouse appreciates that Keats's emendations depict Madeline enjoying a dream in which she actively reciprocates Porphyro's advances, a mutual 'turning to it' that implies that women – whom Woodhouse wished to imagine were as innocent as he professed to be: '*we* innocent ones (ladies & myself)' – are equally capable as men of experiencing, moreover deriving pleasure from, explicit sexual fantasies. Read in these terms, which is exactly how I think Woodhouse reads it, Keats's poem opens the possibility of a realm of unregulated female sexual agency. The letter to Taylor is not so much about protecting Madeline's honour, then, as bound up with an attempt to contain her dream, censoring it in a literal manner at the same time as seeking to reduce the significance of female erotic fantasy per se by reminding Taylor that Madeline's dream is, after all, 'only' a dream. Woodhouse seeks to place checks on Madeline's sexual desire, prompting Taylor to overrule – that is, rule out – Keats's authorial revisions.

The most unsettling change Keats made to his poem was to depict Madeline and Porphyro clasping each other 'breast to breast'. The revision stripped any vestige of doubt regarding the lovers' physical intimacy, prompting Woodhouse to declare: 'I do apprehend it will render the poem unfit for ladies'. Woodhouse casts his objection as a financial consideration: since the rogue (and roguish) stanzas rendered Keats's poem 'unfit for ladies', Taylor could expect his profits to be hit. But still more pressing is his anxiety that Keats is moving towards the production of a literature that invites women to indulge their erotic fantasies, privately, and in a manner Woodhouse regarded as irrefragably 'unfit for ladies'. Male anxieties about women masturbating, rather than any real concern about turnover, is evidently uppermost in Woodhouse's mind, although unarticulated in explicit terms, since only a few sentences later he concedes that 'profanely speaking' Keats's alterations to his poem would result in the 'Interest on the reader's imagination' being 'greatly heightened'. Under normal circumstances, heightened interest would be a positive effect of revision, one that was likely to increase sales: the first thing, of course, that the poem's readers might be expected to do in respect of the racy addition – performing precisely the reading act that Woodhouse asks of Taylor – would be to 'turn to it'.

Cornwall's work offers an additional framing narrative to the spat between Keats and his publisher. Woodhouse, a close bosom-friend of Keats, remembers the gist of Keats's revisions in his letter alerting Taylor to them, but not quite the details. He represents Madeline and Porphyro as clasping each other 'breast to breast'. The actual phrase is 'heart to heart':

> See, while she speaks his arms encroaching slow,
> Have zoned her, heart to heart, – loud, loud the dark winds blow!

In Cornwall's 'Love Cured By Kindness', published in *Dramatic Scenes* (available at book-sellers in the spring of 1819), the sexually knowing King-elect, Don Pedro, attempts to deflect the passion that an artist's daughter has directed at him onto the young courtier whom he knows really loves her. An

intimate episode ensues in which the humane Don Pedro tutors the ingenuous Lisana in affairs of the heart. It concludes in the following manner:

> *Don Pedro.* Mark me, Lisana, this young man may die
> Unless you love and save him ...
> *Lisana.* [*After a pause.*] My Lord, it shall be done.
> *Don Pedro.* And yet, (I'd fain
> Not speak of this) be sure your heart will feel
> No chill when press'd against his: it should be
> All his own ...
> *Lisana.* Sir, you teach me well,
> And I am grateful for it.
> ('Love Cured By Kindness', pp. 71–72)

This passage highlights a vital difference in the way in which sexual
exchange is represented in Keats and Cornwall. Where the sticky excesses
of *The Eve of St Agnes* virtually guaranteed that readers would continue to
perceive Keats as morbidly gauche, comical even, with his intense, onanistic
displays of sexual longing, Cornwall – even when drawing on similar, or
identical, source material and poetic idioms such as hearts pressed against
hearts – appeared worldly wise and experienced, like Don Pedro: a safe pair
of hands. Reading Cornwall's spicy but crucially circumscribed scenes of
ardour involved audiences in a very different, generically less fuzzy mode of
consumption than the act of negotiating Keats's overheated aesthetic. But, to
turn the paradox with which I began this chapter back on itself, Cornwall's
passion did not lack punch. If the boldness of the above cardiacal passage
from 'Love Cured By Kindness' fails to arrest us today, we need only recall
the horrified reaction of Woodhouse and Taylor to the idea of Porphyro
'zon[ing]' Madeline 'heart to heart'.

Cornwall's Cockney publishers, the Ollier bros, were differently
dispositioned, establishing a lucrative relationship with their new prodigy,
appreciating fully that heart-to-heart encounters were exactly what
sensation-hungry audiences were demanding in 1820.[52] We may regard
Cornwall as a weak reflection of Keats; but the point to keep in focus is that
where Keats's erotically charged output was often uncomfortably visceral,
always threatening to dissolve in 'solution sweet', Cornwall's work was
perceived as 'safe', self-censoring, if not wholly sanitized – a perfect mix as
far as poetry-buyers and reviewers alike were concerned. In the early stages
of Cornwall's celebrity, at least, his glossily voluptuous publications represented the acceptable face of Cockney School poetry, which goes a long way
to explaining why Cornwall was able to gather so effectively the plaudits
modern readers feel were Keats's by rights.

Notes

1 *Retrospective Review*, 2, i (1820), pp. 185–206, at p. 194.
2 *Blackwood's Edinburgh Magazine*, 19 (1826), p. xvi.
3 *Blackwood's Edinburgh Magazine*, 3 (1818), pp. 521–22.
4 *John Keats* (London: Palgrave, 2005), p. 56.
5 *New Monthly Magazine*, 14 (1820), pp. 245–48, at p. 246.
6 *Honeycomb*, 9 (1820), pp. 65–72. The phrase used by lawyer, Sir Edward Coke (1552–1634) was 'strong scent of great-swelling phrases'. Coke was lampooning advocates who prided themselves on their lofty style and grammatical precision, but who were often 'at a dead loss of the matter itself'. Coke's phrase had been deployed at the beginning of the *Monthly Review*'s appraisal of *A Sicilian Story*; the *Honeycomb*'s critic is misremembering, or possibly subverting, this quotation. See *Monthly Review*, 91 (1820), pp. 291–96, at p. 296. The *Honeycomb* review is actually of Shelley. The critic complains that whereas a knot of Metropolitan writers had successfully puffed each other's work and secured other favourable reviews with an 'interchange of fulsome compliments and gross flattery' – Cornwall in particular having 'gained certainly a greater reputation than he is entitled to' – Shelley's genius had not been widely enough recognized.
7 *Blackwood's Edinburgh Magazine*, 3 (1818), pp. 519–24, at p. 519. Hunt's story was 'incestuous' only in so far as one brother commits adultery with his sibling's wife.
8 *Examiner*, 23 May 1819, p. 334.
9 For this date (and the erroneous dating of the volume in Armour, *Barry Cornwall*, p. 67), see 'Keats and Procter: A Misdated Acquaintance', *Modern Language Notes*, 66 (1951), pp. 532–36, at p. 533.
10 'Melting' is a euphemism for male orgasm in *Fanny Hill*; Keats is clearly plugging into a more blatant and problematic erotic tradition than Cornwall.
11 Anna Brownwell Jameson, *The Romance of Biography; or, Memoirs of Women Loved and Celebrated by Poets*, 2 vols, 3rd edn (London: Saunders and Otley, 1837), II, 348; *Monthly Review*, 101 (1823), pp. 50–55, at p. 54.
12 Available online at: <http://www.amazon.com/Dramatic-Marcian-Colonna-Romantic-context/dp/0824021940> [date of access: 12.8.7].
13 *1 Esdras*, Chapter 8.
14 William Fulbecke, *Pandectes of the Law of Nations* (1602), p. 78. Interestingly enough in the above context, Shelley's *Homer's Hymn to Moon* from 1818 included the lines: 'The Son of Saturn with this glorious Power / Mingled in love and sleep – To whom she bore / Pandeia'.
15 Byron called Keats a 'miserable Self-polluter of the human Mind' (*BLJ*, VII, 217). Josiah Conder warned Keats not to indulge in 'wasteful efflorescence' in his work; *Eclectic Review*, 2 series, 14 (1820), p. 158.
16 *London Magazine*, 2 (1820), pp. 315–21, at p. 315; *Guardian*, 6 August 1820, p. 2.
17 John Whale, *John Keats* (London: Palgrave, 2005), pp. 56–57.
18 Stuart Curran, 'Women Readers, Women Writers', in *The Cambridge Companion to British Romanticism*, ed. Stuart Curran (Cambridge: Cambridge University Press, 1993), p. 184. See also Lucy Newlyn's study of literacy and reading audiences in chapter 1 of *Reading, Writing and Romanticism: The Anxiety of Influence* (Oxford: Oxford University Press, 2000), especially p. 7. Margaret Homans comments that 'because of changing

patterns of work and leisure, women ... had been replacing the elite group of classically educated men as the chief consumers of literature'; see 'Keats Reading Women, Women Reading Keats', *Studies in Romanticism*, 29 (1990), pp. 341–70, at pp. 346–47.

19 See Chapter 2 of Julia Peakman, *Mighty Lewd Books: The Development of Pornography in Eighteenth-Century England* (London: Palgrave, 2003), especially pp. 35–39, 44.

20 Cornwall's appeal to female book-buyers is an aspect of capital not considered by Kurt Heinzelman in his Keats-oriented comparison of *Isabella*'s complex, self-consciously 'subversive' critique of exchange with *A Sicilian Story*'s 'condescending moralizing' and limited self-reflexivity. See 'Self-Interest and the Politics of Composition in Keats's *Isabella*', *English Literary History*, 55 (1988), pp. 159–93.

21 Review of *The Flood of Thessaly*, *London Magazine*, 7 (1823), pp. 669–72, at p. 669.

22 *The Romance of Biography*, II, p. 348.

23 In April 2008, the letters were available for purchase as a single lot from AbeBooks, priced $475. Keats's letters, by instructive comparison, fetch six-figure sums on today's markets. In 2005, for example, an autograph letter from February 1820, signed with Keats's initials and addressed to Fanny Brawne, sold for $126,500.

24 While Fiona MacCarthy suggests that *Don Juan* lost Byron much of his female readership (*Byron: Life and Legend*, London: Faber, 2003, pp. 365–66), women were evidently still reading Cantos I–II of the scandalous epic, both published in July 1819. In an approbatory review of Felicia Hemans in the *Quarterly Review* in October 1820, William Gifford refers to the fact that 'the most dangerous writer of the present day [Byron] finds his most numerous and most enthusiastic admirers among the fair sex; and we have many times seen very eloquent eyes kindle in vehement praise of the poems, which no woman should have read'. See Gifford, *Quarterly Review*, 24 (1820), pp. 130–39, at p. 131.

25 *Keats: The Critical Heritage*, ed. G. M. Matthews (London: Routledge & Kegan Paul, 1971), p. 241.

26 *New Monthly Magazine*, 14 (1820), p. 444. The journal reviewed *Marcian Colonna* in the same issue.

27 The opening of Book 2 of *Endymion* may owe some of its sexual charge to Keats's memories of meeting his new acquaintance. See Andrew Motion, *Keats: A Biography* (London: Faber, 1997), pp. 180–81.

28 Extract from letter quoted in Edmund Blunden, *Keats's Publisher: A Memoir of John Taylor* (London: Jonathan Cape, 1936), p. 97.

29 *Blackwood's Edinburgh Magazine*, 81 (1857), p. 360.

30 *John Keats*, p. 56.

31 Diego Saglia, *Poetic Castles in Spain: British Romanticism and Figurations of Iberia* (Amsterdam: Rodopi, 2000), p. 245. Saglia argues that *Diego de Montilla* retains the sexual license of *Don Juan* while toning down its political complexities. He adds that 'despite its rigid manipulations of familiar material, the poem succeeds in its repetition of the Byronic mode as it clarifies what is implicit in *Don Juan* ... the balance between subversiveness and containment in Byron's hero', p. 245.

32 *Don Juan*, ed. T. G. Steffan et al. (Harmondsworth: Penguin, 1986), Canto XI, stanza 59.

33 Marilyn Butler, *Romantics, Rebels and Reactionaries: English Literature and its Background, 1760–1830* (Oxford: Oxford University Press, 1981), p. 173.

34 *New Monthly Review*, 13 (1820), pp. 178–83, at p. 182.

35 As Armour notes, although it carried a publisher's date of 1820, *A Sicilian Story* was
    actually in reviewers' hands by early December 1819; see *Barry Cornwall*, p. 63. In all
    probability *The Eve of St Agnes* was begun earlier than *Gyges*, but not published until July
    1820.

36 For a detailed discussion of classical versions of the Gyges story, see Kirby Flower Smith,
    'The Tale of Gyges and the King of Lydia', *The American Journal of Philology*, 23 (1902),
    pp. 361–87.

37 For cognates of the Gyges story, see Ivan M. Cohen, 'Herodotus and the Story of Gyges:
    Traditional Motifs in Historical Narrative', *Fabula*, 45, issues 1–2 (2004), pp. 55–68.

38 There are numerous thematic and semantic convergences between the two poems. As
    they undress, Madeline 'Loosens her fragrant bodice' (l. 229), while Lais stands 'quite
    unloos'd' (stanza 29). Porphyro is led to Madeline's chamber by his 'poor guide', the
    perfidious Old Angela (l. 189), while Gyges is 'guided by the king' to Lais's chamber
    (stanza 29). Moreover, the maidens' chambers are lit with moonbeams: 'Full on this
    casement shone the wintry moon / And threw warm gules on Madeline's fair breast /
    ... Rose-bloom fell on her hands (ll. 217–20); while Lais opens the curtains to 'let in the
    moon, / Which trembling ran around the chamber wide, / Kissing and flooding the rich
    flowers' (stanza 30).

39 In *Isabella; or, The Pot of Basil*, Keats offers a similar pun: 'Great bliss was with them,
    and great happiness / Grew, like a lusty flower in June's caress' (ll. 71–72). See my *Keats's
    Boyish Imagination* (London: Routledge, 2004), p. 113.

40 Cited in Nicholas Roe, *Keats and the Culture of Dissent* (Oxford: Oxford University
    Press, 1997), pp. 274–75.

41 Letter dated 13 July 1820, in *The Letters of John Hamilton Reynolds*, ed. Leonadis M.
    Jones (Lincoln, NE: University of Nebraska Press, 1973), p. 19.

42 *Isis*, 83 (1992), pp. 675–76, at p. 676.

43 See Hermione De Almeida, *Romantic Medicine and John Keats* (Oxford: Oxford
    University Press, 1991; Donald C. Goellnicht, *The Poet-Physician: Keats and Medical
    Science* (Pittsburgh: University of Pittsburgh Press, 1984); William Hale-White, *Keats
    as Doctor and Patient* (London: Oxford University Press, 1938); Hillas Smith, *Keats
    and Medicine* (Newport, Isle of Wight: Cross Publishing, 1995). Nicholas Roe's *Keats
    and the Culture of Disssent* also contains two excellent chapter-length discussions of the
    impact of Keats's medical training on his political and poetical development.

44 Marjorie Levinson, *Keats's Life of Allegory: The Origins of a Style* (Oxford: Basil Black-
    well, 1988), p. 121.

45 William Houlston, *Pharmacopoeia Chirurgica; or, Formulæ for the Use of Surgeons*
    (London: Robinsons, 1794), p. 84. By analogy with my chapter, 'Keats and Feet', in
    Keats's Boyish Imagination, an alternative title for this section would be 'Keats and
    Gleets'.

46 C. T. Andrews has questioned whether Sawrey was indeed Keats's doctor at this time.
    See 'Keats and Mercury', *Keats Shelley Memorial Bulletin*, 20 (1969), pp. 37–43.

47 See Amy Lowell, Robert Gittings and Andrew Motion, as well as Hermione de Almeida.
    For a more recent installment in the debate, see Hillas Smith, 'The Strange Case of Mr
    Keats's Tuberculosis', *Clinical Infectious Diseases*, 38 (2004), pp. 991–93, and Amy Leal,
    'Who Killed John Keats', *The Chronicle of Higher Education*, 53.19 (2007), p. 15.

48 *Edinburgh Medical and Surgical Journal*, 9 (1813), p. 488. The review is of the second,
    1811 edition of Wilson's *Pharmacopoeia*.

49 Goellnicht discusses Keats's possible debts to Stocker's translation in *The Physician-Poet*, pp. 68–69.

50 James Wilson, *Pharmacopoeia Chirurgica; or, A Manual of Chirurgical Pharmacy*, 3rd edition (London: E. Cox, 1814), p. 144.

51 De Almeida thinks it unlikely that Keats saw 'more than a few basic books in the Physical Society Library' (p. 29). I am grateful to Katie Sambrook from the Foyle Special Collections Library, King's College London, for pointing out that while Keats does not appear to have been a member of the Physical Society, and would thus not have been able to borrow books from the library himself, he could have encountered works from the library via colleagues at Guy's who were members.

52 Keats's first publishers, the Ollier brothers, are traditionally supposed to have dropped Keats as a consequence of the disastrous sales of his first volume, *Poems* (1817). John Barnard suggests that the actual situation may, in fact, have been reversed: Keats commissioning the Olliers to print his first volume but hurriedly dispensing with their rather amateurish services as soon as a contract was offered with the more established firm of Taylor and Hessey. See 'A Poet and His Money – A New Look at the Publishing History of Keats's *Poems* (1817), *Times Literary Supplement*, 12 August 2005, p. 12.

5

Metropolitan Commissioners of Lunacy

Situated within a 'common intellectual framework', as Susanna Blumenthal argues, Romantic physicians and lawyers found themselves at the forefront of major conceptual shifts in attitudes towards mental pathology.[1] Solicitor- and doctor-poets Keats and Cornwall were exceptionally well placed, then, to take the temperature of increasingly humane institutional views towards psychiatric illness. However, as well as furnishing them with a fund of shared insights into psychic imbalance, the two men's professional training offered opportunities – or temptations – to use encounters with souls *in extremis* as material for poems designed for audiences with salty appetites for lurid fictions of insanity.

Where Cornwall successfully parlayed his solicitor's knowledge of criminal insanity into spicy mimeographs of emotional calamity, Keats – a surgeon's dresser with 'ample opportunity to observe the effects of madness firsthand', Donald C. Goellnicht suggests – proved less able, or finally unwilling, to turn his fluency with the culture and symptomology of psychic abnormality to comparable account.[2] Indeed, while the transposition of medicine's 'high ideals' to poetry was a self-defining experience for Keats, much as Goellnicht argues in *The Poet-Physician: Keats and Medical Science* (1984), it hampered his efforts to enter market-valuable medical knowledge in the service of the contemporary craze for spectacular mad tales.[3] Once again, Cornwall provides the counter-example for the kind of commercial headway it was possible to make, but which, for a complex of reasons, seemed to elude Keats.

The appeal of Cornwall's perfectly confected verse narratives at a time when institutional attitudes towards psychological illness were undergoing significant realignment opens a fascinating window onto the contours – and ethics – of Romantic taste. Equally, by illustrating how medical familiarity complicates Keats's literary portraits of mental ill-health, new light is thrown on ways in which this ambitious poet negotiates his fraught relation to the marketplace. Finally, this chapter's work concludes my wider investigation into how Cornwall and his popular aesthetic displaced Keats in the public's mind at the same time as they provided an axial, structuring presence in his poetic evolution.

1. 'Lurid Flashes of Desire': Madness and The Literary Marketplace

The belief that higher incidence rates of madness represented an inescapable price for the rapid pace of civilization's progress constituted a significant Enlightenment anxiety. Its spectre haunts an influential *Quarterly Review* essay from 1816 on 'Insanity and Madhouses' by the London City Dispensary physician, David Uwins: 'In proportion as man emerges from his primaeval state, do the Furies of disease advance upon him and would seem to scourge him back into the paths of nature and simplicity.'[4] 'We beat out and expand our minds', Uwins suggests – introducing an extraordinary image that conflates industrial process and psychological vulnerability – 'and thus create a more extended surface of impression'.

Mental illness, which struck unpredictably and across the insulating divide of wealth and education, was a key concern within Romantic medicine. Between 1776 and 1800 alone, no fewer than 52 treatises on the subject were published.[5] Despite the heat of professional debate, however, eighteenth-century pessimism towards the ailment proved difficult to shake. Uwins's essay, which summarized an alarming 1815 parliamentary Select Committee Report on lunacy, confronted *Quarterly Review* subscribers with a singularly inconvenient truth: 'on the medical treatment of madness' there was 'not much to advance' (pp. 398–99). With the exception of obvious organic abnormalities such as lesions and tumours, the mad brain's 'internal mischief' remained a frustrating enigma (p. 401).

The circumscriptions of Romantic knowledge were similarly conceded by Joseph Green, Keats's anatomy instructor at Guy's, whose teaching text *The Dissector's Manual* (1820), a digest of lectures Keats would have heard during his time as a student there, lent authoritative voice to a wide sense of perplexity:

> It is humiliating to the scientific anatomist to reflect, that the dissection of the most important part of the human body [the brain] should yet be that which rewards us with the least satisfying results. The mechanism and the purposes of its several portions are alike obscure.[6]

Even the most basic question, the *London Medical Review* conceded – 'What is the difference between a sane and an insane mind?' – had still to be resolved.[7]

Notwithstanding a sense of settled gloom, attitudes towards psychiatric illness within medical and jurisprudential discourse underwent wide transformation between the 1780s and 1820s. Asylum regimens predicated on the containment of incurable, unindividuated subjectivity, where inmates were routinely condemned to cramped jails, pens, cellars and garrets, ceded to the 'moral' care of patients, newly recognized as uniquely suffering minds and bodies, each with the potential to be rehabilitated into their communities. The mentally infirm were no longer assumed to be in some way responsible for their condition, or lumped together, as Andrew T. Scull puts it, with the 'amorphous class of the morally disreputable' or criminally inclined.[8] At this point, insanity began to be recognized as a defence in law, and in 1800 a purpose-built wing for the criminally insane was constructed at Bethlem Hospital. Treatises on lunacy, including seminal publications such as John Mason Cox's *Practical Observations on Insanity* (1804) and John Haslam's *Observations on Madness and Melancholy* (1809), pioneered new systems of treatment that were structured around an 'intensification of personal contact between physician and patient'.[9]

Despite asylum reforms and more sympathetic attitudes towards mental aberration, however, literary representations of the disease remained largely impervious to progressive trends. In many ways set at ideological right angles to reforms in psychiatric care, one aspect of Romanticism's response to psychological abnormality took the form of a popular literary vogue for sensational romances of derangement, typically boisterous, gaudy tales punctuated by 'shrieks ... and cries, and then short groans' (*Marcian Colonna*, p. 79). In 1820, an exasperated critic for the *Edinburgh Magazine and Literary Miscellany* insisted that de rigueur portraits of agreeable rogues and madmen were best left to Byron, even though the 'whole poetic world are striving hard at it'.[10] The journal lodged a legitimate objection – we gain an impression of the mushrooming market for noisy, unreconstructed tales of emotional catastrophe by glancing at the monthly lists of books advertised in literary journals as 'Preparing for Publication' or 'Just Published'. Equally, we acquire a sense of what Keats and Cornwall were up against, as well as the pressures they felt to conform to the market. In 1819, when Cornwall burst onto the London literary stage with his dazzling début, *Dramatic Scenes*, and Keats was preparing pieces for *Lamia ... and Other Poems* (1820), the roll-call of forthcoming works indexes a contemporary appetite for poems willing to 'up the ante' in their sensationalist portrayals of mental catastrophe. In October 1818, *Blackwood's* includes pre-publication notice of *Charenton; or, The Follies of the Age*, a colourfully insalubrious gothic novel set in 'a well-known establishment in Paris for insane persons'.[11] Also noticed is the imminent publication of Anna Maria Porter's three-volume *The Fast of St Magdalen* (1818), an Italian-flavoured medieval romance, whose protagonists, Ippolita and Rosalia, sport fashionably Tuscan names, and whose rubious lines, like the streets of the small Pisan town in which the tale begins, are 'slippery with blood'.[12] Within this frame of competition, such claustrophobic, dark-cornered poetic romances as Keats's *Isabella; or, The Pot of Basil* and *The Eve of St Agnes* (1820), which combine faddish themes of love and passion with a medieval or Italianate setting, or both, seem strategically well-conceived.

In December 1819, Maga trumpets the imminent appearance of John Roby's *Lorenzo; or, The Tale of Redemption*, a poem that had already been lauded in the *Evangelical Magazine* for surpassing in 'impression' even the romances of Walter Scott and Byron (and at 4s 6d, considerably cheaper than Cornwall's or Keats's 7 or 8s volumes).[13] January's coming attractions include Thomas Grattan's *Philibert, A Poetical Romance*, based on the Martin Guerre story in Gayot de Pitaval's *Cause Célébrès*, featuring self-advertising 'lurid flashes of desire' (Canto 1, line 8).[14] Grattan's female protagonist is called Isabelle, a fashionable appellation for heroines of verse romance in 1820 (in the same year, Charles Lloyd published a flashy novel entitled *Isabel*). In February, *Blackwood's* gives advance notice of Oxford professor of poetry, Henry Hart Milman's *The Fall of Jerusalem*, a blood-soaked tapestry that relayed countless 'circumstances of awful interest' in the *Quarterly Review*'s adulatory appraisal.[15] At the breathtaking climax of Milman's next, equally stupendous dramatic poem, *Belshazzar* (1822), grief-stricken Nitocris, mother of the defeated, titular king, discovers her son expiring among the wrecks of his city:

> Oh, how he used to turn!
> And nestle his young cheek in this full bosom,
> That now he shrinks from! No! It is the last
> Convulsive shudder of cold death. My son,
> Wait – wait, and I will die with thee – not yet –
> Alas! yet this is what I pray'd for – this –
> To kiss thy cold cheek, and inhale thy last –
> Thy dying breath.[16]

Emotionally raucous, convulsively melodramatic, undeniably effective works like these set the bar for long narrative poems in the late-Romantic period. We shouldn't forget, either, the heaviest Romantic hitters in the lists. In December 1818, *Blackwood's* announces the eagerly awaited third series of Scott's *Tales of My Landlord*, a four-volume behemoth showcasing *The*

Bride of Lammermoor, a tale of thwarted love, groans and derangement, at the climax of which the heroine impales her importunate suitor in a violent paroxysm.[17] The following June, *Blackwood's* printed a full-length review of Scott's tale, assuring readers that its 'terrible', 'unforeseen' events were such that they would 'shake the mind'.[18]

This 'snapshot' gives an insight into a commercial rationale that powerfully shaped Cornwall's and Keats's literary representation of emotional calamity. There was, however, an alternative, socially more conscientious model for writing about psychic disorder, which firmly rejected sensationalist portraits of mental infirmity. Between 1795 and 1797, Wordsworth suffered an episode that Joel Faflak terms 'psychological collapse'.[19] Composed during Wordsworth's year of recovery, *Lyrical Ballads* (1798) is closely attuned to the crisis of mental health in England and Wales, in which the treatment of pauper lunatics (maintained out of poor rates) in non-metropolitan contexts was a particular topic of concern. Parliament was slowly turning its attention to the plight of these people: an 1807 Select Committee Report unearthed such horrors as patients 'fastened to the leg of a table', 'chained to a post in an outhouse' or 'shut up chained in an uninhabited ruin'.[20] As a consequence of these disclosures, the 1808 'Act for the Better Care and Maintenance of Pauper and Criminal Lunatics' pushed into legislation an obligation for individual parishes to shoulder the cost of more appropriate provision for rural lunatics. *Lyrical Ballads* shares the reforming impulse, poems like 'The Mad Mother', 'Ruth' and 'The Thorn' eschewing modish tableaux of raving lunacy in an effort to enlist poetry in wider, more humane institutional realignments.

Wordsworth's most radical contribution to the lunacy debate was to argue in the 1800 Preface that contemporary poets had exacerbated the threat to public mental ill-health by supplying readers already addicted to tales of 'extraordinary incident' with an endless supply of 'sickly' romances and mind-blunting tales.[21] Contemporary Romantic medicine seemed to bear out Wordsworth's conviction that the mere act of reading extravagant literatures could cause harmful psychological effects. In *An Inquiry into the Nature and Origin of Mental Derangement*, published the same year as *Lyrical Ballads*, Alexander Crichton – expert witness two years later in the trial of the delusional James Hadfield for the attempted assassination of George III – likewise warned of the deleterious consequences of too-stimulating literature on the health of the imagination. The second volume of Crichton's treatise begins with a section on poetry, which argues that authors had a responsibility to 'restrain' their 'stream of ideas':

In works of genius, not only abstraction and combination, but judgement also, is absolutely necessary. By means of this faculty we make a proper selection of the materials which the representative faculty of the mind yields. The stream of ideas must be restrained, lest they break down the natural banks of reason.[22]

When an 'ardent and well-stored imagination is combined with a correct judgement', Crichton asserted, literature transports its audience into salutary 'new worlds and regions' (p. 24). By contrast, 'too violent' exertions of the mental faculties produce 'fatigue, and debilitate the corporeal parts of the animal' (p. 30). In tune with Crichton's precepts, Wordsworth chastises writers who wrote irresponsibly febrile 'deluges of idle and extravagant stories in verse' (p. 249).

In what Scott Masson red-rings as 'one of the more obscure passages' from the Preface, Wordsworth also insists that poets had a duty to 'sympathize with pain' – even to the extent of 'slip[ping] into an entire delusion' of co-identification with their characters:[23] 'It will be the wish of the Poet to bring his feelings near to those of the persons whose feelings he describes, nay, for short spaces of time perhaps, to let himself slip into an entire delusion, and even confound and identify his own feelings with theirs'. Wordsworth's conviction that writers ought to inhabit the irrational economy of deranged subjectivity for short periods is doubly bold, since medical and legal treatises of the day painted delusion as a species of insanity. Thomas Arnold's influential *Observations on the Nature, Kinds, Causes, and Prevention of Insanity, Lunacy, or Madness* (1783), for example, classed delusion and 'delusive' insanity as sub-categories of 'notional insanity', further sub-divided into 'maniacal' and 'sensitive' presentations.[24] Delusional minds, physicians concurred, were impervious to reason. In his *Description of the Retreat* (1813), even Samuel Tuke, grandson of the founder of the progressive Quaker institution at York (praised by the *Edinburgh Review* for his 'good sense and humanity'), found 'no advantage' in attempting to empathize with aberrant states of mind or 'reason with them, on their particular hallucinations'.[25] Rather, mad-doctors preferred to jolt inmates back into rational being, using Leyden jars to pass electrical currents through their temples, or administering cold plunges, 'suddenly immersing the maniac in the very acmé of his paroxysm', as governor of Fishponds Asylum, John Mason Cox, recommended in *Practical Observations on Insanity*.[26]

In spite of its humane underpinnings, the 'moral' cure came to hold terrors of its own. Cox himself was an evangelizing advocate of the 'Swing', a fearsome contraption 'easily constructed', Cox assured readers, 'by suspending a Windsor chair from a hook in the ceiling' (p. 137). Tightly strapped in, alarmed patients were rotated at velocities varying from somnambulant to stomach-wrenching.[27] 'Improvements' on the basic design were fitted with windlasses and were capable of reaching 100 rotations per minute. Along with the aim of inspiring salutary fear, the principle objective was to induce bodily evacuations of such 'magnitude and fetor' sufficient to quell lunatic symptoms.[28] Wordsworth's insistence on psychological border-crossings, then, gestures towards a genuinely radical economy of feeling, predicated on a logic that was, medically speaking, fugitive.

The concept of slipping into an 'entire delusion' powerfully inflects individual poems in *Lyrical Ballads*, notably 'The Idiot Boy'. Here, Geoffrey Hartman detects a deranged quality in the language of the poem itself, as diction comes to embody dictum: 'In the "Idiot Boy", even though it is night, the idiot boy thinks the moon is the sun which shines so cold, and the owls hooting are the cocks crowing. So the metafelicity of this, the distortion, the coloration – what one could call strong, crazy metaphors – is sunk into the specific instance'.[29] Betty Foy's devotion to her hapless son, her determination to care for him at home, is presented as a salutary display of socialization; the idiot boy's safe return to his community (a narrative component signally absent from 'sickly' tales of madness) focuses a moment of joy and gratitude equal in intensity to the tearful stanzas that conclude 'Simon Lee'. Wordsworth's sentiments in 'The Idiot Boy' could hardly have been at greater odds with conservative views on the treatment and management of insanity, epitomized by Eldon's notorious anti-reforming speech to parliament in 1819. Rejecting the Commons' attempt to tighten licensing restrictions for 'houses built for the reception, care, treatment or confinement of lunatics', Eldon declared: 'There could not be a more false humanity than an over-humanity with regard to persons afflicted with insanity'.[30]

Wordsworth's conceptual centre of gravity in 'The Thorn' is again the problem of rural lunacy. Strongly self-reflexive, the poem assembles itself out of village prejudice and hearsay, the rustic community providing various readings of Martha's monomaniacal 'doleful cry', 'Oh woe is me! oh misery!' (a 'too parodyable mimetics', Susan Wolfson notes, drawing Wordsworth's bad faith with the poem's gothic diction into sharp relief).[31] The most pernicious tittle-tattle, relayed through the uncritically nodal figure of the mariner, implies that the outcast mother has killed her baby in a psychotic fit.[32] In 1798, Wordsworth distances himself from his 'loquacious' narrator, adding a rare second layer of paratextual clarification in 1800 to label him 'credulous and talkative' (p. 288). The Mariner's sensationalist opining, Wordsworth is at lengths to stress, is as equally under scrutiny as the gossiping of Martha

Ray's own community, the poem's potential to excite 'idle' interest quickly becoming a sharp critique of that potential.

A shorter first version of Bethlem apothecary John Haslam's ground-breaking psychiatric case notes, *Observations on Madness* (1809), also appeared in 1798. One of its 'cases' described a severely distressed female villager, 'E. D.', admitted to hospital in 1795 following the death of her baby. Martha Ray's monomaniacal self-hatred parallels that of Haslam's patient, similarly assumed to have destroyed her own child:

> [E. D.'s] insanity came on a few days after being delivered ... Under the impression that she ought to be hanged, she destroyed her infant, with the view of meeting with that punishment. When she came into the house, she was very sensible of the crime she had committed, and felt the most poignant affliction for the act. She frequently spoke about the child: great anxiety and restlessness succeeded ... Her tongue became thickly furred, the skin parched, her eyes inflamed and glassy, and her pulse quick. (pp. 102–03)

Much as parliamentary reforms and medical treatises drew pauper lunacy into the frame of reform, 'The Thorn' conducts an analogous investigation into psychic aberrance and social intolerance.

If Wordsworth's poems are conditioned by a context of medical inquiry, reverse intersections trouble Haslam's case studies. A palpable flicker of sentimental idiom interrupts the account of E. D.'s self-consuming remorse: '[She] felt the most poignant affliction for the act ... her eyes inflamed and glassy ... her pulse quick'. The adjective 'poignant', together with 'glassy' eyes and a 'quick' pulse, signal beyond clinical registers. Something similar occurs in Cox's own notes on female patients, as Helen Small dilates in her book *Love's Madness: Medicine, the Novel, and Female Insanity 1800–1865*. Case VII of *Practical Observations* documents the grief of a 19-year-old, seduced and abandoned by her 'deceitful lover'. Departing from his usual modus operandi with male patients, Cox lingers over the woman's appearance, describing her 'fair skin, dark hair and eyes'. The medical report picks up a 'familiar sentimental narrative', Small notes, as it tips like Haslam's into 'stylistic exuberance'.[33]

'The Thorn' isn't wholly insulated from 'sickly' sentimentalism, either. Wordsworth borrowed his protagonist's name from real-life Covent Garden singer and celebrity, Martha Ray, or Reay (1741–1779), whose scandalous affair with John Montagu, fourth Earl of Sandwich, and her subsequent violent death had gripped the public's imagination a generation earlier.[34] Unhinged with sexual jealousy, solicitor and clergyman James Hackman lay in wait for Ray in the foyer of the Royal Opera House, and when she emerged shot the singer through the head. The murder inspired poems and pamphlets on both sides of the Atlantic. Philip Morin Freneau (1752–1832) commemorated the deed in 'Under the Portraiture of Martha Ray' – reprinted in 1795 – the final couplets representative of a 'tabloid' aesthetic far removed from the self-interrogating sophistication of 'The Thorn':

> Like Juno, she, in spangles drest,
> By *Lords* would only be carress'd;
> 'Till, grown a rival to the skies,
> An earthly lawyer seiz'd the prize.'[35]

As an intriguing coda to this discussion, in 1824 the historical Martha Ray's step-granddaughter, celebrated beauty Anne Skepper, married none other than Barry Cornwall, whose racily readable *Marcian Colonna* ends with its psychotic 'hero' echoing Hackman's crime by murdering his lover.[36]

2. The Internal Mischief

The icon of the poet-fanatic or genius loon belongs to a governing set of Romantic self-representations – the idea that the genuine poet's overheated imagination had to push itself to, or beyond, the brink of insanity before it could produce authentic works, cohering as an authorizing myth of creative genius. In fact, several prominent literary figures including Blake, Coleridge, Shelley, Lamb, Hazlitt, Clare and Charles Lloyd experienced all too real bouts of depression, anxiety, delusion or psychosis, their work decisively marked by episodes of emotional disequilibrium. What, then, was the scope of Keats's and Cornwall's personal encounter with madness?

Neither poet, fortunately, experienced protracted phases of mental ill-health. To be sure, Keats claimed a 'horrid Morbidity of Temperament';[37] but this self-diagnosis needs to be read against J. H. Reynolds' rather more upbeat report on his friend's character: 'I know of no one who ... with rich personal abuse, as he has suffered, could be so cheerful & so firm.'[38] In less sentimental mien, Keats conceded: 'I do not think I shall ever come to the rope or the Pistol: for after a day or two's melancholy ... I see by little and little more of what is to be done, and how it is to be done' (*LJK*, II, 32). Cornwall was likewise prone to bouts of mild depression; but as with Keats these brief seasons of moroseness were balanced by a general resilience of spirit.

In terms of professional encounter, however, both men's experience of insanity was far more extensive. As a practising solicitor, Cornwall would have known about celebrated cases such as Hackman's, nemesis of his future wife's step-grandmother – 'too well remembered to require much preface', as James Ridgway noted in his edition of the *Speeches of Lord Erskine* (1812).[39] We know for certain that other legal treatises on insanity provided Cornwall with material for poems. A footnote to *The Girl of Provence* – a taut étude in erotic delusion singled out by Thomas Campbell in the *New Monthly Review* for its 'spirited description'[40] – acknowledges that the central incident was suggested by a prurient passage in George Dale Collinson's *A Treatise on the Laws Concerning Idiots, Lunatics, and other Persons Non Compotes Mentis* (1812) recounting the morbid erotic obsession of a young Parisian woman with a naked statue of Apollo in the National Museum.[41] Most reviewers strongly disapproved of the tale. *Blackwood's* sniped that it savoured 'more of the drivelling of idiotcy than of the rage of madness'; while the *British Magazine* wondered that Cornwall 'could bestow so much pains on so worthless a subject'.[42]

The issue at stake in this intensely self-conscious poem is poetry itself, especially dazzling verses like Cornwall's own. Eva becomes addicted to Apollo's 'burning lines' (p. 89), to precisely that species of overheated, admiration-kindling poetry which Wordsworth cautioned against:

... beautiful is great Apollo's page:
But they who dare to read his burning lines
Go mad, – and ever after with blind rage
Rave of the skiey secrets and bright signs:
But all they tell is vain: for death entwines
The struggling utterance, and the words expire
Dumb, – self-consum'd, like some too furious fire.
      (*The Girl of Provence*, p. 89)

Far from registering tremors of uncertainty about the ethical basis of his project, Cornwall sublimates the reality-distorting effects of overwrought poetry on the imagination, as identified by Wordsworth and Crichton, into a virtual manifesto of sensation. The act of reading febrile, erotic poetry overwhelms Eva in waves of unreality, until gazing on Apollo's unadorned form she convinces herself that the god has descended to carry her off. Although Gill Gregory discerns a sympathetic frame to Cornwall's explorations of female desire, such a reading may be excessively buoyant. Leaving no hermeneutic lacuna to allow for good faith in Eva's vision, the nudges and winks of Cornwall's parenthetical note – locating his source in a legal tract on insanity, of all things – work to compromise Eva's narrative from the outset. Unlike Martha Ray's, her story isn't offered to readers to petition sympathy for sufferers of delusions, but rather as a shallow, even shabby, entertainment in which the reader, 'in the know' from the beginning, is encouraged to dismiss the holiness of Eva's heart's affections as mere ravings.

The Girl of Provence exploits a further Romantic staple of lurid tales about mad women: erotomania. As discussed in Chapter 4, the auto-referential act itself of reading lifts Eva to a climax of 'intolerable joy', an irresistible flush of pleasure that causes the poem to dissolve altogether into lines of asterisks in stanza 37 (an aposiopesis that abashed contemporary reviewers).[43] The rapidly oxidizing story, like its protagonist, is 'self-consuming', a fire Cornwall deliberately allows to burn at too high a temperature.

Incidentally, 'self-consuming' was exactly how Cornwall – quoting, appropriately enough, from his own poem 'Echoes' – described Keats in the obituary which he contributed to Baldwin's *London Magazine* in April 1821. The image of self-consuming fire occurs a further time in the *Olio* tribute to Keats in 1828, lending significant support to McGillivray's and G. M. Matthews's conjecture that the piece was authored by Cornwall:

> He who could perceive the inner-workings, who could estimate the wear and wasting, which an ardent, restless, and ambitious intellect makes in the 'human form divine', must have felt persuaded that the flame burning within would shortly consume the outward shell. His spirit was like burning oil in a vessel of some precious and costly wood, which when the flame has consumed its nutrients, will then burn that which contained it.[44]

Following the Mad Acts of 1828 and the formation of the Metropolitan Lunacy Commission from the previous governing body, the Royal College of Physicians, Cornwall's long-standing interest in the relation of law to insanity helped him to a position as one of the government inspectors of asylums for England and Wales.[45] He would shortly know more about the culture of psychiatric management than virtually anyone in the country. Even prior to becoming a Metropolitan Commissioner for Lunacy, Cornwall had gained significant insights into the social and personal impact of mental illness. Long amity with Charles and Mary Lamb presented ample opportunity to observe the horrors of domestic lunacy at close hand. As a 20-year-old, Charles spent six weeks in Hoxton asylum. Mary's own fits of psychosis were even more alarming.[46] On 23 September 1796, shortly after her brother's release, she seized a 'case-knife' from the kitchen and rushed through the family home. Before Charles could snatch away the knife, Mary had injured her father and aunt and fatally stabbed her invalid mother. Declared temporarily insane, she was spared a trial and sent instead to an asylum to recuperate. During his sibling's calmer intervals, Charles did his best to care for her at home – offering, as Cornwall records, 'an arm that never shook nor wavered' (*Charles Lamb: A Memoir*, p. 28):

> [Mary's] relapses were not dependent on the seasons; they came in hot summers and with the freezing winters. The only remedy seems to have been extreme quiet when any slight symptom of uneasiness was apparent. Charles (poor fellow) had to live, day and night, in the society of a person who was – mad! If any exciting talk occurred, he had to dismiss his friend with a whisper. If any stupor or extraordinary silence was observed, then he had to rouse her instantly. He has been seen to take the kettle from the fire and place it for a moment on her head-dress, in order to startle her into recollection. He lived in a state of constant anxiety; – and there was no help. (*Charles Lamb: A Memoir*, p. 73)

At other times, even Lamb's resourcefulness with a hot kettle was insufficient to ward off the more extreme phases of Mary's illness. Cornwall's portrait of the pair walking hand-in-hand to the local asylum, Mary carrying her own straitjacket, stands as one of Romanticism's most poignant records of insanity:

> Whenever the approach of one of her fits of insanity was announced by some irritability or change of manner, he would take her, under his arm, to Hoxton Asylum. It was very afflicting to encounter the young brother and his sister walking together (weeping together) on this painful errand; Mary herself, although sad, very conscious of the necessity for temporary separation from her only friend. They used to carry a strait jacket with them. (*Charles Lamb: A Memoir*, p. 25)

Keats's encounters with madness were equally acute, and formative. In 1675, the first purpose-built institution for the insane, Robert Hooke's newly designed Bethlem Hospital, opened in Moorfields (now Finsbury Park), dominating the entire district. Over 500 feet long, the edifice was dubbed the 'palace for lunatics'. By 1800, the building's structure was decaying, and between 1812 and 1815 the hospital was re-sited at St George's Fields, Southwark.[47] The Swan and Hoop Inn, where Keats spent his boyhood, was in Moorfields: 24 Moorfields Pavement Row. As a boy, Keats would have been familiar with Caius Cibber's sinister shaven-headed statues, 'Raving and Melancholy Madness', which adorned the hospital's broken gateposts. It is possible that he was remembering these figures when he imagined scenes of mentally agitated Titans in the *Hyperion* poems. Perhaps he passed inmates on the streets begging for the cost of their maintenance, and saw queues of psychiatric 'tourists' at the hospital's daunting gates, many of whom carried long prodding poles for goading patients through the cell bars into fits or fights. It's sobering to remember that while mad-doctors such as Pinel and Cox pioneered new models of therapy, displacing older notions of insanity as an incurable metaphysical disease of mind or spirit, the public could still purchase tickets at Bethlem for the pandemonious spectacle of inmates raving, weeping or engaging in sexual acts.[48]

Between October 1815 and March 1817, Keats enrolled to train as an apothecary-surgeon at the United Hospitals of Guy's and St Thomas's. Site of a 20-bed 'lunatic house', Guy's was originally conceived as a refuge for the 'incurables' and 'hopelessly insane' who were refused admittance by St Thomas's. Keats received instruction from several of the leading medical figures of the day, including Astley Cooper, John Haighton and Joseph Green. Tuition at Guy's included practical experience of wound-dressing and bleeding, as well as long hours in the putrefying atmospheres of the hospital's dissecting rooms.[49] After passing his apothecary's examination with credit on 25 July 1816, thus obtaining his certificate, Keats served as surgeon's 'dresser' to the infamously clumsy William Lucas, Jr, thereby gaining even closer access than ordinary pupils to seriously ill patients. As De Almeida notes, during this period Keats would have had 'ample opportunity to observe, study, and sometimes treat the full complement of dreaded diseases, physical and mental, known to human life in early nineteenth-century England'.[50] A resolution passed by the institution's governors in 1783 required hospital physicians 'to attend the Lunatic Patients': as a dresser, Keats, Goellnicht notes, would therefore 'have been in attendance at the mental ward from time to time' (p. 167).

Training was also 'theoretically comprehensive'.[51] Keats's surviving lecture notes confirm his fluency with neuropathological discourse. In addition to sketching contemporary theories of the blood and circulation, his medical *Note Book* preserves annotations on the 'Physiology of the Nervous System', as well as detailed descriptions of nerves, ganglions and brain structure that inform the striking image of Hyperion's enormous mental pain being 'portioned to a giant nerve'.[52] On top of this, Keats had access to the library of the Physical Society, now part of the Foyle Special Collection, King's College, London (the catalogue is available online).[53] In 1816, this rich storehouse was stocked with over 600 medical volumes, containing such authoritative treatises on mental illness as Arnold's *Observations on the Nature, Kinds, Cause, and Prevention of Insanity, Lunacy, or Madness* (1782), Cox's *Practical Observations on Insanity* (1804), and Haslam's *Observations on Madness and Melancholy* (1809). Unfortunately, no borrowing records for the library survive.

Alan Ingram's pioneering work, *The Madhouse of Language*, shows that mental illness at this transitional point was increasingly understood in materialist terms as a 'disease of the brain, not of the mind' (p. 27). Romantic mad-doctors began to look to the scalpel rather than to metaphysics to reveal insanity's 'internal mischief', and 'overladen' veins, heart pains and raised or retarded pulses were considered significant symptoms or triggers of madness. One of the foundational medical publications in the period, William Cullen's *First Lines of the Practice of Physic* (1776–83), linked fits of insanity explicitly to the physical cause of 'increased impetus of blood in the vessels of the brain' and recommended bleeding as a palliative.[54] Goellnicht argues that Keats would have known Cullen's work (p. 20). It's certainly true that Guy's medical library contained copies of the fourth, fifth and sixth updated editions of Cullen's textbook (1784, 1788 and 1796), and most Romantic doctors took their lead from Cullen's emphases. William Babbington's and James Curry's *Outlines of a Course of Lectures on the Practice as Delivered in the Medical School of Guy's Hospital*, for example, pointed to 'congestion, extravasation or effusion of blood' as one of the 'appearances' of insanity, whose 'exciting causes' included 'disappointed ambition', 'sudden elevation' or 'reversal of fortune'.[55] Similarly, describing the dissected brain of a mad drummer from a 'recruiting party', Haslam posited a relation between the veins of the pia mater, which he thought were excessively 'loaded with blood', and the patient's disturbing symptomology.[56] Crichton concurred, arguing that during fits of insanity the heart and arterial system became 'loaded and distended with blood' (II, 178). In similar terms, Cox linked lunacy to an 'increased force or unnatural quantity of blood sent to the head' (p. 27).

Materialist assumptions about blood in contemporary medical publications can be heard in Keats's overladen image of the defeated Titans' 'sanguine feverous boiling gurge of pulse' (*Hyperion*, II, 26–28). Medically inflected notions of the role of congested blood in aetiologies of madness are also legible in Keats's comment to Richard Woodhouse, made during the composition of *Hyperion* in October 1818, that the maddening thought of 'Poems to come brings the blood frequently into my forehead'. Fearing for his sanity, Keats even worried that his poetic ambitions might cause him to lose 'all interest in human affairs' (*LJK*, I, 387–88).[57]

Scenes of human suffering witnessed in Guy's lunatic house thread their way, too, into the imaginative work. Goellnicht argues that lines from *Sleep and Poetry*, composed in late 1816, depicting a group of distressed figures, amount to 'a description of patients in a mental ward' (p. 167):

Lo! How they murmur, laugh, and smile, and weep:
Some with upholden hand and mouth severe;
Some with their faces muffled to the ear
Between their arms; some, clear in youthful bloom,
Go glad and smilingly athwart the gloom.
  (*Sleep and Poetry*, ll. 137–49)

Importantly, these relatively muffled lines avoid sensationalism. Where Cornwall fully exploited his professional *entrée* into the rhetoric of psychiatry, Keats's poetry often fails – or reluctantly declines – to make capital out of the opportunities afforded by his medical training to depict psychic disorder in the mind-shaking vein of popular writers such as Grattan, Roby and Porter. The unsettling *vérité* of *Sleep and Poetry* also troubles scenes from the first *Hyperion* (conceived as early as September 1817 – that is, shortly after Keats left Guy's Hospital). In Book 2, for instance, an impressive tableau of mental distress, conventionally histrionic viewed in generic terms, is shadowed by darker scenes of commotion witnessed on Guy's lunatic ward:

    some groaned;
Some started on their feet; some also shouted;
Some wept, some wailed, all bowed with reverence;
And Ops, uplifting her black folded veil,
Showed her pale cheeks, and all her forehead wan,
Her eye-brows thin and jet, and hollow eyes.
  (*Hyperion*, II, 110–15)

More so even than the passage from *Sleep and Poetry*, these pandemonious lines appear to be in two minds, wavering between a painful consciousness of insanity's all too real terrors and the desire to emulate more popularist portrayals of derangement characterized by wails, groans and weeping. In Wolfson's phrase, elsewhere Keats may indeed have 'rather liked camping it up'; but his efforts in this vein here seem to be more conflicted.[58] Any commercially promisingly lurid tints are finally interrupted by Ops's tragic 'hollow eyes' and 'forehead wan', Keats's evident familiarity with a cramped city lunatic ward investing his portraits of madness with the sobering realism that Cornwall strategically avoids. We need look no further for the garish contrast than Marcian's stagy eyeballs, which are permitted to 'roll / Wildly and fiery red'.

A similarly instructive opportunity for comparison can be found in *Marcian Colonna*. In his convent asylum, the unhinged protagonist chafes inwardly at his thwarted prospects, his psychological collapse described with characteristic Cornwallean punch:

> distrust and bitter hate,
> And envy, like the serpent's twining coil,
> Ran 'round his heart and fixed its station there,
> And thro' his veins did lurking fevers boil
> Until they burst in madness; –
>   (*Marcian Colonna*, p. 13)

This furuncular passage contains instructive parallels with *Hyperion*'s medically inflected, though more conflicted, sketch of overthrown Titans, who brood on their own seismic reversals of fortune:

> ... clenched teeth still clench'd, and all their limbs
> Lock'd up like veins of metal, crampt and screw'd;
> Without a motion, save of their big hearts
> Heaving in pain, and horribly convulsed
> With sanguine feverous boiling gurge of pulse.
>   (*Hyperion*, II, 26–28)

Keats's gurge of pulse strives to compete on generic ground with Cornwall's racing idiom, reaching for a similar palette of effects. It's decisively out-done, however, by *Marcian Colonna*'s black phantoms and 'lurking' fevers, despite – although equally *because* of – the fact that the physical and emotional mayhem that so delighted Cornwall's readers is carefully disengaged from the more recognizably, more troublingly, human dimensions of pain in Keats's thematically contiguous poem.

The opening of *Hyperion*, which depicts Saturn sitting motionless in an advanced state of catatonic depression, possibly also owes a debt to Keats's experience in the lunatic house:

> Deep in the shady sadness of a vale
> Far sunken from the healthy breath of morn,
> Far from the fiery noon, and eve's one star,
> Sat gray-hair'd Saturn, quiet as a stone,
> Still as the silence round about his lair;
> ...
> Along the margin-sand large foot-marks went,
> No further than to where his feet had stray'd,
> And slept there since. Upon the sodden ground
> His old right hand lay nerveless, listless, dead,
> Unsceptred; and his realmless eyes were closed;
>   (*Hyperion*, I, 1–19)

Moreover, this strikingly sympathetic portrait of Saturn's symptoms is intriguingly consonant with prevailing Romantic medical opinion, as outlined in a section on 'Grief and Melancholy' in Crichton's *An Inquiry into the Nature and Origin of Mental Derangement* (1798), a volume available to Keats in Guy's Physical Society library:

> When a person is suddenly informed of some melancholy event that deeply affects his life, fortune, or fame, his whole strength seems at once to leave him; the muscles which support him are all relaxed ... In many cases he actually sinks down ... Causes of deep grief, when not clearly forseen, may, in certain habits, exhaust the irritability and power of the nerves so much, as to produce all the phenomena of sleep. This sleep is generally of the comatose kind, or misted with catalepsy ... I have seen very remarkable instances, in which this state of torpor has continued several days. (II, 183–84)[59]

It is of course difficult to parse Keats's exact influences here: the description of Saturn's mental ailments, recorded with all the precision of hospital notes, deploys a medical register that may be found in numerous volumes of psychiatry from the period. All the same, the confluence of *deep/deep*, *sink/ sunken* and *nerves/nerveless* is suggestive.

3. 'A maniac, full of love, and death, and fate': Marcian Colonna

Coleridge admired Cornwall's colour-brave dramatizations of emotional distress and psychological disintegration, but with laudatory comments inscribed in Charles Lamb's personal copy of *Dramatic Scenes*, running to some 600 words, he also sounded a prescient note of caution. Counselling the literary newcomer to be 'economic and withholding in similies, figures, &c.', Coleridge insists that dramatic poetry 'must be Poetry *hid* in Thought and Passion, not T. or P. disguised in the dress of Poetry' (p. 116). In Coleridge's eyes, the tendency to confuse 'Passion' with 'Poetry' in the pursuit of mind-shaking lines, while welcomed by readers, threatened to disqualify Cornwall's writing for serious consideration by future audiences. Cornwall's lack of economy is nowhere more apparent than in the chromatic 'maniac extravagancies' of his best-selling *Marcian Colonna*.

The poem's plot is voguishly horrible. The prince of Colonna has two sons, one of whom is destined to succeed him in title and estate. The younger son Marcian, displaying signs of hereditary insanity, is hidden by his ambitious politician parents in a distant asylum where he is looked after by monks. Every night Marcian is tormented by phantom members of his family's male line, who reveal that his fate is to murder the one whom he most loves. Marcian's sole comforts are pleasant memories of his childhood companion

Julia. On the death of his older brother, Marcian is summoned back to
Rome, where he is reunited with Julia, whose husband Orsini has reportedly drowned in a shipwreck. Marcian and Julia marry. After a brief interval
of tranquility, Marcian begins to drift in and out of madness. He relates his
recurring dream of lunacy and murder to Julia. Shortly afterwards, news
reaches them that 'black Orsini' is, in fact, still alive. The lovers flee Rome.
Surviving a shipwreck themselves, they take refuge in a cave, but on being
discovered are forced to take flight again. Psychologically exhausted, Julia
decides to return to her implacable first husband. Her decision tips Marcian
over into a permanent state of lunacy. Cold-bloodedly, he puts into action
his plan to poison Julia and thus prevent her from returning to Orsini.

Everything about Cornwall's visceral étude in madness bulges and strains.
The ghastly parade of Marcian's mad ancestry early in the poem sets the tone:

> A grim array,
> Like spectres from the graves of buried men,
> Came by in silence ...
> ...
>   'Look', the phantom said,
> 'Upon thine ancestry departed – dead.
> 'Each one thou seest hath left his gaping tomb
> 'Empty, and comes to warn thee of thy doom:
> 'And each, whilst living, bore within his brain
> 'A settled madness: start not – so dost thou:
> 'Thou art our own, and on thy moody brow
> 'There is the invisible word ne'er writ in vain.
> 'Look on us all: we died as thou shalt die,
> 'The victims of our heart's insanity.
> 'From sire to son the boiling rivers ran
> 'Thro' every vein, and 'twas alike with all:
> 'It touched the child and trampled down the man;
> 'And every eye that, with its dead dull ball,
> 'Seems as it stared upon thee now, was bright
> 'As thine is, with the true transmitted light.
> 'Madness and pain of heart shall break thy rest,
> 'And she shall perish whom thou lovest the best.
>   (*Marcian Colonna*, p. 52)

Lugubrious arrays of phantoms are practically obligato in such generic territory, and Cornwall could summon spectres more vividly than most of his
peers. Modern readers balk at *Marcian*'s gothic hokery, at the corniness of
'boiling' rivers and 'gaping' tombs. Indeed, this instinctive recoil is part of

the problem: we have lost the ability to read Cornwall at face value, while
keeping a straight face. Nevertheless, the poem was widely celebrated in its
own day, and it laid the path for even bolder poetic experiments in terms of
representing psychological states – in particular sexual psychosis – such as
Browning's 'Porphyria's Lover' (first published as 'Porphyria' in 1836), and
Tennyson's spasmodic tour-de-force, *Maud* (1855).[60]

Little more than 'the history of the ravings of a lunatic', according to the
sceptical *Monthly Review, Marcian Colonna* sharply illustrates Cornwall's
feeling for the market, his 'nous'.[61] Delivering precisely the kind of 'tremen-
dous agitations of the breast' that Francis Jeffrey worried were overvalued
in modern literature, Cornwall's tale is peppered with such gurning descriptions as the following:[62]

> She saw his soul
> Rising in tumult, and his eyeballs roll
> Wildly and fiery red, and thro' his cheek
> Deep crimson shot: he sighed but did not speak.
> Keeping a horrid silence there he sate,
> A maniac, full of love, and death, and fate.
> (*Marcian Colonna*, p. 88)

Oddly, Charles Lamb thought Cornwall's macabre Italian tale 'dainty'. The
Eclectic Review, on the other hand, professed to a sense of shock on encountering the 'disgustingly horrible and unnatural story', denounced as devoid
of 'moral substance'.[63]

In one sense, Cornwall could hardly have hoped for better publicity;
particularly since he had been scrupulous to ensure that while his work
pushed at the boundaries of what book-buyers, of both sexes, could
purchase with propriety, it stopped short of trespassing beyond them.
Robert's Semi-Monthly Magazine captures the point, musing as it does
on the suitability of inherited insanity as a theme for poetic entertainment: 'Perhaps such a subject is not the happiest for poetry; yet no-one
can deny, that in 'Marcian Colonna' as much has been made of it, without
shocking the feelings of the reader or violating propriety, as it was possible
to make'.[64] Similarly, in 1825, Amédée Pichot, reassured those readers not
yet familiar with Cornwall's poem that despite its gothic tints there was
'nothing Satanic' in its 'dulcet breathings'.[65] The *Eclectic Review* was scathing,
however, and insisted that Cornwall's latest pot-boiler lacked any credible
design on posterity: 'If he wishes to write poetry that shall not only sell but
live', the reviewer argued, such morally disposable tales should be left 'to the
inimitable and detestable Author of Don Juan' (p. 330). Cornwall's unease at

suggestions of disposability is palpable in the letter he tucked in with Keats's presentation copy of *Marcian Colonna* in late June 1820, which implores his rival to 'Think of it as well as you can'.[66]

For all its generic spectres, star-crossed lovers, turned brains and palsied limbs, *Marcian Colonna* depends for its more visceral impact on Cornwall's professional insights into mental disintegration, which are seamlessly incorporated into a commercialized idiom. Cox's *Practical Observations on Insanity*, one of the period's most popular books on the subject, is a possible source for key ideas and images found at the beginning of the poem. In a section that discourses on the topic of inherited mental disease, Cox identifies the 'baneful and detestable habit of Monkish seclusion' as a further 'prolific source of diseased intellect' (p. 14). Both maladies are central to Cornwall's story.

Cornwall is also medically current in his dramatic exploration of the concept of lucid intervals, a contested category of psychological experience in the Romantic era. With the news that Julia's first husband has – it appears – died, Marcian is free to marry his childhood companion. During the initial stages of their reunion, Marcian's symptoms seem to subside. Ashby Bland Crowder dismisses *Marcian Colonna* for offering what he sees as merely a simplistic treatment of a 'conventional lunatic'.[67] The poem, he argues, is concerned solely with 'uncontrolled passion' and 'lack of rationality'; Browning, by contrast, adopts a more sophisticated approach to criminal madness in 'Porphyria's Lover', which explores the Victorian concept of 'rational lunacy'. Crowder perhaps misses Cornwall's fascination with the Romantic notion of lucid intervals, a subject that was being vigorously debated in legal publications as well as tested in court. In *Commentaries on the Laws of England* (1765–1769), William Blackstone defined a lunatic, or *non compos mentis*, as 'one who hath had understanding, but by disease, grief, or other accident, has lost the use of his reason. A lunatic is indeed properly one that hath lucid intervals, sometimes enjoying his senses, and sometimes not.'[68] This definition had important implications for the management of a lunatic's estate, and also impacted on the determination of culpability in trials for criminal insanity. Several Romantic clinicians took issue with Blackstone's definition of 'interval'; Romantic psychiatry, indeed, harboured a profound scepticism towards the concept of the lucid interval itself. Haslam and Crichton cautioned that apparent intermissions in symptoms merely disguised a more insidious, deep-seated malaise. Haslam objected that the term 'interval' was too vague, since it could denote a brief moment or equally a period of several years. Lunatics, he added, might be capable of appearing sane for long stretches, while their underlying illness was in fact only hidden. 'As the law requires a precise development of opinion', he explained, 'I should define a lucid interval to be the complete recovery of the patient's intellects'.[69]

Cornwall's pioneering poem dramatizes this legal ambivalence, depicting Marcian's lunacy, which lies 'hidden for a while', as something that might be called to the surface by 'a mere glance, a word, a sound':

> ... Colonna's mind forgot,
> In the fair present hour, his future lot.
> To those o'er whom pale Destiny with his sting
> Hangs, a mere glance, a word, a sound will bring
> The bitter future with its terrors, all
> Black and o'erwhelming.
> ...
> The soul can never fly itself, nor mask
> The face of fate with smiles. –
>   (*Marcian Colonna*, p. 43)

Rejection of the lucid interval proved decisive in Erskine's landmark defence of James Hadfield in 1800 for the attempted assassination of George III, a sensational trial that, as Dana Rabin notes, 'catapulted ... the debate surrounding the insanity defence into the headlines and into statutory law'.[70] If Hadfield's attempt on the monarch's life had been conducted during an interval of lucidity, as hitherto defined, the defendant would have had to have been considered sane at the time of the attack and thus accountable for his actions. Erskine assembled a field of expert witnesses to testify to the impossibility of the ex-dragoon having been of sound mind during the assault, whatever appearances to the contrary, due to serious brain injuries sustained while fighting in the Napoleonic wars. Erskine's defence hinged on the testimony of two expert witnesses. The first, Henry Cline, an authority on brain anatomy, was a surgeon at Keats's hospital, St Thomas's. Erskine asked Cline: 'Have you frequently observed persons that were lunatics, whether from hereditary taint, wounds in the brain, or other circumstances that are invisible ... capable of conversing and appearing rational?' Cline's answer was unequivocal: 'In every respect rational'.[71] Westminster Hospital surgeon and expert on criminal insanity, Alexander Crichton, broadly concurred with Cline: 'When any question concerning a common matter is made to [Hadfield], he answers very correctly; but when any question is put to him which relates to the topic of his lunacy, he answers irrationally'.[72] Crichton's perspective on the matter paralleled Haslam's own: 'Insane people will often, for a short time, conduct themselves, both in conversation and behaviour, with propriety ... [However,] let the examiner protract the discourse, until the favourite subject shall have got afloat in the madman's brain, and he will be convinced of the hastiness of his decision' (*Observations*, p. 27).

The Hadfield jury's 'special verdict' found the ex-soldier 'not guilty' of treason, judging the defendant to have been 'under the influence of insanity when the act was committed'. Spared the gallows, he was sent directly to Bethlem Hospital. Undoubtedly humane, the verdict discomforted parliament. Four days after Hadfield's acquittal, a bill was introduced to the House of Commons, the resulting 'Act for the Safe Custody of Insane Persons Charged with Offences' providing for the automatic detainment of the criminally insane.[73]

By the 1820s, the view endorsed by Crichton, Cline and Haslam had become legal and medical orthodoxy. In *Hints for the Examination of Medical Witnesses* (1829), John Gordon Smith, professor of medical jurisprudence at the University of London, modified Blackstone's standard definition of lunacy accordingly:

> Lunatics are people who are said to have *lucid intervals* – occasional remissions of the complaint, during which their conduct may be unexceptionable. But during these intervals they are no more to be considered *well*, than a person subject to epileptic fits may be considered fit to be trusted in dangerous situations between the occurrence of one paroxysm and that of another.

There's little doubt that Cornwall would have approved of the compassionate nature of the Hadfield verdict. In a letter to his fellow Commissioner, John Forster, on 27 August 1856, he rails against a renewed lack of sympathy towards the criminally insane among juries:

> There appears to be a Crusade against Lunacy, at present. The argument seems to be that a Jury of 12 ignorant men must know more about diseases of the brain than Physicians or Surgeons, and that Madhouses are prisons and not hospitals. I suppose the fever will subside.[74]

During the composition of 'Porphyria's Lover', Robert Browning – a close friend who dedicated *Columbe's Birthday* to Cornwall in 1844 – discovered a rich fund of lurid idiom in *Marcian Colonna*, also drawing on John Wilson's 'Extracts from Gosschen's Diary', published in *Blackwood's Edinburgh Magazine* in 1818.[75] Marcian's cold act of murder was also inspired by the calculated criminality of Wilson's psychotic narrator, who calmly describes to a prison chaplain his frenzied sexual attack on a 'poor infatuated wretch' (p. 597):

I grasped her by that radiant, that golden hair, – I bared those snow-white breasts, – I dragged her sweet body towards me, and, as God is my witness, I stabbed, and stabbed her with this very dagger, ten, twenty, forty times, through and through her heart. She never so much as gave one shriek, for she was dead in a moment, – but she would not have shrieked had she endured pang after pang, for she saw my face of wrath turned upon her, – she knew that my wrath was just, and that I did right to murder her who would have forsaken her lover in his insanity.

I laid her down upon a bank of flowers, – that were soon stained with her blood. I saw the dim blue eyes beneath the half-closed lids, – that face so changeful in its living beauty was now fixed as ice, and the balmy breath came from her sweet lips no more. My joy, my happiness, was perfect. (*Tales of Terror*, p. 21)

Cornwall's debt to Wilson is most evident in his description of Marcian's final, chilling act of sexual delinquency:

... his heart hardened as the fire withdrew,
Like furnaced iron beneath the winter's dew.
He gained – he gained (why droops my story?) then,
An opiate deadly from the convent men,
And bore it to his cave: she drank that draught
Of death, and he looked on in scorn, and laughed
With an exulting, terrible joy, when she
Lay down in tears to slumber, silently.
– She had no after sleep; but ere she slept
Strong spasms and pains throughout her body crept,
And round her brain, and tow'rds her heart, until
They touched that seat of love, – and all was still.
Away he wandered for some lengthened hour
When the black poison shewed its fiercest power,
And when he sought the cavern, there she lay,
The young, the gentle, – dying fast away.
He sate and watched her, as a nurse might do,
And saw the dull film steal across the blue,
And saw, and felt her sweet forgiving smile,
That, as she died, parted her lips the while.
Her hand? – its pulse was silent – her voice gone,
But patience in her smile still faintly shone,
And in her closing eyes a tenderness,
That seemed as she would fain Colonna bless.
She died, and spoke no word; and still he sate
Beside her like an image. Death and Fate
Had done what might be then: The morning sun

Rose upon him: on him? – his task was done.
The murderer and the murdered – one as pale
As marble shining white beneath the moon,
The other dark as storms, when the winds rail
At the chafed sea ...
   (*Marcian Colonna*, pp. 89–90)

Robert Morison plays down Cornwall's part in the genesis of 'Porphyria's Lover', emphasizing Browning's debt to Wilson's 'reprehensibly commercial' tale of terror instead.[76] However, as Michael Mason points out, key elements in Browning's poem were actually introduced to the narrative genotype in *Marcian Colonna*: 'Procter omits some important features of Wilson's piece that survive in "Porphyria" ... Some of Procter's additions, however, are taken up by Browning: notably the traits of survival on the victim's face, and the all-night vigil throughout which the murderer is so immobile.'[77] Prejudice against Cornwall is ingrained. Keats himself has been preferred as a more legitimate starting place for Browning than Cornwall. Noting that Browning's title recalls Keats's hero Porphyro from *The Eve of St Agnes*, Catherine Maxwell perceives a Bloomian struggle in 'Porphyria's Lover' between two strong poets (Browning and Keats, emphatically not Browning and Cornwall). Notwithstanding her acknowledgement of Mason's work on 'near sources' for 'Porphyria's Lover' in Wilson's and Cornwall's own psychotic texts, these 'secondary' filaments of influence are largely discounted in favour of Keats, Maxwell insisting that any connections between Browning and Cornwall (or Browning and Wilson) 'seem less important' than Browning's 'determining revision of a great precursor in Keats'.[78] In my view, Browning was sufficiently canny to look to the audience-pleasing Cornwall, rather than to the decidedly unpopular Keats, when it came to giving readers what they wanted.

4. 'The Manias of this Mad Age'

Not all contemporary reviewers agreed with the popular adjudication on *Marcian Colonna*. The *Eclectic Review* saw its demented Cockney rhymes as proof that the poem had given the author's governing rationality the slip:

Sometimes, we have the conjunction *and* made to sustain the weight of the rhyme:
   'The masters of the world have vanished, *and*
   Thy gods have left or lost their old command.'

Sometimes, the relative:
————————— 'save some sad few
(Like him imprison'd and devoted,) *who* –'
Or still better, a preposition:
'He was the youngest of his house, and *from*
His very boyhood a severer *gloom* –
Again:
'Her shape and voice fell like a balm upon
His sad and dark imagination'
'————————— His mother fondly kissed
Her eldest born, and bade him on that day
Devote him to the dove-eyed Ju-li-A!!'[79]

Byron also thought that eccentric rhymes 'quite spoiled' his ex-classmate's Cockney epic.[80] The *Eclectic* didn't balk at manipulating words from the 'Advertisement' to make Cornwall appear to confess: 'The poem is not what I intended to make it, – I could not manage the thing' (p. 331).[81] For the *Eclectic*, Cornwall's portrayal of ungovernable madness itself finally proves ungovernable.

And yet it was Keats who was accused of displaying symptoms of *actual* madness. In the 'Cockney School of Poetry, No. IV' review, Lockhart suggests that the former medical pupil who once attended lunatics had himself been 'reduced to a state of insanity' through overwheening poetic ambition:

> Of all the manias of this mad age, the most incurable, as well as the most common, seems to be no other than the *Metromanie* ... His friends, we understand, destined him to the career of medicine, and he was bound apprentice some years ago to a worth[y] apothecary in town. But all has been undone by a sudden attack of the malady to which we have alluded ... We hope, however, that in so young a person, and with a constitution originally so good, even now the disease is not utterly incurable. Time, firm treatment, and rational restraint do much for many apparently hopeless invalids.[82]

Jennifer Wallace points out that *Blackwood's* criticism of Keats's poetry was frequently 'expressed metaphorically in comments on his physical health.'[83] Here, it is Keats's *mental* rather than physical health that is at stake in Z's mugging. Just as Keats made use of Romantic medical language in concocting his portraits of insanity, Lockhart deploys similarly precise vocabularies to ridicule his Cockney quarry. Keats's apparent compulsion to write is figured as an incurable psychic malady, 'Metromanie'. Nicholas Roe suggests that Lockhart uses this term as a way of snidely invoking the 'mania for writing poetry that allegedly accompanied the French Revolution and shared its democratic impetus.'[84] Such strategy would certainly be consonant with Lockhart's politically sprung remarks elsewhere. However, a secondary, equally legible – and just as damaging – gynopsychiatric meaning may be in play, which seeks to link Keats's work with a mental disorder typically associated with women: *erotomamia* or *nymphomania*.

Just as madness was thought to originate in an overload of blood in the vessels of the brain, *nymphomania* – 'nymphs', the seventeenth- and eighteenth-century anatomical denotation for vaginal labia continued to be an accepted medical term throughout the Romantic period, deployed in such publications as *The London Dissector* (1804) and *The Dissector's Manual* (1820) – was conjectured to originate in an excess of blood to the female genitals. According to *OED*, the first use of *metromania* in the sense of *nymphomania* doesn't occur in an English publication until Dunglison's *Medical Lexicon* (1848). All the same, used as a sub-species of *erotomania* (and, after 1771, of the freshly minted *nymphomania*), the term was common in French medical volumes from the 1720s onwards.[85] The connection is made, for instance, in the fifth edition of Pinel's *Nosographie Philosophique; ou, la Méthode de l'Analyse Appliquée la Médicine* (1813), where it is included in a list of synonyms for *nymphomania*: *metromania*, *furor uterinus* and *melancholia uterina* (Astruc, Cullen, Sauvages and Linnaeus are cited as authorities).[86]

Lockhart may well have been aware of a gendered dimension to 'metromania'; elsewhere in the review he is meticulous in deploying psychiatric terms, distinguishing carefully between a 'violent fit or two', the 'phrenzy' of Keats's *Poems* (1817), and the 'calm, settled, imperturbable drivelling idiocy' of *Endymion*. He was also shortly the author of a novel set in a madhouse, *The History of Matthew Wald* (1824), which displays a technical facility with medical terminologies.[87] Lockhart, then, not only suggests that the madness of Keats's poetic diction reflects more irradicable authorial derangement; by utilizing the language of illness familiar from conventional tales of grief-stricken maidens unhinged by desire for their dead or demon lovers, he configures Keats as a sexually unstable heroine of the kind found in the poet's own anxious, gothicky-sentimental romances.

5. 'Substantially insane': Cornwall and *Liber Amoris*

Cornwall's capacity for tolerating the kinks, quirks and foibles of character helped him to form an enduring friendship with the notoriously querulous essayist, William Hazlitt. P. G. Patmore remarked that Cornwall was 'among the very few – "some two or three" – to whom Hazlitt knew and felt that he might always resort, at a moment of real need or difficulty'.[88] Hazlitt's 'personal intimacy' with the poet, Patmore recollected, began almost immediately after the appearance of *Dramatic Scenes* in 1819, and 'endured, without breach, till Hazlitt's death'. Cornwall, it seems, was the only person with whom Hazlitt, who could 'quarrel upon a look, a movement, a shadow', never fell out (III, 161–62).[89] Privately, Cornwall conceded to J. W. Dalby that Hazlitt was the 'keenest critic England ever possessed – but the *strangest* man!'[90]

As Patmore remembered things, Cornwall had been 'pleased to listen, with attention and interest, to all the little insignificant details of [Hazlitt's] daily life ... which must have seemed, to ordinary hearers, the most utter and empty common-place' (III, 87):

> To P[rocte]r, and to him alone (except myself) Hazlitt could venture to relate, in all their endless details, those "affairs of the heart" in one of which his *head* was always engaged, and which happily always (with one fatal exception) evaporated in that interminable talk about them of which he was so fond. (III, 87–88)

The 'fatal exception' alludes to the dangerous infatuation that Hazlitt developed with Sarah Walker, 19-year-old daughter of his Holborn landlady. The one-sided 'liaison' began in 1820 and continued until 1823, by which time Hazlitt, as his friends testify, had worked himself up into a state of wild-eyed derangement. In his memoirs, Cornwall pronounced him as 'substantially insane; certainly beyond self-control.'[91] This diagnosis reflects Romantic medical orthodoxy, which regarded severe frustration in matters of love as a potential trigger for mental pathology, sexual jealousy in particular being considered a significant 'exciting cause' of madness. As John Mason Cox outlined in his *Practical Observations on Insanity*:

> Disappointment, Jealousy, and particularly Seduction, as consequences of this passion [love], are too often the cause of insanity of the most deplorable species. In men, disappointed love may induce this effect by driving its victim to various kinds of dissipation, such as intoxication, excessive venereal gratifications, or solitary indulgences, which, debilitating both body and mind, have a direct tendency to produce mental diseases ... The corroding suspicion that constitutes the passion of jealousy is also a very common origin of madness, and unhappily its subjects are too frequently stimulated to the commission of the most atrocious crimes. (p. 24)

This paragraph serves as a condensed narrative of what Cornwall termed Hazlitt's 'insane passion' for Walker, which ended in Hazlitt orchestrating an episode of scarcely conceivable sexual conspiracy, and in which Cornwall and his poetry played a central (and discreditable) role.[92] Hazlitt critics fail to make much of the fact, but lines from Cornwall's tragedy *Mirandola* (1821) maintain a fomenting presence in *Liber Amoris* (1823), as I wish to discuss. Cornwall's poetry also figures in the essayist's darker, viscerally misogynistic journal between 4 and 16 March 1823. Indeed, *Marcian Colonna* – appropriately enough, the tale of a jealous psychopath – has an important function in Hazlitt's attempt first to court Walker, then sadistically to 'try' her virtue.

Cornwall's initial impressions of Sarah Walker were not favourable. Describing their first encounter in her mother's lodging-house at 9 Southampton Buildings, Holborn, where Hazlitt holed up following the disintegration of his marriage to Sarah Stoddart, Cornwall remembered Walker's visage as unsettling, 'round and small' with eyes that seemed 'motionless, glassy, without any speculation (apparently) in them'. Walker is constructed as a Lamia figure, Cornwall recalling her 'steady, unmoving gaze upon the person she was addressing' as 'exceedingly unpleasant', and her gait as 'wavy, sinuous ... like the movement of a snake' (pp. 82–83). The description parallels a feverish passage in *Liber Amoris* which relates a nightmarish vision of Walker ('S.'), metamorphosing before Hazlitt's eyes into a serpent-woman (an image that might itself owe a debt to Keats's *Lamia*):

> She started up in her own likeness, a serpent in place of a woman. She had fascinated, she had stung me, and had returned to her proper shape, gliding from me after inflicting the mortal wound, and instilling deadly poison into every pore; but her form lost none of its original brightness by the change of character, but was all glittering, beauteous, voluptuous grace. Seed of the serpent or of the woman, she was divine![93]

Hazlitt's representations of Walker in *Liber Amoris* are perilously unstable, and competing versions of her jostle for space. She is configured alternatively as a living Greek statue or goddess, as a 'queen' and 'common adventurer' (Mark McCutcheon has recently drawn out the contemporary early nineteenth-century resonance of 'common' within a widely understood vocabulary of prostitution).[94] A passionate playgoer, Hazlitt also imagined his unwilling muse as a Covent Garden heroine, linking Walker in his reveristic devotion to Isadora, the duped duchess in Cornwall's then almost completed tragedy *Mirandola* (1821).[95] Hazlitt even managed to persuade Cornwall to include a portrait of Isadora that served to verify his private fantasy of Walker. Obligingly, the loyal (or mischievous) Cornwall sublimated the teenager's reportedly snaky motor skills into something more flatteringly fawnlike:

Farewell! With what a waving air she goes
Along the corridor. How like a fawn;
Yet statelier. – Hark! no sound however soft
(Nor gentlest echo) telleth when she treads;
But every motion of her shape doth seem
Hallowed by silence. Thus did Hebe grow
Amidst the Gods, a paragon; and thus –
Away! I'm grown the very fool of love.
  (*Mirandola*, I, iii, 102–09)

Mirandola's plot turns, fittingly in the context of the Walker affair, on sexual jealousy, portraying the emotional turmoil of an older man obsessed with a woman half his age. Believing her betrothed Guido killed in the wars, Isadora is induced through a serious of political machinations to marry her lover's father, the Duke of Mirandola. After the union, however, Guido returns safely from his military campaigns (a well-seasoned, sensational plot device that Cornwall also exploits in *Marcian Colonna*). The ensuing patri-filial drama reaches a pitch of melodrama when Guido is executed at his father's behest, the order to rescind the sentence arriving too late:

Casti.
My lord!
Where is your son?

Duke.
My son? Ha! death and haste.
Fly, fly and save him. Bring him hither ...
... O, my heart!
Fly some one! fly again, and bring my son.
Oh! mercy, mercy!

Casti.
Where is he – his son?

Officer.
Led out to death.

Casti.
Ha! where?

Officer.
In the western court.
[Casti rushes out.]

Duke.
My son! where is my son? Is no one gone

To stop my orders? ...
[*Sinks down.*]

(*After a short pause, Casti re-enters.*)

...

Duke.
Ha! my good messenger, a word, a word;
But one: I'll give my Dukedom to you, – all.
Tell me he lives. Swear it. 'Tis my command.

Casti.
Alas! it was too late. We can but pray.

...

Duke.
Sulphur and blistering fire. I want to die.
Unloose me here, here: I'm too tight. – Some one
Has tied my heart up; no, no; here, Sir, here.
All round my heart, and round my brain, – quick, quick –
I'm burning. – Hush! a drug – a –

Casti.
Hold him up.

Duke.
Some dull – some potent drink. I'll give – I'll give
The world away for peace. Oh! round my heart,
And – Ah! unloose this cord about my throat.
Has no one mercy here? I am the Duke, –
The Duke. Ha! I am – nothing.

Casti.
Raise his head.
Now, my dear lord, –

Duke.
O my poor son, my son!
Young victims – both so young, – so innocent.
But they are gone. I feel as I could sleep –
Sleep – hush! for ever. My poor son! –
[*Dies.*]

(*Mirandola*, V, ii, 280–318)

Cornwall's sulphurous denouement, with its echoes of *Richard III* and Lear's discovery of his hanged daughter Cordelia, throws Keats's rival tragedy *Otho the Great* decisively into the shade.

By consenting to write Sarah Walker into *Mirandola*, Cornwall enables
Hazlitt's self-flagellating erotic imagination to sustain an alternate, 'unsul-
lied' version of the teenager. (In the last line of the commissioned panegyric,
however, Cornwall inserts an altogether more candid commentary on
the nature of his friend's fixation: 'I'm grown the very fool of love'.)[96] His
diagnosis of Hazlitt's insanity, too, was not made flippantly, and was offered
years later when, as long-serving Lunacy Commissioner, he could draw
on a wealth of first-hand observations of mental illness. Benjamin Robert
Haydon had reached a similar conclusion in a letter of 7 August 1822:
'Hazlitt called last night in a state of absolute insanity about the girl who
has jilted him'.[97] The incontrovertibly psychotic tones of Hazlitt's private
journal in March 1823 certainly appear to bear out Cornwall's and Haydon's
individual verdicts on Hazlitt's mental state. The journal, which contains
passages of astonishing sexual frankness subsequently censored by Hazlitt's
grandson, William Carew Hazlitt, chronicles a conspiracy to test Walker's
virtue through a shadowy emissary known only as 'Mr. F.'.[98] The shady task
of Hazlitt's confederate was to seduce Walker; if she rebutted the handsome
'F.', Hazlitt told himself, he would know that the 'sole queen and mistress of
[his] thoughts' was faithful to him (*Liber Amoris*, Part II, letter X).

Hazlitt's journal entry for 9 March describes how 'F.', posing as a lodger,
probed Sarah about her reading tastes. As she poured tea, oblivious to the
wider angles of conspiracy, 'F.' inquired if she was familiar with the poetry of
Byron or Cornwall – authors known for skirting decorum:

> Had she read Don Juan? "No, for her sister said it was impious" F. repeated
> the word "impious" and laughed, at which she laughed. "Had Mr. F. read any
> of Mr. Procter's poetry?" He could not say. On which she explained Mr. Barry
> Cornwall's. Oh yes. Had she. Yes: she had Marcian Colonna and Mirandola and
> had seen Mirandola. Mr. Procter was a particular friend of Mr. Hazlitt's, and had
> very gentle and pleasing manners.[99]

Acquaintance with Byron's poetry would be interpreted as shorthand for
an admission of sexual knowledge, and Walker wisely denies having read
it. Indeed, she parries with a secret of her own: Procter's identity as 'Barry
Cornwall', which was apparently unknown to Hazlitt's agent.[100] There's
something gratifying about how the young woman seeks to turn the tables
on 'F.', countering the bare face of Byron 'impious' eroticism with Cornwall's
more acceptable cheek.

Naturally, Hazlitt was aware that Walker had seen *Mirandola*, since he
had himself accompanied her to Convent Garden. Equally, he knew she'd
read at least part of Cornwall's tragedy; it was he who directed her attention

to Cornwall's eulogizing passage. On 11 March, after debriefing his scurrilous agent, Hazlitt recorded how Sarah led 'F.' to 'her' lines: 'She took [*Mirandola*] and turning to the place where was the description of herself, said – "This was Mr. H.'s favourite passage." F. said he could hardly believe his eyes when he saw it, for she seemed perfectly unmoved. He then read [it] off ...

A day later, Cornwall's tale of 'grief and crime', *Marcian Colonna*, whose protagonist's descent into unalloyed madness and sexual violence uncannily mirrors Hazlitt's own, figured as an additional prop in Hazlitt's delinquent scheme:

> F. had got his Marcian Colonna [Sarah Walker's copy] lying on the chair beside him and when she came in, read her some lines, and asked if she remembered them. No: but she had read the whole. He then asked her to look at them, and for that purpose she came round the table to his side, and on his asking her, she sat down. After looking them over, the book was laid aside, and he laid his hand upon her thigh, to which she made not the slightest objection. He then put his own around her neck, and began to play with her necklace and paddle in her neck, all which she took smilingly. (p. 386)

The presence of Cornwall's dark tale of erotic obsession in Hazlitt's fanatical diary of 'insane passion' sets up a dizzying *mise-en-abyme* in which life and art resonate mutually. At any rate, Cornwall's under-acknowledged but pivotally supportive – at times perhaps even guiding – role in the insalubrious episode between Hazlitt and Walker complicates the nineteenth-century belief that the 'amiable' poet's work and his apparently uneventful life lacked any vital confluence.

Notes

1 Susanna Blumenthal, 'The Mind of a Moral Agent: Scottish Common Sense and the Problem of Responsibility in Nineteenth-Century American Law', *Law and History Review*, 26 (2008), pp. 99–159, at p. 101.

2 Donald C. Goellnicht, *The Poet-Physician: Keats and Medical Science* (Pittsburgh: University of Pittsburgh Press, 1984), p. 191.

3 According to Goellnicht, it was this transference that enabled Keats to 'leave the service of the former discipline for that of the latter' (p. 263).

4 *Quarterly Review* (1816), 388–417, at pp. 398–99.

5 See Torrey and Miller, *The Invisible Plague: The Rise of Insanity from 1750 to the Present* (Rutgers University Press: London, 2001), p. 40.

6 Joseph Green, *The Dissector's Manual* (London: Cox, 1820), p. 87. This volume constituted an expanded version of Green's *Outlines of a Course of Dissections for the Use of Students at St. Thomas's Hospital* (1815).

7 *London Medical Review*, 1 (1808), p. 42.

8 Andrew T. Scull, *Museums of Madness: The Social Organization of Insanity in Nineteenth-Century England* (Penguin: Harmondsworth, 1982), p. 13.

9 'Shaping Psychiatric Knowledge: The Role of the Asylum', in *Medicine in the Enlightenment*, ed. Roy Porter (Amsterdam: Rodopi, 1995), p. 257.

10 *Edinburgh Magazine and Literary Miscellany*, 7 (1820), pp. 7–14, at p. 13.

11 *Blackwood's Edinburgh Magazine*, 4 (1819), p. 105.

12 Anna Maria Porter, *The Fast of St Magdalen*, 3 vols (London: Longman, 1818), I, p. 2.

13 *Blackwood's Edinburgh Magazine*, 4 (1819), p. 347. In a biographical sketch of her husband, Roby's widow concedes that despite energetic advertizing puffs, the volume ultimately 'met with a limited sale'. See E. Roby, *The Legendary and Poetical Remains of John Roby* (London: Longman, 1854), p. 16.

14 *Blackwood's Edinburgh Magazine*, 4 (1819), p. 471. See *Philibert: A Poetical Romance*, p. 13. The *New Monthly Review*, 14 (1820) was captivated by *Philibert's* 'fearful' plot (p. 532).

15 *Blackwood's Edinburgh Magazine*, 6 (1820), p. 585. The *Quarterly* promised Milman 'whatever immortality the English language can bestow'; *Quarterly Review*, 23 (1820), pp. 198, 225.

16 Henry Hart Milman, *The Fall of Jerusalem: A Dramatic Poem* (London: Murray, 1820), p. 157.

17 *Blackwood's Edinburgh Magazine*, 4 (1818), p. 367.

18 *Blackwood's Edinburgh Magazine*, 5 (1819), p. 342.

19 Joel Faflak, 'Analysis Interminable in the Other Wordsworth', *Romanticism on the Net*, 16 (November 1999) <http://users.ox.ac.uk/~scat0385/otherww.html> [date of access: 2.7.7].

20 Charles Watkin Williams-Wynn, *Report from the Select Committee Appointed to Enquire into the State of Lunatics*, 15 July 1807, p. 21.

21 *Lyrical Ballads*, eds. R. L. Brett and A. R. Jones (London: Methuen, 1965), p. 249.

22 Alexander Crichton, *An Inquiry into the Nature and Origin of Mental Derangement, Comprehending a Concise System of the Physiology and Pathology of the Human Mind*, 2 vols (London: Cadell, 1798), II, p. 24.

23 Scott Masson, *Romanticism, Hermeneutics and the Crisis of the Human Sciences* (Aldershot: Ashgate, 2004), p. III.

24 Thomas Arnold, *Observations on the Nature, Kinds, Causes, and Prevention of Insanity, Lunacy, or Madness*, 2 vols (Leicester: Robinson, 1793), I, pp. 172–73.

25 Samuel Tuke, *Description of the Retreat, an Institution Near York, for the Treatment of Insane Persons of the Society of Friends* (York: Alexander, 1813), p. 151. Review of Tuke by Sydney Smith, *Edinburgh Review*, 24 (1814), pp. 189–98, at p. 190.

26 John Mason Cox, *Practical Observations on Insanity* (London: Baldwin, 1804), p. 123.

27 For more information on Cox's swings, see Nicholas J. Wade, U. Norrsell, and A. Presly, 'Cox's Chair: "A Moral and a Medical Mean in the Treatment of Maniacs"', *History of Psychiatry*, 16 (2005), pp. 73–88.

28 *The Eclectic Repertory and Analytical Review, Medical and Analytical*, 9 (Philadelphia, 1819), p. 520.

29 See *Romantic Circles*, Available online at: <http://www.rc.umd.edu/praxis/bloom_hartman/hartman/hartman.html> [date of access: 15.3.8].

30 See *The History of Bethlem*, p. 416.
31 Susan J. Wolfson, 'Sounding Romantic: the Sound of Sound', *Romantic Circles* (April, 2008): Available online at: <http://www.rc.umd.edu/praxis/soundings/wolfson/wolfson.html> [date of access: 12.4.8]. As James Chandler has recently argued – his insight is particularly resonant in the context of 'The Thorn' – the sentimental is both 'a language of emotion' and 'about a language of emotion'; 'The Language of Sentiment', *Textual Practice*, 22 (2008), pp. 21–39, at p. 21.
32 Following Romantic conventions, John Haslam's *Observations on Insanity* (1798) divided insanity into two categories: *mania* and *melancholia*.
33 See Helen Small, *Love's Madness: Medicine, the Novel, and Female Insanity, 1800–1865* (Oxford: Clarendon Press, 1996), pp. 45–46.
34 Wordsworth was friendly with Ray's son, barrister Basil Montagu; but as Brett and Jones point out, in another, deeper sense, Wordsworth's use of the name is 'completely inexplicable', p. 291. Montagu's own son Basil is also mentioned in *Lyrical Ballads*, as 'Edward' in 'To my Sister' and 'Anecdotes for Fathers'.
35 See Philip Morin Freneau, *Poems, Written Between the Years 1768 and 1794* (Monmouth, NJ: author, 1795), p. 330 (misnumbered as p. 320). A rather better poem by Freneau, 'The Indian Student', reprinted along with 'Under the Portraiture of Martha Ray' in the author's 1795 volume, anticipates certain features of 'Ruth', another poem in *Lyrical Ballads* focused on the theme of 'mad' women.
36 Martha Ray lived as the mistress of John Montagu, 4th Earl of Sandwich; one of their five illicit children was Basil Montagu, Skepper's stepfather and Cornwall's future father-in-law.
37 Letter to B. R. Haydon, dated May 1817, *LJK*, I, 142.
38 Letter dated 13 July 1820. See *The Letters of John Hamilton Reynolds*, ed. Leonidas M. Jones (Lincoln, NE: University of Nebraska Press, 1973), p. 19.
39 *Speeches of Lord Erskine, When at the Bar on Miscellaneous Subjects*, ed. John Ridgway (London: Ridgway, 1812), p. 1.
40 *New Monthly Review*, 7 (1823), pp. 388–84, at p. 384.
41 Collinson reprints the account printed in *The Times* on 11 May 1807, advertised as a case of 'Singular Insanity' (p. 4). Gill Gregory conjectures that the 'girl' was also in some sense Cornwall's daughter, Adelaine Anne Procter. See *The Life and Work of Adelaide Anne Procter: Poetry, Feminism and Fathers* (Aldershot: Ashgate, 1998), p. 53.
42 See *Blackwood's Edinburgh Magazine*, 13 (1823), pp. 532–41, at p. 538; and the *British Magazine* (1823), pp. 99–108, at p. 106.
43 *Monthly Review*, 101 (1823), pp. 50–55, at p. 54.
44 *The Olio*, 1 (1828), pp. 391–94, at p. 392; signed 'Illuscenor'. See G. M. Matthews, pp. 256–57.
45 His expertise was widely acknowledged by literary peers: as Helen Small suggests, Cornwall – the dedicatee of *The Woman in White* (1859) – was almost certainly 'the source of much of Wilkie Collins's knowledge of contemporary asylum conditions and laws' (p. 186).
46 At the end of his incarceration, Lamb wrote to Coleridge: 'I am got somewhat rational now, & *don't bite any one*. But *mad* I was'. See *The Letters of Charles Lamb*, ed. E. V. Lucas, 3 vols (1935), I, 4.
47 Andrew Motion confuses dates in his biography of Keats when he suggests that the

redesigned Bethlem Hospital opened in Moorfields in 1815. See *John Keats* (London: Faber and Faber, 1997), p. 7.

48 After 1770, visits to Bethlem Hospital were ticketed and restricted to Mondays. For a history of visiting this hospital during the Romantic period, see Jonathan Andrews et al., *The History of Bethlem* (London: Routledge, 1997), pp. 190–93.

49 For a detailed recent discussion of Keats's medical routine, see John Barnard, '"The Busy Time": Keats's Duties at Guy's Hospital from Autumn 1816 to March 1817', *Romanticism*, 13.3 (2008), pp. 119–218.

50 Hermione De Almeida, *Romantic Medicine and John Keats* (Oxford: Oxford University Press, 1991), p. 28. De Almeida's important book limns out numerous ways in which Keats's medical experience authenticates his poetic imagery.

51 *Romantic Medicine and John Keats*, pp. 24–25, 29.

52 John Keats, *Anatomical and Physiological Note Book*, ed. Maurice Buxton Forman (London: Oxford University Press, 1934), pp. 52–67.

53 See: <http://library.kcl.ac.uk>.

54 William Cullen, *First Lines of the Practice of Physic* (1776–1783), new edn, 2 vols (1808), I, 313.

55 William Babbington and James Curry, *Outlines of a Course of Lectures on the Practice as Delivered in the Medical School of Guy's Hospital* (London: Bensley, 1802–1806).

56 John Haslam, *Observations on Madness and Melancholy*, 2nd edition (London: Callow, 1809), pp. 90–91. Also see p. 167. Haslam's minute observation produced the first clinicopathological description of general paresis, a type of paralysis resulting from a form of neurosyphilis involving changes to the structure of the brain. See George E. Vaillant, 'John Haslam on Early Infantile Autism', *American Journal of Psychiatry*, 119 (1962), p. 376.

57 Interestingly, when Keats informs his brother and sister-in-law in December 1818 that he intends to return to the abandoned poem, he uses a blood metaphor, describing the difficulty of 'get[ing] into the vein again' (*LJK*, II, 12).

58 See 'Sounding Romantic: the Sound of Sound', *Romantic Circles* (April, 2008).

59 The volume Keats would have been able to consult has its original Physical Society library shelfmark 407 tooled on the spine, with its subsequent revised shelfmark 824–825 written in ink on the front pastedown.

60 In the 'Advertisement' to *Marcian Colonna*, Cornwall explains that his aim was to 'paint the fluctuations of a fatalist's mind, – touched with insanity – alternately raised by kindness and depressed by neglect or severity' (p. v). Compare this to Tennyson's rhetorically similar description of *Maud*, as recalled by Henry van Dyke in 1892: '[*Maud*] shows the unfolding of a lonely, morbid soul, touched with inherited madness, under the influence of a pure and passionate love'. See Henry van Dyke, *The Poetry of Tennyson* (New York: Charles Scribner's Sons, 1889), p. 123.

61 *Monthly Review*, 92 (1820), pp. 310–18.

62 *Edinburgh Review*, 34 (1820), p. 450.

63 Letter dated 22 June 1829; see Charles Lamb, *Works: Including His Most Interesting Letters*, ed. Thomas Noon Talfourd, new edn (London: Bell and Daldy, 1852), p. 156. *Eclectic Review*, n.s. 14 (1820), pp. 323–33, at pp. 330, 332.

64 *Robert's Semi-Monthly Magazine*, 1 (1841), pp. 149–60, at p. 150.

65 Amédée Pichot, *Historical and Literary Tour of a Foreigner in England and Scotland*,

2 vols (London: Saunders and Otley, 1825), II, p. 228.
66 'Keats and Procter: A Misdated Acquaintance', p. 532.
67 Ashby Bland Crowder, 'Porphyria's Lover: A Reason for Action', *The South Central Bulletin*, 37, Studies by Members of the SCMLA (1977), pp. 145–46, at p. 146.
68 William Blackstone, *Commentaries on the Laws of England in Four Books*, 16th edn (London: Strahan, 1825), I, 304.
69 Cox, by contrast, insisted that although many 'ingenious arguments' had been offered to prove that insanity did not permit of lucid intervals, 'a multitude of facts have occurred in my own practice ... to controvert the assertion'. See *Practical Observations on Insanity*, p. 199.
70 Dana Rabin, *Identity, Crime, and Legal Responsibility in Eighteenth-Century England* (London: Palgrave, 2004), p. 162.
71 *A Complete Collection of State Trials*, compiled by T. B. Howell (London: Hansard, 1820), XXVII, 1333.
72 *State Trials*, XXVII, 1334.
73 See Rabin, p. 156. For an excellent discussion of the 'special verdict', see Arnie Loughnan, '"Manifest Madness": Towards a New Understanding of the Insanity Defence', *Modern Law Review*, 70 (2007), pp. 379–401, at pp. 398–99.
74 Letter printed by Armour, pp. 244–46.
75 *Blackwood's Edinburgh Magazine*, 3 (1818), pp. 596–98.
76 'Porphyria' appeared in the *Monthly Repository* in January 1836. It was reprinted with slight revisions under the title 'Madhouse Cells' in Browning's self-published *Dramatic Lyrics* (1842). See Robert Morrison, '*Blackwood's* Berserker: John Wilson and the Language of Extremity', *Romanticism on the Net*, 20 (2000) <http://users.ox.ac.uk/~scat0385/20morrison.html> [date of access: 3.7.7].
77 Michael Mason, 'Browning and the Dramatic Monologue', in Isobel Armstrong (ed.), *Robert Browning* (Athens: Ohio University Press, 1975), pp. 260–61, at p. 257.
78 Catherine Maxwell, 'Browning's Pygmalion and the Revenge of Galatea', *ELH*, 60 (1993), pp. 989–1013, at p. 1009 (n. 10).
79 *Eclectic Review*, n.s. 14 (1820), p. 331.
80 Letter to John Murray, 4 January 1821 (*BLJ*, VIII, 56).
81 As originally printed, the 'Advertisement' states that Cornwall's 'intention ha[d] in some measure been departed from ... [and that] the story gradually took the form in which it now stands' (*Marcian Colonna*, p. v).
82 *Blackwood's Edinburgh Magazine*, 3 (1818), 519–24, at p. 519.
83 Jennifer Wallace, 'Keats's Frailty: The Body and Biography', in *Romantic Biography*, ed. Arthur Bradley and Alan Rawes (Aldershot: Ashgate, 2003), p. 141.
84 Nicholas Roe, *Keats and the Culture of Dissent* (Oxford: Oxford University Press, 1997), p. 20.
85 For more details about the use of these terms in eighteenth-century French medicine, see George Rousseau's essay on erotomania in *Cultural History After Foucault*, ed. John Neubauer (Somerset, NJ: Aldine Transaction, 1999), p. 8n.
86 Philippe Pinel, *Nosographie Philosophique; ou, la Méthode de l'Analyse Appliquée la Médicine*, 5th edn (Paris: J. A. Brosson, 1813), I, 287n.
87 As Mason notes, some of the most impressive experiments in 'conveying the quality of madness from the victim's point of view' were conducted by writers associated with

Blackwood's, like Lockhart and Wilson (p. 265).

88 P. G. Patmore, *My Friends and Acquaintances*, 3 vols (London: Saunders and Otley, 1854), III, 163.

89 For an excellent article on Patmore's role in Romantic magazine culture, see David G. Steward, 'P. G. Patmore's Rejected Articles and the Image of the Magazine Market', *Romanticism*, 12.iii (2006), pp. 200–11.

90 Recorded by S. R. Townshend Mayer, *Gentleman's Magazine*, 237 (1874), pp. 555–68, at p. 559.

91 *The Literary Recollections of Barry Cornwall*, ed. Richard Willard Armour (Boston: Meador, 1936), p. 83.

92 *Literary Recollections*, p. 81.

93 *Liber Amoris: or, The New Pygmalion* (London: Hogarth, 1985), pp. 155–56.

94 See Mark McCutcheon, '*Liber Amoris* and the Lineaments of Hazlitt's Desire', *Texas Studies in Literature and Language*, 46 (2004), pp. 432–451, at p. 437.

95 See Heskereth Pearson, *The Fool of Love: A Life of William Hazlitt* (London: Hamish Hamilton, 1934), p. 119.

96 Hazlitt reprinted the excerpt from *Mirandola* at the beginning of Part III of *Liber Amoris*, addressed to J. S. K. (James Sheridan Knowles): 'What do you think of those [lines] in a modern play, which were actually composed with an eye to this little trifler (though that's a secret) [Hazlitt then quotes lines from *Mirandola*, I, iii]'. Intriguingly, the next two editions of *Liber Amoris*, privately printed in 1893 and 1894 with an introduction by Richard le Gallienne, silently reinstate the 'secret', modifying the above passage to read, with dizzying new causality: 'a modern play, which might actually have been composed with an eye to this little trifler'. The Hogarth Press's 1985 edition of *Liber Amoris*, introduced by Michael Neve, uses the 1893 text. The 'publishers' note' claims that the 1893 edition is 'an accurate rendering of the 1823 text' (p. 282). Where Hazlitt's reference to Cornwall's *Mirandola* is concerned, it is in an important respect inaccurate.

97 *Diary*, II, 375.

98 See '*Liber Amoris* and the Lineaments of Hazlitt's Desire', p. 437.

99 The unexpurgated journal is appended to *The Letters of William Hazlitt*, ed. Herschel Moreland Sikes (Macmillan: London, 1979), p. 382.

100 Unless, of course, 'Mr F.' feared that to reveal knowledge of Cornwall's real identity would be to risk arousing Sarah Walker's suspicion of a possible connection between himself, Cornwall and Hazlitt.

Afterword – Afterlives

On 19 March 1821, Cornwall wrote to Byron to keep him abreast of 'book news'. 'Poor Keats is at Rome', he reported – 'dying, I hear'.[1] Although the news had not yet reached England, Keats was already a month dead. It was Cornwall who composed one of the earliest obituaries, printed in April in Baldwin's *London Magazine*, a literary journal to which Cornwall regularly contributed. Cornwall appears sensitive to the fact that his own work had received the plaudits that posterity was likely to reassign to his disregarded peer: '[Keats] has been suffered to rise and pass away almost without a notice; the laurel has been awarded (for the present) to other brows: the bolder aspirants have been allowed to take their station on the slippery steps of the temple of fame'.[2] As Samantha Matthews points out, this passage alludes to the poet-dreamer's agonized struggle to ascend the steps of Moneta's temple in Canto 1 of Keats's *The Fall of Hyperion*.[3]

Cornwall also composed a sentimental poetic tribute, 'An Elegy on the Death of the poet Keats', which was published in the four-penny *Athenaeum* in 1832, signed 'B':

Pale Poet, in the solemn Roman earth,
   Cold as the clay, thou lay'st thine aching head!
Ah! what awaits thy genius – what thy worth, –
   Or what the golden fame above thee spread?
      Thou art dead, – dead!

Too early banished from thy place of birth,
   By tyrant Pain, thy too bright Spirit fled!
Too late came love to show the world thy worth!
   Too late came Glory for thy youthful head!

Mourn; poets! mourn; – he's lost! O minstrels, grieve!
   And with your music let his fame be fed!
True lovers, 'round his verse your sorrows weave
   And maidens! mourn, at last, a poet dead!
      He is dead, – dead, – dead![4]

It is, perhaps, symptomatic of our neglect of Cornwall that this heartfelt, if clumsy, commemoration is not included with other (often equally indifferent) poems on Keats's death collected by Jeffrey Robinson in *Reception and Poetics in Keats: 'My Ended Poet'* (1998). Its absence in an otherwise excellent book underscores our wider failure to 'see' Cornwall. Cornwall's elegy is itself clear-eyed, however, and looks back to the day when 'Ode on a Grecian Urn' and the sonnet 'To Michel Agnolo' had been 'place[d] beside' each other in *Annals of Fine Art*. In Elmes's prestigious journal, Keats had instructed the 'Bold Lover' and 'maidens' chiselled into the urn's relief: 'do not grieve'. Cornwall responds by enjoining all 'True lovers' and 'maidens' to 'grieve' now for a poet dead.

The pitch of pathos achieved in Cornwall's 1832 portrait of Keats as the 'pale poet', his 'too bright' spirit 'too early banished', recalls, of course, Shelley's own elegy on Keats's death, *Adonais*, which raised this sentimental version of the fated poet to the status of cult.' In fact, Cornwall's 1821 obituary in the *London Magazine*, which pre-dates Shelley's great poem, already anticipates the rhetoric of *Adonais* in its depiction of Keats as a delicate, neglected, tragic genius who had been 'suffered to rise and pass away almost without a notice'. Just as Cornwall's review in the *Edinburgh Magazine and Literary Miscellany* was instrumental in recalibrating contemporary attitudes towards Keats's work in the Summer of 1820, his early obituary, penned barely six months later, was equally decisive in promulgating a powerfully appealing myth of the young poet, giving Keats's posthumous reputation a significant boost.

Intriguingly, exaggerated reports of Cornwall's own constitutional delicacy had also attracted reviewers' attentions. Indeed, at one curious juncture the narrative of Cornwall's contemporary reception was constructed in terms that strikingly prefigure the conditioning tropes of tragedy and fragility that were soon to shape Keats's afterlife. In the *New Monthly Review*'s warm appraisal of *A Sicilian Story* in February 1820 – the month of Keats's lung haemorrhage – the anonymous critic broached the subject of melancholia in Cornwall's work. It had pleased several poets, the reviewer observed, to brood in print; but their posturing merely aped the fashionably misanthropic Byron. Cornwall's pensiveness, on the other hand, seemed to have its origins in genuine physical malaise. Citing *A Sicilian Story*'s dedicatory sonnet, 'To –' ('It may be that the rhymes I bring to thee / ... are my last'), the *New Monthly Review* alluded ominously to rumours concerning the precarious state of Cornwall's health:

We fear that the writer, who is only known to the generality of his readers by the name of Barry Cornwall, assumes no poetic license when he indulges in the same tone of despondency. We believe we are not mistaken in ascribing the cause to ill-health. One of his beautiful occasional poems intimates, if we read it rightly, an intention of leaving this country, for a period not expressed,

> To see the blue and cloudless day
> Shine on the fields of Italy.[6]

... We cannot conclude without expressing our humble wishes that the benign climate he is about to visit, will restore to his fame that vigor of which, if we may judge from these specimens, his mind has lost nothing, and we shall then be content to sacrifice some portion of that deep feeling which now, if our suspicions be correct,

> Like the gay glories of the tulip's flower,
> Springs from disease engendered at the root.

The *New Monthly* thus portrays Cornwall as a doomed poet in terms that are presciently identical to those with which Keats would shortly be returned to the public.

Although Cornwall frequently worried about his physical condition in letters to friends, when it came to it his health was vigorous enough. His star would continue to rise for another three years, cresting with the publication of *Marcian Colonna* (1820), followed by *Mirandola*'s creditable run at Covent Garden just six weeks before Keats's death in Rome.[7] It is possible that the critic for the *New Monthly* had heard about Keats's ill-health (which was about to reach its crisis point), and for his own reasons transferred the pathos of the situation to Keats's Cockney School stablemate. Given the extent to which the literary ambitions, political lives and poetic receptions of both writers were imbricated in readers' imaginations, such a poignant blurring at the edges of identity now scarcely surprises.

Notes

1 Letter printed in *The Works of Lord Byron: Letters and Journals*, ed. Ernest Hartley Coleridge, 7 vols (London: Murray, 1901), V, 38.
2 Cornwall signs himself 'L'. See *London Magazine*, 3 (1821), at p. 426. For attribution of authorship, see Joanne Shattock (ed.), *The Cambridge Bibliography of English Literature*, 3rd edn (Cambridge: Cambridge University Press, 1999), IV, 388; and Olive M. Taylor, 'John Taylor, Author and Publisher', *London Mercury*, 13 (1925), p. 260.
3 Samantha Matthews, *Poetical Remains: Poets' Graves, Bodies and Books in the Nineteenth Century* (Oxford: Oxford University Press, 2004), pp. 113–14.

4　*Athenaeum*, 10 March 1832, No. 228, p. 162. For attribution of authorship, see *The Cambridge Bibliography of English Literature*, IV, 389.

5　On 8 June 1821, Shelley wrote to Ollier to inform him that he had finished his panegyric on Keats (*LPBS*, II, 297).

6　The lines quoted by the reviewer are from Cornwall's 'When Shall We Three Meet Again', one of the 'Miscellaneous' poems included in *A Sicilian Story* (1820).

7　Cornwall never visited Italy.

Select Bibliography

The London Dissector; or, System of Dissection, Practised in the Hospitals and Lecture Rooms of the Metropolis, Explained by the Clearest Rules, for the Use of Students, 4th edn (London: Longman, 1813).

The London Dissector; or, System of Dissection, Practised in the Hospitals and Lecture Rooms of the Metropolis, Explained by the Clearest Rules, for the Use of Students (Philadelphia, 1818; based on the 5th London edition of 1816).

Andrews, C. T., 'Keats and Mercury', *Keats Shelley Memorial Bulletin*, 20 (1969), pp. 37–43.

Andrews, Jonathan et al., *The History of Bethlem* (London: Routledge, 1997).

Applyby, John H., 'Sir Alexander Crichton, F. R. S. (1763–1856), Imperial Russian Physician at Large', *Notes and Records of the Royal Society of London*, 53 (1999), pp. 219–30.

Armour, Richard Willard, *Barry Cornwall: A Biography of Bryan Waller Procter* (Boston: Meador, 1935).

——, *The Literary Recollections of Barry Cornwall*, ed. Richard Willard Armour (Boston: Meador, 1936).

Arnold, Thomas, *Observations on the Nature, Kinds, Causes, and Prevention of Insanity, Lunacy, or Madness*, 2 vols (Leicester: Robinson, 1793).

Babbington, William and James Curry, *Outlines of a Course of Lectures on the Practice as Delivered in the Medical School of Guy's Hospital* (London: Bensley, 1802–1806).

Baker, Thomas N., *Sentiment and Celebrity: Nathaniel Parker Willis and the Trials of Literary Fame* (Oxford: Oxford University Press, 1999).

Baldwin, James, *The Book-Lover: A Guide to the Best Reading* (London: Putnam, 1893).

Barnard, John, *John Keats* (Cambridge: Cambridge University Press, 1987).

——, 'A Poet and His Money – A New Look at the Publishing History of Keats's *Poems* (1817)', *Times Literary Supplement*, 12 August 2005, p. 12.

——, '"The Busy Time": Keats's Duties at Guy's Hospital from Autumn 1816 to March 1817', *Romanticism*, 13.3 (2008), pp. 119–218.

Bate, Walter Jackson, *John Keats* (London: Hogarth, 1992).

Becker, Franz, *Bryan Waller Procter (Barry Cornwall)* (Wien: Braumüller, 1911).

Benedict, Barbara M., *Making the Modern Reader: Cultural Mediation in Early Modern Literary Anthologies* (Princeton, NJ: Princeton University Press, 1996).

Bennett, Andrew, *Keats, Narrative and Audience: The Posthumous Life of Writing* (Cambridge: Cambridge University Press, 1994).

——, *Romantic Poets and the Culture of Posterity* (Cambridge: Cambridge University Press, 1999).

Bentley, G. E., 'Leigh Hunt's "Literary Pocket-Book" 1818–22: A Romantic Source Book', *Victorian Periodicals Newsletter*, 8 (1975), pp. 125–28.

Blackstone, William, *Commentaries on the Laws of England in Four Books*, 16th edn (London: Strahan, 1825).

Blumenthal, Susanna, 'The Mind of a Moral Agent: Scottish Common Sense and the Problem of Responsibility in Nineteenth-Century American Law', *Law and History Review*, 26 (2008), pp. 99–159.

Blunden, Edmund, *Keats's Publisher: A Memoir of John Taylor* (London: Jonathan Cape, 1936).

——, *Leigh Hunt: A Biography* (1930; Hamden, CT: Archon, 1970).

Brown, Charles, *Life of John Keats*, ed. D. H. Bodurtha and W. B. Pope (Oxford: Oxford University Press, 1937).

Brown, Hilary, 'German Women Writers in English Short Story Anthologies of the 1820s', *Modern Language Review*, 97 (2002), pp. 620–31.

Burton, Robert, *The Anatomy of Melancholy*, ed. T. Faulkner, N. Kiessling and K. Blair, 3 vols (Oxford: Clarendon Press, 1984).

Burwick, Frederick, *Poetic Madness and the Romantic Imagination* (1996).

Butler, Marilyn, *Romantics, Rebels and Reactionaries: English Literature and its Background, 1760–1830* (Oxford: Oxford University Press, 1981).

Byron, George Gordon, *The Works of Lord Byron*, ed. Ernest Hartley Coleridge, 7 vols (London: Murray, 1901).

——, *Byron's Letters and Journals*, ed. Leslie A. Marchand, 12 vols (London: Murray, 1973–1982).

——, *Don Juan*, ed. T. G. Steffan et al. (Harmondsworth: Penguin, 1986).

Caldwell, James Ralston, 'The Meaning of *Hyperion*', *PMLA*, 51 (1936), pp. 1080–97.

Chandler, James, 'The Language of Sentiment', *Textual Practice*, 22 (2008), pp. 21–39.

Chilcott, Tim, *A Publisher and his Circle: The Life and Work of John Taylor, Keats's Publisher* (London: Routledge & Kegan Paul, 1972).

Cohen, Ivan M., 'Herodotus and the Story of Gyges: Traditional Motifs in Historical Narrative', *Fabula*, 45, issues 1–2 (2004), pp. 55–68.

Coleridge, Samuel Taylor, *Collected Letters of Samuel Taylor Coleridge*, ed. Earl Leslie Griggs, vol. 3, 1807–1814 (Oxford: Clarendon Press, 1959).

——, *A Book I Value: Selected Marginalia*, ed. H. J. Jackson (Princeton, NJ: Princeton University Press, 2003).

Colvin, Sidney, *John Keats: His Life and Poetry, His Friends, Critics and After-Fame*, 2nd edn (London: Macmillan, 1918).

Conder[?], Josiah, Review of *Lamia, Isabella, the Eve of St Agnes, and other Poems*, *Eclectic Review*, 2nd series, 14 (1820).

Cornwall, Barry [Bryan Waller Procter], *Dramatic Scenes, and Other Poems* (London: C. & J. Ollier, 1819).

——, *A Sicilian Story, with Diego de Montilla and Other Poems* (London: C. &. J. Ollier, 1820).

——, *Marcian Colonna, An Italian Tale with Three Dramatic Scenes* (London: Warren, and C. & J. Ollier, 1820).

——, *Mirandola: A Tragedy* (London: Warren, 1821).

——, *The Flood of Thessaly, The Girl of Provence, and Other Poems* (London: Henry Colburn, 1823).

——, *Essays and Tales in Prose* (Boston: Ticknor, 1853).

——, *Charles Lamb: A Memoir* (London: Moxon, 1866).

——, *An Autobiographical Fragment and Biographical Notes, With Personal Sketches of Contemporaries, Unpublished Lyrics, and Letters of Literary Friends*, ed. Coventry Patmore (London: Bell, 1877).

——, *Dramatic Scenes and Marcian Colonna* (1819), repr. in Donald H. Reiman (ed.), *Romantic Context, Poetry, Significant Minor Poetry 1789–1830* (London: Garland, 1978).

Cox, Jeffrey N., *Poetry and Politics in the Cockney School: Keats, Shelley, Hunt and their Circle* (Cambridge: Cambridge University Press, 1998).

Cox, John Mason, *Practical Observations on Insanity* (London: Baldwin, 1804).

Cramer, Maurice Browning, 'Browning's Friendships and Fame Before Marriage (1833–1846)', *PMLA*, 55 (1940), pp. 207–30, at pp. 214–15.

Crichton, Alexander, *An Inquiry into the Nature and Origin of Mental Derangement*, 2 vols (London: Cadell, 1798).

Crowder, Ashby Bland, 'Porphyria's Lover: A Reason for Action', *The South Central Bulletin*, 37, Studies by Members of the SCMLA (1977), pp. 145–46.

Cullen, William, *First Lines of the Practice of Physic* (1776–1783), new edn, 2 vols (1808).

Curren, Stuart (ed.), *The Cambridge Companion to British Romanticism* (Cambridge: Cambridge University Press, 1993).

De Almeida, Hermione, *Romantic Medicine and John Keats* (Oxford: Oxford University Press, 1991).

Dobell, Bertram, *Sidelights on Charles Lamb* (London: Dobell, 1903).

Elfenbein, Andrew, *Byron and the Victorians* (Cambridge: Cambridge University Press, 1995).

Erickson, Lee, *The Economy of Literary Form: English Literature and the Industrialization of Publishing, 1800–1850* (London: Johns Hopkins, 1995).

Erskine, Thomas, *Speeches of Lord Erskine, When at the Bar on Miscellaneous Subjects*, ed. James Ridgway (London: Ridgway, 1812).

——, *The Speeches of the Hon. Thomas Erskine*, ed. James Ridgway (New York: Eastburn, Kirk & Co., 1813).

Everest, Kelvin (ed.), *Shelley Revalued: Essays from the Gregynog Conference* (Leicester: Leicester University Press, 1983).

Faflak, Joel, 'Analysis Interminable in the Other Wordsworth', *Romanticism on the Net*, 16 (1999), <http://users.ox.ac.uk/~scat0385/otherww.html>.

Fields, James Thomas, *Old Acquaintance: Barry Cornwall and Some of his Friends* (Boston, MA: Cambridge University Press, 1876).

Fischer, Hermann, *Romantic Verse Narrative: The History of a Genre*, trans. Sue Bollans (Cambridge: Cambridge University Press, 1991).

Fisher, Judith L., '"In the Present Famine of Anything Substantial": Fraser's "Portraits" and the Construction of Literary Celebrity; or, "Personality, Personality Is the Appetite of the Age"', *Victorian Periodicals Review*, 39 (2006), pp. 97–135.

Flynn, Philip, 'Beginning *Blackwood's*: The First Hundred Numbers (April 1817–May 1825)', <http://www.english.udel.edu/Profiles/flynn_blackwood.htm>

——, 'Beginning *Blackwood's*: The Right Mix of Dulce and Ùtile', *Victorian Periodicals Review*, 39 (2006), pp. 136–57.

Ford, G. H., 'Keats and Procter: A Misdated Acquaintance', *Modern Language Notes*, 66 (1951), pp. 532–36.

Freneau, Philip Morin, *Poems Written Between the Years 1768 & 1794* (Monmouth, NJ: author's press, 1795).

Genette, Gerard, *Paratext: Thresholds of Interpretation* (Cambridge: Cambridge University Press, 1997).

Goellnicht, Donald C., *The Poet-Physician: Keats and Medical Science* (Pittsburgh, PA: University of Pittsburgh Press, 1984).

——, 'Keats on Reading: "Delicious Diligent Indolence"', *Journal of English and Germanic Philology*, 88 (1989), pp. 190–210.

Gonsalves, Joshua, 'Reading Idiocy: Wordsworth's "The Idiot Boy"', *Wordsworth Circle*, 38 (2007), pp. 121–30.

Gordon, Mary, *'Christopher North': A Memoir of John Wilson* (New York: Widdleton, 1863).

Goulding, Christopher, 'An Unpublished Shelley Letter', *The Review of English Studies*, 52 (2001), pp. 233–37.

Grayling, A. C., *The Quarrel of the Age: The Life and Times of William Hazlitt* (London: Phoenix Press, 2001).

Green, Joseph Henry, *Outlines of a Course of Dissections, for the Use of Students of Anatomy at St. Thomas's Hospital* (London: Cox, 1815).

——, *The Dissector's Manual* (London: The Author, 1820).

Gregory, Gill, *The Life and Work of Adelaide Anne Procter: Poetry, Feminism and Fathers* (Aldershot: Ashgate, 1998).

Guy, Thomas, *Armigero Fundati, ad normam recensitæ editionis Pharmacopoeiæ Collegii Regalis Medicorum Londinensis* (London: n.p. 1791).

Hale-White, William, *Keats as Doctor and Patient* (London: Oxford University Press, 1938).

Harris, Katherine (ed.), hypertext of *The Forget-Me-Not*, <http://www.orgs. muohio.edu/anthologies/FMN/Index.htm>.

Haslam, John, *Observations on Madness and Melancholy*, 2nd edn (London: Callow, 1809).

Hayden, John O., *The Romantic Reviewers, 1802–1824* (London: Routledge, 1969).

Haydon, Benjamin Robert, *Autobiography of Benjamin Robert Haydon*, 3 vols (London: Longman, 1853).

Hazlitt, William, *Lectures on the English Poets, Delivered at the Surrey Institution* (London: Taylor and Hessey, 1818).

——, *Select British Poets; or, New Elegant Extracts from Chaucer to the Present Time* (London: Hall, 1824).

——, *Select Poets of Great Britain* (London: Tegg, 1825).

——, *William Hazlitt: The Complete Works*, ed. P. P. Howe, 21 vols (London, 1930–34).

——, *The Letters of William Hazlitt*, ed. Herschel Moreland Sikes (London: Macmillan, 1979).

——, *Liber Amoris: or, The New Pygmalion* (London: Hogarth, 1985).

Heinzelman, Kurt, 'Self-Interest and the Politics of Composition in Keats's *Isabella*', *English Literary History*, 55 (1988), pp. 159–93.

Hill, George, *An Essay on the Prevention and Cure of Insanity* (1814).

Hofkosh, Sonia, *Sexual Politics and the Romantic Author* (Cambridge: Cambridge University Press, 1998).

Homans, Margaret, 'Keats Reading Women, Women Reading Keats', *Studies in Romanticism*, 29 (1990), pp. 341–70.

Hood, Thomas, *The Gem, A Literary Annual*, 4 vols (London: Marshall, 1829).

Houlston, William, *Pharmacopoeia Chirurgica; or, Formulæ for the Use of Surgeons* (London: Robinsons, 1794).

Howell, T. B. (ed.), *A Complete Collection of State Trials* (London: Hansard, 1820).

Howitt, William, *Homes and Haunts of the Most Eminent English Poets*, 2 vols (London: Bentley, 1847).

Hunt, Leigh, *A Sicilian Story* (London: Murray, 1816).

——, *The Literary Pocket-Book; or, Companion for the Lover of Nature and Art* (London: Ollier, 1819).

——, *The Correspondence of Leigh Hunt*, ed. Thornton Hunt, 2 vols (London: Smith, Elder and Co., 1862).

——, "Leigh Hunt Digital Collection," ed. Sid Huttner et al., *Iowa Digital Library*, <http://www.lib.uiowa.edu/spec-coll/leighhunt/index.html>.

——, *Leigh Hunt: A Life in Letters*, ed. Eleanor M. Gates (Essex, CT: Falls River, 1998).

Ingram, Allan, *The Madhouse of Language: Writing and Reading Madness in the Eighteenth Century* (London: Routledge, 1991).

Ingram, Allan and Michelle Faubert, *Cultural Constructions of Madness in Eighteenth-Century Writing: Representing the Insane* (Basingstoke: Palgrave Macmillan, 2005).

Jackson, Heather, *Marginalia: Readers Writing in Books* (Yale, CT: Yale University Press, 2001).

Jaffe, Aaron, *Modernism and the Culture of Celebrity* (Cambridge: Cambridge University Press, 2005).

James, Clive, 'Cultural Amnesia', *Times Literary Supplement*, 19 May 2007, p. 23.

Jameson, Anna Brownwell, *The Romance of Biography; or, Memoirs of Women Loved and Celebrated by Poets*, 2 vols, 3rd edn (London: Saunders and Otley, 1837).

Jerdan, William, *The Autobiography of William Jerdan*, 4 vols (London: Arthur Hall, 1852–1853).

Jones, Leonidas M., The Life of John Hamilton Reynolds (London: University Press of New England, 1984).

Jordan, John O. and Robert L. Patten (eds), *Literature in the Marketplace: Nineteenth-century British Publishing and Reading Practices* (Cambridge: Cambridge University Press, 1995).

Keach, William, *Arbitrary Power* (Princeton, NJ: Princeton University Press, 2004).

Keats, John, *John Keats's Anatomical and Physiological Note Book*, ed. Maurice Buxton Forman (Oxford: Oxford University Press, 1934).

——, *The Letters of John Keats, 1814–1821*, ed. Hyder Edward Rollins (Cambridge, MA: Harvard University Press, 1958).

——, *The Poems of John Keats*, ed. Miriam Allott (London: Longman, 1970).

——, *John Keats: The Complete Poems*, ed. John Barnard, 2nd edn (Harmondsworth: Penguin, 1977).

——, *The Poems of John Keats*, ed. Jack Stillinger (Cambridge, MA: Belknap Press, 1978).

Kemble, Frances, *Records of a Girlhood* (1878; New York, NY: Cosimo, 2007).

Klancher, Jon, The *Making of English Reading Audiences, 1790–1832* (Madison, WI: University of Wisconsin Press, 1987).

Kucich, Greg, 'Gendering the Canons of Romanticism' in Tony Pinkney, Keith Hanley and Fred Botting (eds.), *Romantic Masculinities* (Keele: Keele University Press, 1997).

Lamb, Charles, *The Letters of Charles Lamb: To which are Added Those of His Sister Mary Lamb*, ed. E. V. Lucas, 3 vols (London: Dent, 1935).

——, *The Prose Works of Charles Lamb*, 3 vols (London: Moxon, 1838).

——, *Final Memorials of Charles Lamb: Consisting Chiefly of his Letters, not before Published, with Sketches of some of his Companions*, ed. Thomas Noon Talford, 2 vols (London: Moxon, 1848).

——, *Works: Including His Most Interesting Letters*, ed. Thomas Noon Talfourd, new edn (London: Bell and Daldy, 1852).

Leal, Amy, 'Who Killed John Keats', *The Chronicle of Higher Education*, 53.19 (2007), p. 15.

Leary, Lewis, 'Wordsworth in America: Addenda', *Modern Language Notes*, 58 (1943), pp. 391–93.

ELECT BIBLIOGRAPHY 181

L'Estrange, A. G., *Life of Mary Russell Mitford*, 3 vols (London: Bentley, 1870).

Levinson, Marjorie, *Keats's Life of Allegory: The Origins of a Style* (Oxford: Basil Blackwell, 1988).

Loughnan, Arnie, '"Manifest Madness": Towards a New Understanding of the Insanity Defence', *Modern Law Review*, 70 (2007), pp. 379–401.

MacCarthy, Fiona, *Byron: Life and Legend* (London: Faber, 2003).

Madden, R. R. (ed.), *The Literary Life and Correspondence of the Countess of Blessington*, 3 vols (London: T. C. Newby, 1855).

Marggraf Turley, Richard, *The Politics of Language in Romantic Literature* (London: Palgrave, 2002).

——, *Keats's Boyish Imagination* (London: Routledge, 2004).

Marshall, P. David, *Celebrity and Power: Fame in Contemporary Culture* (Minneapolis: University of Minnesota Press, 1997).

Marvell, Andrew, *Andrew Marvell*, eds. Frank Kermode and Keith Walker (Oxford: Oxford University Press, 1990).

Mason, Michael, 'Browning and the Dramatic Monologue', in Isobel Armstrong (ed.), *Robert Browning* (Athens: Ohio University Press, 1975).

Masson, Scott, *Romanticism, Hermeneutics and the Crisis of the Human Sciences* (Aldershot: Ashgate, 2004), p. 111.

Matthews, G. M., *Keats: The Critical Heritage* (London: Routledge & Kegan Paul, 1971).

Matthews, Samantha, *Poetical Remains: Poets' Graves, Bodies and Books in the Nineteenth Century* (Oxford: Oxford University Press, 2004).

Maxwell, Catherine, 'Browning's Pygmalion and the Revenge of Galatea', *English Literary History*, 60 (1993), pp. 989–1013.

McCutcheon, Mark, 'Liber Amoris and the Lineaments of Hazlitt's Desire', *Texas Studies in Literature and Language*, 46 (2004), pp. 432–451.

McGann, Jerome, *The Poetics of Sensibility: A Revolution in Literary Style* (Oxford: Clarendon Press, 1996).

Mellor, Anne K, *Romanticism and Gender* (London: Routledge, 1993).

Milnes, Richard Monckton, *Life, Letters, and Literary Remains of John Keats*, 2 vols (London: Moxon, 1848).

Mizukoshi, Ayumi, '"The Cockney Politics of Gender: The Cases of Hunt and Keats", *Romanticism on the Net*, 14 (1999), <http://users.ox.ac.uk/~scat0385/cockneygender.html>.

——, *Keats, Hunt and the Aesthetics of Pleasure* (London: Palgrave, 2001).

Mole, Tom, *Byron's Romantic Celebrity: Industrial Culture and the Hermeneutic of Intimacy* (London: Palgrave Macmillan, 2007).

Monckton Milnes, Richard (ed.), *Life, Letters, and Literary Remains of John Keats*, 2 vols (London: Moxon, 1848).

Morehead, Charles, *Memorials of the Life and Writings of the Rev. Robert Morehead, D.D.* (Edinburgh: Edmonstone and Douglas, 1875).

Morrison, Robert, 'Blackwood's Berserker: John Wilson and the Language of Extremity', *Romanticism on the Net*, 20 (2000), <http://users.ox.ac.uk/~scato385/20morrison.html>.

Motion, Andrew, *Keats* (London: Faber and Faber, 1997).

Neubauer, John (ed.), *Cultural History After Foucault* (Somerset, NJ: Aldine Transaction, 1999).

Newlyn, Lucy, *Reading, Writing and Romanticism: The Anxiety of Influence* (Oxford: Oxford University Press, 2000).

O'Neill, Michael, *Literature of the Romantic Period: A Bibliographical Guide*, ed. Michael O'Neill (Oxford: Clarendon Press, 1998).

Paine, Thomas, *Paine: Political Writings*, ed. Bruce Kuklick (Cambridge: Cambridge University Press, 1989).

Patmore, P. G., *My Friends and Acquaintances*, 3 vols (London: Saunders and Otley, 1854).

Peacock, Thomas Love, *Peacock's Four Ages of Poetry*, ed. H. F. B. Brett-Smith (Oxford: Blackwell, 1921).

——, *The Letters of Thomas Love Peacock*, ed. Nicholas A. Joukovsky, 2 vols (Oxford: Clarendon Press, 2001).

Peakman, Julia, *Mighty Lewd Books: The Development of Pornography in Eighteenth-Century England* (London: Palgrave, 2003).

Pearson, Heskereth, *The Fool of Love: A Life of William Hazlitt* (London: Hamish Hamilton, 1934).

Phillips, Richard, *An Experimental Examination of the Last Edition of the Pharmacopoeia Londinensis* (London: Phillips, 1811).

Pichot, Amédée, *Historical and Literary Tour of a Foreigner in England and Scotland*, 2 vols (London: Saunders and Otley, 1825).

Pinel, Philippe, *A Treatise on Insanity in which are Ccontained the Principles of a New and More Practical Nosology of Maniacal Disorders*, trans. D. D. Davis (Sheffield: Cadell and Davies, 1806).

——, *Nosographie Philosophique; ou, la Méthode de l'Analyse Appliquée la Médicine*, 5th edn (Paris: J. A. Brosson, 1813).

Pite, Ralph, 'The Watching Narrator in *Isabella*', *Essays in Criticism*, 40 (1990), pp. 287–302.

Porter, Roy, *Mind-Forg'd Manacles: A History of Madness in England from the Restoration to the Regency* (Cambridge, MA: Harvard University Press, 1987).

—— (ed.), *Medicine in the Enlightenment* (Amsterdam: Rodopi, 1995).

——, *Madness: A Brief History* (Oxford: Oxford University Press, 2003).

Pyle, Forest, 'Keats's Materialism', *Studies in Romanticism*, 33 (1994), pp. 57–80.

Rabin, Dana, *Identity, Crime, and Legal Responsibility in Eighteenth-Century England* (London: Palgrave, 2004).

Reiman, Donald H. (ed.), *The Romantics Reviewed: Contemporary Reviews of British Romantic Writers*, 9 vols (New York: Garland, 1972).

Reynolds, John Hamilton, *The Letters of John Hamilton Reynolds*, ed. Leonidas M. Jones (Lincoln, NE: University of Nebraska Press, 1973).

Robertson, Daniel N., 'Madness, Badness, and Fitness: Law and Psychiatry (Again)', *Philosophy, Psychiatry, & Psychology* 7 (2000), pp. 209–22.

Robinson, Charles E., 'Percy Bysshe Shelley, Charles Ollier, and William Blackwood: The Contexts of Early Nineteenth-Century Publishing', in Kelvin Everest (ed.), *Shelley Revalued: Essays from the Gregynog Conference* (Leicester: Leicester University Press, 1983).

Robinson, Jeffrey C., *Reception and Poetics in Keats: 'My Ended Poet'* (London: Macmillan, 1998).

——, 'Romantic Passions: Passion and Romantic Poetics', *Romantic Circles* (1998), <http://www.rc.umd.edu/praxis/passions/robinson/rbsn.html>.

Roe, Nicholas, '"Bright Star, Sweet Unrest": Image and Consolation in Wordsworth, Shelley, and Keats', in Stephen C. Behrendt (ed.) *History and Myth: Essays on English Romantic Literature* (Detroit, MI: Wayne State University Press, 1990).

—— (ed.), *Keats and History* (Cambridge: Cambridge University Press, 1995).

——, *John Keats and the Culture of Dissent* (Oxford: Clarendon, 1997).

—— (ed.), *Leigh Hunt: Life, Poetics, Politics* (London: Routledge, 2003).

——, *Fiery Heart: The First Life of Leigh Hunt* (London: Pimlico, 2005).

Rojek, Chris, *Celebrity* (London: Reaktion, 2001).

Rollins, Hyder Edward (ed.), *The Keats Circle: Letters and Papers, 1816–1878*, 2 vols (Cambridge, MA: Harvard University Press, 1948).

——, *The Letters of John Keats, 1814–1821* (Cambridge, MA: Harvard University Press, 1958).

Rousseau, George, *The Languages of Psyche: Mind and Body in Enlightenment Thought* (Berkeley, CA: University of California Press, 1990).

Rowland, Jr. William G., *Literature and the Marketplace: Romantic Writers and their Audience in Great Britain and the United States* (Lincoln: University of Nebraska Press, 1996).

Saglia, Diego, *Poetic Castles in Spain: British Romanticism and Figurations of Iberia* (Amsterdam: Rodopi, 2000).

Scott, Grant F. and Sue Brown (eds), *New Letters from Charles Brown to Joseph Severn, Romantic Circles Electronic Edition* <http://www.rc.umd.edu/editions/brownsevern/>.

Scull, Andrew T., *Museums of Madness: The Social Organization of Insanity in Nineteenth-Century England* (Harmondsworth: Penguin, 1982).

Shattock, Joanne (ed.), *The Cambridge Bibliography of English Literature*, 3rd edn (Cambridge: Cambridge University Press, 1999).

Shelley, Mary Wollstonecraft, *Proserpine and Midas*, ed. André Henri Koszul (London: Milford, 1922).

——, *The Journals of Mary Shelley, 1814–1844*, 2 vols, eds. Paula R. Feldman and Diana Scott-Kilvert (Oxford: Clarendon Press, 1987).

Shelley, Percy Bysshe, *The Letters of Percy Bysshe Shelley*, ed. Frederick L. Jones, 2 vols (Oxford: Clarendon Press, 1964).

Simcox, George Augustus, 'Barry Cornwall', *Fortnightly Review*, n.s. 20 (1876), pp. 708–18.

Sitter, John, 'Introduction: The Future of Eighteenth-Century Poetry', in John Sitter (ed.), *The Cambridge Companion to Eighteenth-Century Poetry* (Cambridge: Cambridge University Press, 2001).

Small, Helen, *Love's Madness: Medicine, the Novel, and Female Insanity 1800–1865* (Oxford: Clarendon Press, 1996).

Smith, Hillas, *Keats and Medicine* (Newport, Isle of Wight: Cross Publishing, 1995).

—, 'The Strange Case of Mr Keats's Tuberculosis', *Clinical Infectious Diseases*, 38 (2004), pp. 991–93.

Smith, Kirby Flower, 'The Tale of Gyges and the King of Lydia', *The American Journal of Philology*, 23 (1902), pp. 361–87.

Smith, Leonard D., *Cure, Comfort and Safe Custody: Public Lunatic Asylums in Early Nineteenth-Century England* (London: Leicester University Press, 1999).

St Clair, William, *The Reading Nation in the Romantic Period* (Cambridge: Cambridge University Press, 2004).

Steward, David G., 'P. G. Patmore's Rejected Articles and the Image of the Magazine Market', *Romanticism*, 12.iii (2006), pp. 200–11.

Stillinger, Jack, 'Keats and Romance', *Studies in English Literature, 1500–1900*, 8 (1968), pp. 593–605.

Sun, Emily, 'Facing Keats with Winnicott: On a New Therapeutics', *Studies in Romanticism*, 46 (2007), pp. 57–75.

Suzuki, Akihito, *Madness at Home: The Psychiatrist, The Patient, and the Family in England 1820–1860* (London: University of California Press, 2006).

Sweet, Nanora, 'The *New Monthly Magazine* and the Liberalism of the 1820s', in *Romantic Periodicals and Print Culture* (London: Frank Cass, 2003).

Torrey, E. Fuller and Judy Miller, *The Invisible Plague: The Rise of Insanity from 1750 to the Present* (Piscataway, NJ: Rutgers University Press, 2002).

Tuke, Samuel, *Description of the Retreat, an Institution Near York, for the Treatment of Insane Persons of the Society of Friends* (York: Alexander, 1813).

Turner, Graeme, *Understanding Celebrity* (London: Sage, 2004).

Uwins, David, 'Insanity and Madhouses', *Quarterly Review* (1816), pp. 388–417.

Vaillant, George E., 'John Haslam on Early Infantile Autism', *American Journal of Psychiatry*, 119 (1962), p. 376.

Van Dyke, Henry, *The Poetry of Tennyson* (New York: Charles Scribner's Sons, 1889).

Vickers, Neil, *Coleridge and the Doctors, 1795–1806* (Oxford: Clarendon Press, 2004).

Vitale, Serena, *Pushkin's Button*, trans. Ann Goldstein and Jon Rothschild (Chicago, IL: University of Chicago Press, 2000).

Wade, Nicholas J. et al., 'Cox's Chair: "A Moral and a Medical Mean in the Treatment of Maniacs"', *History of Psychiatry*, 16 (2005), pp. 73–88.

Wallace, Jennifer, 'Keats's Frailty: The Body and Biography', in Arthur Bradley and Alan Rawes (eds.), *Romantic Biography* (Aldershot: Ashgate, 2003).

Walmsley, Robert, *Peterloo: The Case Reopened* (Manchester: Manchester University Press, 1969).

Wardle, Ralph M., *Modern Language Notes*, 57 (1942), pp. 459–62.

Watts, Alaric Alfred, *Alaric Watts: A Narrative of his Life*, 2 vols (London: Bentley, 1884).

Whale, John, *John Keats* (London: Palgrave, 2005).

Whipple, Edwin P., *Recollections of Eminent Men* (Boston: Ticknor, 1886).

Williams-Wynn, Charles Watkin, *Report from the Select Committee Appointed to Enquire into the State of Lunatics*. 15 July 1807 (London: House of Commons, 1807).

Willis, Nathaniel Parker, *Melanie and Other Poems*, ed. with a Preface Barry Cornwall (London: Saunders and Otley, 1835).

——, *Pencillings by the Way: Written During Some Years of Residence and Travel in Europe* (New York: Scribner, 1852).

Wilson, James, *Pharmacopoeia Chirurgica; or, A Manual of Chirurgical Pharmacy*, 3rd edn (London: E. Cox, 1814).

Wolfson, Susan J., 'Feminising Keats', in Peter J. Kitson (ed.), *Coleridge, Keats, and Shelley* (Houndmills: Macmillan, 1996).

——, 'Representing some Late Romantic-Era, Non-Canonical Male Poets: Thomas Hood, Winthrop Mackworth Praed, Thomas Lovell Beddoes', *Romanticism On the Net*, 19 (2000), <http://users.ox.ac.uk/~scat0385/19hood.html>.

——, *Felicia Hemans: Selected Poems, Letters, Reception Materials* (Princeton, NJ: Princeton University Press, 2000).

——, 'Sounding Romantic: the Sound of Sound', *Romantic Circles* (2008), <http://www.rc.umd.edu/praxis/soundings/wolfson/wolfson.html>.

Wordsworth, William, and Samuel Taylor Coleridge, *Lyrical Ballads*, eds R. L. Brett and A. R. Jones (London: Methuen, 1965).

——, *William Wordsworth*, ed. Stephen Gill (Oxford: Oxford University Press).

Wu, Duncan, *Wordsworth's Reading, 1770–1799* (Cambridge: Cambridge University Press, 1993).

——, 'Hazlitt's "Sexual Harassment"', *Essays in Criticism*, 50 (2000), pp. 199–214.

Yost, George, 'Keats's Poignancy and the Fine Excess', *South Atlantic Bulletin*, 45 (1980), pp. 15–22.

Ziegenhagen, Timothy, 'Keats, Professional Medicine, and the Two Hyperions', *Literature and Medicine*, 21 (2002), pp. 281–305.

Index